TOWARD A JUST WORLD

TOWARD A JUST WORLD

JUST WORLD

———

THE CRITICAL YEARS

IN THE SEARCH FOR

INTERNATIONAL JUSTICE

Dorothy V. Jones

THE UNIVERSITY OF CHICAGO PRESS

CHICAGO AND LONDON

DOROTHY V. JONES is a scholar-in-residence at the Newberry Library and an associate in the history department at Northwestern University. Among her books are *Code of Peace: Ethics and Security in the World of the Warlord States* (1991) and *License for Empire: Colonialism by Treaty in Early America* (1982), both published by the University of Chicago Press.

The University of Chicago Press, Chicago 60637
The University of Chicago Press, Ltd., London
© 2002 by The University of Chicago
All rights reserved. Published 2002
Printed in the United States of America
11 10 09 08 07 06 05 04 03 02   1 2 3 4 5

ISBN: 0-226-40948-1 (cloth)

Library of Congress Cataloging-in-Publication Data
Jones, Dorothy V.
   Toward a just world : the critical years in the search for
international justice / Dorothy V. Jones.
      p.   cm.
Includes bibliographical references and index.
   ISBN: 0-226-40948-1 (cloth : alk. paper)
   1. Peace—History.   2. World politics—20th century.   3. Justice.
   I. Title.
   JZ5560 .J66   2002
   341—dc21

                                    2002004968

♾ The paper used in this publication meets the minimum requirements of the American National Standard for Information Sciences—Permanence of Paper for Printed Library Materials, ANSI Z39.48-1992.

Dedicated to Robert R. Jones

who has walked with me every step of the way
and whose life I am privileged to share.

CONTENTS

ACKNOWLEDGMENTS

This book has had a long gestation. If by this point I have not made clear my gratitude to the people who have helped me see it to completion, a listing of names in this acknowledgments section would hardly make up for that lack. Many people have helped. They have been generous with time and resources, critical of defective argument, and patient with authorial floundering on the way to finding out what the book is really about. Without their help, the book would have been much poorer. Indeed, there might not have been any book at all. Although reluctant to burden readers with a list of names, I am, nonetheless, extremely grateful for all the help I have received. Beyond that, there are some debts to institutions that need to be publicly acknowledged.

First among these is a debt to the Newberry Library. This privately endowed research library on Chicago's north side has for many years offered scholars an intellectual home base and the stimulus of contacts with other scholars from many different disciplines. It is my good fortune to be one of the scholars with a long-term association with the Newberry. This has given me access to their unparalleled collections of manuscripts and rare books, enabled me to draw on the knowledge and helpfulness of their reference librarians and staff, and given me a place to test out ideas while they were still in the formative stage. This has been of incalculable assistance in my work. It has also been a continuing pleasure.

Further, I have benefited greatly from my appointment as a History Department Associate at Northwestern University. The associate program is intended to give scholars without a regular teaching position an institutional home and identification, inclusion in History Department activities, and access to the resources of the several Northwestern University libraries including the Law Library. Without these, my work on the search for international justice would have been more difficult, and I might well have missed some of the important, little-known aspects of that search that I found.

Finally, I owe much to the New York–based Carnegie Council on Ethics and International Affairs. My association with scholars, policymakers, and members of international organizations, both at the council and at council-sponsored programs, has widened my outlook on international affairs while deepening my understanding of the ethical questions involved in making choices in the international sphere. My service on the Editorial Advisory Board of the council's journal, *Ethics & International Affairs*, and on the council's Board of Trustees, has done much to overcome my Midwest parochialism, and the reaction to my presentations at several council-sponsored conferences has helped me revise and strengthen my arguments. All this has made for richer scholarship and a better book. The friendships that have resulted from this association are the lovely frosting on the cake.

This is the story of a remarkable journey. The focus of the journey is an idea, the idea of international justice. The pursuit of this idea throughout the twentieth century provides a motif for the century that goes beyond its obvious wars and power struggles. Yet the idea of international justice is intimately connected with those wars and struggles. Part of the excitement of the journey lies in people's efforts to sever that connection, to make war a thing of the past because justice has been given an international meaning and presence. But what meaning? And what kind of presence? This book explores some of the answers given and actions taken as people have worked toward that elusive, contested, and long-sought goal: a just world.

The critical years in the pursuit of international justice were those of the first half of the twentieth century. The actions and definitions of those years of effort set the tone and direction for the efforts made in the second half of the century and on into the next century as well. People who made no pretense of being philosophers had, by midcentury, achieved a philosophic tour de force. Not justice alone but justice *and something else* formed the key to giving this ancient concept a place in international affairs. Little by little, through years of struggle by many different people, linkages began to form, until by midcentury there were three pairings that tied justice to basic international concerns:

- justice and peace
- justice and rights
- justice and law

This compound concept, made up of three separate linkages in shifting relations to each other, is too complex to be captured by the traditional female symbol of justice with her sword and balance scales. Yet the concept fits, at the same time as it reflects, the shifting relations and emphases of the international system.

How these linkages came about, the steps and missteps along the way, the successes and failures of people struggling against their own limitations in times that sometimes hampered and sometimes enabled their efforts—these form the subject of this book. To keep the subject in focus, the events presented are set within the overall context of efforts to determine exactly what happens to the concept of justice when *international* is added to its already formidable baggage of meaning. Events both familiar and unfamiliar contribute to the account. The many unfamiliar events recounted in this book add richness and complexity to the story of the pursuit of international justice. Familiar events, on the other hand, take on new shades of meaning when set within a context different from that in which they are usually seen.

Take, for example, the Lytton Commission. There is near-unanimous agreement that the commission was an unmitigated failure. Dispatched by the League of Nations in the early 1930s to investigate Japanese aggression in Manchuria, it had no effect on the aggression and its report provided the impetus for Japanese withdrawal from the League. The whole episode has come to be seen as a symbol of the weakness and failure not only of the commission but of the League of Nations itself.

In a context of wars and power struggles this might well be a sufficient treatment of the Lytton Commission. Change the context to the pursuit of justice, however, and all else is changed. Then there is much more to be said about the Lytton Commission and its place in the search for a justice that would have presence and meaning in a world of contending national states. Then it can be seen that the commission's journeyings and recommendations and Japan's subsequent withdrawal from the League were important markers in the history of those times. They were signs of profound changes that were taking place in the international system. The changes were subtle and slow-moving. They would not show up on anybody's map of potential zones of international conflict. But they were there. And when, as is done in this book, the Lytton Commission is compared with other little-known international commissions of inquiry, the changes can clearly be seen.

In the context of a search for international justice, even the 1930s take on a different look. Generally seen as a decade of disastrous and unending international crises, the '30s were also a period of bold experimentation on the international level. They helped forge the bond between justice and peace that is so strong today. In those years, valuable experience was gained in peaceful methods of dispute settlement and in testing the potential and limits of international administration. There were some notable successes, now all but forgotten. In this book those successes are brought back into the light of historical memory as part of the ongoing search for international justice.

Although the examples given in this introduction are highly simplified, they are enough to indicate the book's method of presentation. The prologue gets the narrative under way by showing how the delegates to the 1899 Peace Conference at The Hague in The Netherlands wrought considerably more than they knew or have been given credit for. Their accomplishments were not, however, in the realm of power. That realm defied their efforts to bring it under control through arbitration procedures and a limitation on arms. Where the delegates staked out new ground was in the linkage of justice and law. Not until 1945 would this linkage make much of an impact on the international scene, but the linkage itself depended heavily on the intellectual and institutional resources provided by the delegates of 1899. Subsequent developments on the legal path of international justice—the International Criminal Tribunal for the former Yugoslavia, the International Criminal Tribunal for Rwanda, and the International Criminal Court—are still in debt to the delegates of 1899.[1] The delegates were very much people of their times. As they thought about the world and their attempts to bring justice to that world, they thought along conventional lines of state dominance and independence of action. These conventions provided both a secure framework for thought and a barrier to different approaches to thought and political organization. This duality was a constant in efforts to define and achieve international justice in the first half of the twentieth century—as it still is today. For that reason, part 1 sets out the conditions within which people had to operate as they pursued the idea of international justice. They did not have the luxury of extended debate without practical consequences. A decision made, an action taken, could not be recalled for refinement and revision. Consequences, intended or not, had to be lived with, which raises the question: Who were these people who cared so passionately about the idea of international justice?

They not only did not claim to be philosophers. They were *not* philosophers. They were heads of state, diplomats, military leaders, government officials, international civil servants, and concerned private citizens from many countries and professions. They acted with few guidelines, often in response to crises, and in so doing made paths into the unknown. The preceding centuries of thought about justice provided inspiration but little direct help. Justice might well be the perfect virtue, as Aristotle had said, but when justice was claimed by both sides in a war—as frequently happened in the first half of the twentieth century—perfection was not the issue. Possession was the issue, and what were the searchers for international justice going to do about it?

What they did about it is set out in part 2. That there was some connection between justice and peace had, for many years, been assumed in a general kind of way. Early in the twentieth century it became clear that this vague assumption was not adequate to the pressures that were building from events that no one seemed able to control. Nineteenth-century procedures of great power balancing were no longer effective. International difficulties seemed to call for some sort of international response, but what that should be remained unclear. Justice was involved, and peace as well, since the two were somehow connected. But how was this connection to be applied? Which should prevail? Should justice be pursued at any cost, even if that meant war? People such as Alfred Thayer Mahan, the American proponent of naval power, certainly thought so. But if the result of this action was wholesale destruction, as in World War I, then the idea of justice that was the reason for war in the first place hardly seemed adequate to the cost that had had to be paid.

And that was the nub of the problem: the idea of justice. When this group or that acted on its own idea of justice, that idea was, more often than not, narrowly based and exclusionary. It was justice for that group, and that one alone, with little care for those who stood in the way and no care at all for the system of which the group was a part. This was the deeply entrenched habit of thought and action that came under scrutiny in the twentieth century as people struggled to adjust to the unprecedented in international affairs. They invested great hopes in the new institutions and procedures that are discussed in part 2 of this book. The collapse of those hopes at the end of the 1930s should not be allowed to obscure what had been accomplished before the collapse. Most strikingly, in this period the idea of justice began to take on an international flavor. Slowly, painfully, its definitional base was being widened to include more groups and more of the world, and the previous vague connection between justice and peace was gradually being transformed into the strong link that persists to this day.

And what of the other two linkages, justice and rights, and justice and law? These are dealt with in part 3. The path to these linkages lies through terrain so familiar that it might seem there is nothing to be gained by walking that path again. But the assumption that studying the run-up to World War II and the subsequent war crimes trials would yield nothing new is false. Context is again the key. These events were not simply about power, national grievances, the desire for an imperial reach, or attempts to assess individual guilt for state-sponsored actions. They were that, but they were also about something else as well.

That something else was a reaction to the international ideas and institutions that had been quietly gathering strength since the beginning of the century—a reaction that was both violently against and passionately for. From the mid-1930s through the war itself and on into the period of the war crimes trials that reaction was played out: in diplomacy, in public initiatives, on battlefields, and in courtrooms. At the core of these struggles was a profound disagreement over the definition and reach of justice. With that as the context, known events appear in a different light, and many little-known events move to the fore. It then becomes clear that there is much that has not been said about the period from the mid-thirties to the mid-forties. And there is much to be learned from the actions of people whose contributions have, for the most part, been left out of accounts where the context is of war and the struggle for power.

Part 4 deals with the working out of the trends that are detailed in the bulk of the book. By that point they can be recognized as trends, but there was no guarantee along the way that the protracted conflicts of loyalties and thought in the earlier period would have this particular outcome. Nobody was well prepared for the struggle to define and achieve the just world that still eludes both final definition and successful establishment. Yet there were successes along the way, and much was achieved. Later generations have at least a broader definition of justice on which to stand and more varied institutional tools with which to work than were available at the beginning of the twentieth century. Those later generations will need them all as they face the challenges of their times: in particular, the challenge of militants whose demands fall outside even expanded definitions of justice and whose methods put intolerable pressure on the linkages between justice and peace, justice and rights, and justice and law. Add to that the shrinking of the areas of effective state action, for good or ill, and it can be seen that efforts toward a just world are as problematic at the beginning of the twenty-first century as they were at the beginning of the twentieth—as problematic, yes, but also as promising, and, thanks to the people and efforts described in this book, much better situated for the task.

Prologue

The modern search for international justice began at an international conference in The Netherlands at the end of the nineteenth century. There in the homeland of Hugo Grotius, the great Dutch legal scholar, the conference delegates felt that they were picking up and continuing the task that Grotius had begun so long before in his masterwork on the laws of war and peace. The elaborate style of his work made it difficult for moderns to read, but the issues that Grotius had addressed in the seventeenth century were just as pressing at the end of the nineteenth. Chief among them were two: the effort to restrain and limit the international use of force and the effort to resolve disputes in accordance with justice.[1]

The word *justice* was much on the lips of the delegates at The Hague in 1899 as they wrestled with the seemingly intractable problems of their day. Theirs were the first hesitant steps on a search-and-define mission that was to continue throughout the coming century. The mission challenged and eventually transformed traditional thought as successive generations tried to determine what justice might consist of in an international context. By the end of the twentieth century, justice had become a key concept in international affairs and had acquired so many different meanings that it would have been unrecognizable to people in 1899—unrecognizable and, in many respects, unacceptable. The journey to that outcome was long and difficult, and there were many conflicts and outbreaks of violence along the way.

International. That was the stumbling block. The traditional views of justice had, through the centuries, found symbolic expression in a figure that was of very little help when it came to international affairs. In that setting what was the use of Justice—that full-busted female, classically draped, sword and scales in hand, who presided blindfolded over established courts of law—as traditionally portrayed? Was she for the Protestants or the Catholics in the Thirty Years' War, which had prompted Grotius to write his great work? What about the nineteenth-century Italian struggles for independence? Was she for the Italians or the Austrians? To ask this question was, in effect, to ask if Justice was on the side of liberty or on the side of order. Did Justice cheer when Bismarck's wars unified fractious Germany? Or did she weep for the victims of those deliberately provoked conflicts? And what of the Boers and the British, at sword's point even as the delegates of 1899 drove confidently to the opening session of the conference?

Representatives of the Boers had come to The Netherlands to get a hearing for their case against the British in southern Africa. But the Boers, like the Finns, the Poles, and the Armenians who had also come seeking international support, had no official standing. They were outsiders at The Hague, where the meetings were held, and their grievances were not on the conference agenda. As one delegate put it, "Their proposals, if admitted, would simply be bombshells sure to blow all the leading nations of Europe out of the conference and bring everything to naught."[2]

Unfair as that might have seemed to the Boers who had traveled to The Hague so that justice, as they understood it, might be served, that evaluation was exactly correct. The situation at The Hague in 1899 exemplifies some of the difficulties of the search for justice in an international setting. Those difficulties only increased in the years to come as new states, each with its claims and grievances, entered the international system. A further complication in the years ahead was the role of the public in international affairs. The twentieth century saw drastic changes in that role, from a tolerated nuisance, to be kept at arm's length, to a valued resource on which diplomats could draw but whose criticisms were increasingly hard for diplomats to ignore. And what of sovereignty, that concept to which the delegates of 1899 paid such deference? By century's end sovereignty retained, at least in principle, much the same high position it had had in 1899, but there was a practical difference. The barriers that protected sovereignty from outside interference had been considerably weakened by the sobering experiences of the intervening years.

The second thoughts of harrowing experience were not a problem for the delegates of 1899. They lived in a confident time, and they were confident of the importance of their task. From May 18 to July 29 they labored to continue the work of Hugo Grotius. The accomplishment of which they were the most proud, the one which most, they felt, carried on the Grotian tradition, was an agreement to establish a Permanent Court of Arbitration. Here they were able to pay tribute to Grotius in an innovative and lasting way. They had paid a more traditional tribute on July 4 at the Nieuwe Kerk in Delft, where Grotius was buried, in a ceremony replete with organ music, oratory, and anthems from the church choir. Impressive as the ceremony was, it was only for that one day. The Permanent Court of Arbitration was for all time, an especially fitting tribute to the man who had said, "As in making peace, it scarcely ever happens that either party will acknowledge the injustice of his cause, or of his claims, such a construction must be given as will equalize the pretensions of each side."[3] By providing an institutional means of arbitration, the delegates felt that they had done exactly what Grotius had advised.

They had also kept intact the high status of state sovereignty. The Permanent Court of Arbitration left sovereignty full and free. It was not a court in the usual sense but a panel of experts of different nationalities who could be called on to arbitrate a dispute, should the disputants be so inclined. Even that limited end was difficult to achieve. Arguments about commissions of inquiry, or the right to suggest that a dispute be submitted to arbitration, were prolonged and bitter and threatened to wreck the conference. Only a special mission to Berlin kept German representatives at The Hague. The problem was to provide arbitration guidelines for states without stepping on the extended, tender toes of that most cherished attribute of statehood: sovereignty. It was a delicate and demanding task.

It remained so throughout the coming century, a fact that is central to any account of the search for justice in international affairs. It is impossible to understand why the journey has been so long and difficult without a clear understanding of the intellectual baggage that has had to be carried along the way—carried, shifted about, repackaged, and partially jettisoned as changing circumstances have forced attitudes toward justice to change. The struggle for definition and achievement of a justice that is truly international has been a vast, collective twentieth-century effort. It has often been hampered by the very beliefs on which people have based their efforts, and it has occasionally been helped forward by the reluctant realization that some beliefs are not adequate to the times in which they flourish. This book tells the story of that grand, protracted struggle.

THE CAGE OF CUSTOM

The struggle began in a setting of outward opulence and inward doubt. The first session of the 1899 conference at The Hague took place in the luxurious surroundings of the Dutch summer palace, The House in the Wood. Here, on May 18, delegates from the twenty-six countries involved in the conference gathered in the elaborate room known as the Orange Salon. Many of the delegates were career diplomats, men who were socially adroit, professionally cautious and, if truth were known, profoundly skeptical that any good could come out of such a gathering. It would not have done, of course, to come out publicly against the stated purposes of the conference. One could hardly argue against an attempt to slow the arms race—an upward spiral that gained speed with every improvement in weapons design— but one could certainly have private reservations about the possibility that states would agree to any significant reduction. As for the rules of warfare, which were to be rationalized at the conference, it might indeed be beneficial to continue the work of the Brussels Conference of 1874, which had made a start on setting out those rules. But surely that was a matter for a small private gathering of military specialists, not for this assemblage of diplomatic luminaries whose every public word and gesture was being scrutinized by the world's press.

And what of arbitration, another stated goal of the conference? The very word was misleading to those outside the inner circle of experienced diplomats. It was not a cure-all for conflicts, not the high road to peace that some envisioned when they heard the word. It was a highly specialized procedure to be used only under very specific circumstances, and only by those—such as diplomats—with extensive knowledge of international affairs. It was true that the recent arbitration of the dispute between Great Britain and the United States in the *Alabama* affair had been a success. But these two countries had not been about to go to war over the damage wrought to Union shipping by the British-built Confederate cruiser the *Alabama* during the American Civil War. Not every dispute could be brought within reach of arbitration procedures. And even then there were disadvantages not obvious to the uninformed. As the German delegates at the conference kept pointing out, the delays occasioned by arbitration could be costly to the country that was prepared to test its concept of justice on the field of battle. Germany could mobilize quickly. Other states were not nearly so well prepared. In case arbitration should fail, any delays benefited those other states and put Germany at a disadvantage.[4]

But these were thoughts expressed chiefly in private conversations or in committee meetings where the bulk of the conference work was done. Officially, these meetings were secret, a rule that had been adopted by the conference over the objections of delegates from Sweden and the United States. The main effect of the rule was to antagonize the journalists who had come to The Hague from far and near to keep their readers abreast of ne-gotiations. The journalists' presence and their insistent interest in what was, after all, a gathering not concerned with any urgent matters of peace and war confounded the traditionalists among the delegates. Somehow journal-ists, church groups, student associations, peace organizations, and worthy folk of every persuasion had the idea that the conference at The Hague was set to do away with war altogether and usher in the new century with a new age of peace. People outside official circles had even taken to calling the meeting a peace conference. So persistent and widespread was this misun-derstanding of the original purposes of the conference that the delegates felt obliged to make some acknowledgment of public expectations. On the opening day, Baron de Staal, the newly installed president of the confer-ence, accepted the name that the public had bestowed: "The name 'Peace Conference,' which the popular mind, outstripping a decision by the Gov-ernments in this respect, has given to our meeting, well indicates the essen-tial object of our labors. The Peace Conference cannot fail in the mission incumbent upon it; its deliberations must lead to a tangible result which the whole human race confidently expects."[5]

Willem Hendrik de Beaufort, foreign minister of The Netherlands, took the same theme of peace and related it to the grand setting where the dele-gates met on opening day: an octagonal room with towering walls topped by a windowed cupola, the whole adorned by immense paintings in Rube-nesque style. One painting, he said, deserved the delegates' special attention. There, over the entrance, was a representation of the Peace of Westphalia in which the figure of Peace was shown entering the salon to shut up the tem-ple of Janus—a temple traditionally kept open in time of war and closed in time of peace. It was Beaufort's hope that this classical allegory was a good omen for the conference and that when the delegates had completed their work they would "be able to say that Peace, which art brought into this hall, has sallied forth to shower her blessings upon the whole human race." To this hope, according to the official record of the conference, there was "unanimous assent."[6]

Beaufort's graceful allusion to Peace and the Roman god Janus was just that: an allusion, a rhetorical device. Not Beaufort nor any other delegate in the hall could recapture the depth of meaning that a classical reference had had for the seventeenth-century artists whose work covered the walls and the cupola of the room where the delegates sat. For those artists, the specifics of the signing of the Treaties of Westphalia or, in other paintings, the life of Prince Frederick Henry of Orange (in whose honor the palace had been built) were not, by themselves, sufficient to express the full meaning of what was happening. That meaning could only be shown by placing the events within a larger framework. Since they were working in the tradition of the late Renaissance, the framework that came naturally to their minds was a classical one. So the nineteenth-century delegates, in their sober suits of black and brown, were surrounded by the romping gods and goddesses of ancient Greece and Rome, and Prince Frederick Henry himself—an astute and powerful Dutch leader of the mid-seventeenth century—appeared in classical mode: driving out the Vices, parading in a Roman triumph. It was a lost world of meaning that surrounded the delegates in the Orange Salon, and they might well congratulate themselves on their modern sensibilities, free of these trammels of the past.

They were not, however, free of trammels of their own. They might not relate in any meaningful way to the painted Muses sporting on the sacred heights of Parnassus, but they had their own sacred sites, their own allegiance to a modern Parnassus of thought whose validity they did not question. No less than the artists of the mid-seventeenth century were they people of their time whose ideas and expressions were shaped by the conventions of their time. For them, the Peace of Westphalia had no allegorical resonance. Its significance lay in the fact that its date—1648—was usually taken as the date for the start of the European state system, and to this system of states they were bound by a hundred ties. Their gods and goddesses were rolled into one single figure, the State. To it they gave an unquestioned allegiance that, in some cases, bordered on worship and that, in every case, colored the words spoken and the actions taken at the conference.

The delegates were exactly what their name implied: representatives of a power not their own, deputed to defend and, if possible, secure the interests of that power in the meetings at The Hague. If that could be done through cooperation with the representatives of other states, well and good. If not— as in the case of the limitation of armaments—that was too bad. But in no case and in no wise must the state and the power of the state be diminished or undercut. For these heirs of nineteenth-century thought about nationalities, independence, sovereignty, interests, and freedom, there was no doubt whatsoever where these different strands of thought led. They culminated in the state. Only through the state could nationality be protected, independence be maintained, sovereignty be exercised, interests be pursued, and freedom be kept free. And, given the late nineteenth-century system of mutually suspicious and competing states, this was not an unreasonable conclusion. It did, however, make for difficult negotiations.

Take the attempt to agree on rules for land warfare. The delegates were building on centuries of effort to restrain and control the use of force. Hugo

Grotius was only one of the eminent authorities who could have been cited on the subject. The delegates saw their task as giving these efforts a practical base in contemporary international affairs. To this end they took a declaration of 1874 as their starting place. The benefit of this action was that a number of states had already been involved in drawing up the rules that the declaration contained. The drawback was that none of the states represented at the conference in Brussels, where the declaration had been worked out in 1874, had done anything with it since. Indeed, Great Britain had remained aloof from the whole proceeding, and the British representative at Brussels had had strict instructions to observe but not to participate. The idea seemed to be that British soldiers were only to be guided by rules based on a British assessment of what was right and proper in warfare.

By 1899 national pride had climbed down enough to allow a British military representative, Sir John Ardagh, to participate in the conference's efforts to modernize and harmonize the 1874 rules for land warfare. But this was an arm's-length kind of participation, as if too close an association, too deep an involvement, would somehow denigrate the power he represented. He objected first of all to the idea of a convention or treaty, saying that the rules ought rather to be expressed as guidelines for the states' instructions to their troops. As for Great Britain, it would, of course, cooperate even if the rules were embodied in a treaty, but it reserved to itself the right to choose which rules it would make part of its own manual of instructions. It could not bind itself to rules it might later find inappropriate or even dangerous to the safety of the military forces for whom it was responsible. "This full liberty to accept or modify the articles is of supreme importance to us."[7]

In the event, Ardagh's assertion of Britain's freedom of judgment and adherence to its own standards and responsibilities did not prevent final British agreement to the Convention with Respect to the Laws and Customs of War on Land.[8] Even national pride could see some advantage in coming to general agreement on rules for the conduct of war. But the British argument, with its insistence on British freedom of judgment, served notice of the difficulties that lay ahead as people struggled to work out a satisfactory relation between national and international claims on their lives and loyalties. Here, in little, were the arguments of the coming century against other assertions of an international presence, cautious as those assertions might be: the activities of the League of Nations, the efforts after World War II to give international expression to human rights, the late-century drive to establish courts of international criminal law.

The delegates of 1899 rested on the certainties of the nineteenth century regarding the rights of the state (extensive), the role of the public in international affairs (minor), and the responsibility of the great powers for the maintenance of Europe's political balance (major). The world that engendered these certainties was disappearing even as the delegates gathered at The Hague, but the ideas they held did not follow that world into history. Their ideas lingered far into the twentieth century, during which they at times bedeviled and at times lent force to the century's effort to define and achieve justice in an international setting. Of particular importance in that struggle were the ideas associated with the rights of the state. Each new state that came into the system—and there were many—was eager to claim the widest possible scope for the exercise of the sovereignty it had just won. When that desire came up against the continuing attempt to place individual human beings in some direct relation to international standards of behavior, conflict immediately ensued and continued throughout the century.

In this attempt to add a focus on human beings to the traditional emphasis on states, the delegates of 1899 wrought more than they knew. Paradoxically, it was where they were the most traditional that they were the most innovative—at least in the long term. Their effort to reach agreement on a limitation of armaments and restraint on the development of new weapons was a complete failure, as skeptics had predicted it would be. Their steps toward an arbitration "court" were so tentative as to offer an ample target for criticism. It was in consideration of that most traditional of subjects, rules for warfare, that they provided material for an extraordinary assertion of individual rights in the future. In the war crimes trials conducted by the Allied powers following World War II, the Hague Convention with Respect to the Laws and Customs of War on Land was a bulwark of the case for the prosecution, and it was cited in the judgment at the Nuremberg trial of the major German war criminals. Clearly this was beyond anything the delegates would have been able to conceive, given the central position of the state in their thinking, and yet they had laid the groundwork for this assertion of individual rights against the rights of the state.[9]

So traditional was the subject of rules for warfare, and so abundant was the work that had been done on it, that the delegates of 1899 were comfortable with the subject. It fit their frame of reference even though, at bottom, it shifted their focus from state actions and responsibilities to the actions, responsibilities, and protection of individual human beings. Their conceptual cover for this shift, the idea that allowed them to do it without apparent mental dissonance, was the expectation that the states that signed the treaty would incorporate the rules it embodied into their instructions to their own armed forces. Thus the burden of execution was transferred back to the states, where, in the delegates' thinking, it properly belonged. The rules still had to be agreed on, however, and it was in the effort to come to agreement that the delegates found themselves considering what international standards ought to guide the actions of human beings—individual human beings, not states—in actual combat and in collateral wartime activities such as care of the sick and wounded, the treatment of prisoners of war, and the behavior of military personnel in occupied territory.

Two principles of great future importance emerged from these discussions. The first was that individuals had international rights that were to be protected even in wartime. The discussions at The Hague and the Hague Convention itself were very specific as to the wartime circumstances in which these rights were relevant. Their purpose was to extend protection to prisoners of war and, especially, to the civilian population of occupied territories. The intended effect of these protective rules was the limitation of the activities of the occupying forces. Victory was not to confer complete freedom of action on the victorious power. Although in command of an area and possessed of destructive capabilities, the victors were yet to stay their hands from certain actions. They were not to force either prisoners or the population to fight against their own country or to take an oath to the occupying power. They were not to hold the civilian population collectively responsible for the hostile acts of individuals, nor punish them on that account. And, of primary importance in the war crimes trials and in later arguments that individuals did indeed have international rights, not just in wartime but in general, was the following: "Family honour and rights, individual lives and private property, as well as religious convictions and liberty, must be respected."[10] Much was built on this slender but critical foundation.

The second principle was that certain international laws and customs were inviolable. They could not be changed even by treaty action. This principle effectively limited what the delegates felt they could do in their task of bringing the rules of land warfare up to date. The issue first arose in a rather obscure discussion of the right to send an agent (a *parlementaire*) from one contending force to another to communicate directly with the force commander. The Brussels Declaration, which the delegates were using as a model, gave the commander the right to set a period when he would refuse to receive such an agent. If a parley was sought anyway, the parlementaire would lose the inviolability that otherwise protected him. The delegates of 1899 struck out this provision on the grounds that the right to send a parlementaire was grounded in the law of nations as was the inviolability of his person in his role as messenger. The conference could not give legal standing to the proposition that this right and this protection could be changed at the will of a belligerent.

When the issue arose again, this time in connection with an attempt to make military necessity a limiting factor on the rule to protect the honor and rights of civilians, the delegates refused to sanction the change. As one delegate put it: military necessity might, as a special case, override this protective rule, but "it is impossible to admit the destruction of human rights as a legal thesis."[11] There were, in other words, limits to the changes that even states could make in the treaties that bound them. Such fidelity to overarching standards beyond immediate contemporary desires was important in 1899 and was to assume even greater importance in the years ahead, particularly in the search for international justice.

In one other respect the discussions of the delegates at the 1899 conference at The Hague foreshadowed the future. They took an initial step in the differentiation of justice in an international setting, a differentiation that was one of the hallmarks of the twentieth century. The century-long process was a complicated one, involving as it did the many concepts of justice that had been developed through the ages, the attempts to fit those concepts to prevailing ideas about the state and at the same time to adjust those ideas to the rapid changes in a century that seemed to make obsolescence the norm—in ideas, weapons, artistic expression, and political and economic institutions. By the end of the century, the general term *international justice* had acquired an abundance of differentiating adjectives: racial justice, labor justice, economic justice, generational justice, ecological justice, and gender justice. Nor were those all the permutations of meaning. There were changes across time as well, each change adding to what had gone before, until the term became a vehicle for the deepest hopes and desires of the century. At first the hope was for the fair settlement of international disputes, peaceful, if possible, but by force, if necessary, so that justice might be served. Then, following World War I, the goal was peace itself—peace that was seen as so absolute a requirement for the functioning of justice that the two were conceptually merged. Another war and another change: justice as retribution, as deserved punishment for acts that had plunged the world into war and outraged accepted standards of behavior. While efforts were under way to give lasting institutional expression to this conception of justice, other meanings were pushed to the fore. Distributive justice was the key virtue for the new states that entered the international system in increasing numbers following the World War II. This period also saw the remarkable differentiation of the blanket term *social justice* into many component parts—such as those mentioned above—a process that seems likely to continue as new groups seek international recognition for the justice of their claims.

All of this lay in a future that the delegates of 1899 could scarcely foresee.

Yet they, too, found the term *justice*—although an essential ingredient of their work—an inadequate guide for what they were trying to do. To have any resonance in an international setting the term had to be refined and given more subtle shades of meaning. The delegates working on the establishment of the Permanent Court of Arbitration made a start at this differentiation. In establishing the court as a means for the peaceful settlement of international disputes, they were concerned, they said, with a special kind of justice. The justice they had in mind was arbitral justice. As one delegate explained it, since the international system had neither courts nor law comparable to those within a state, arbitral justice "provides for the absence of all jurisdiction and tends directly to prevent recourse to force." It was the kind of justice that sovereign states could understand and accept, reserving to themselves, as they did, the final decision on whether to seek arbitration of any dispute in which they were involved. So arbitral justice was, in the delegate's words, "an enlightened utilization of the sovereignty of States." [12]

This "enlightened utilization" was not, of course, enough to prevent recourse to force by the very sovereign states represented at the conference. But, for the purposes of this study, that is not the point of the delegates' attempt to take the general concept of justice and try to make it fit the international context in which they were living. Here was an effort, albeit hesitant and restricted, to take justice out of its national-domestic context and make it an active player in the turbulent world of international politics. Hugo Grotius had tried the same move nearly three hundred years earlier in his celebrated work on the laws of war and peace. But the exiled Grotius was without political power and, in that work, he represented no one but himself. At The Hague in 1899 and throughout the century that followed, those engaged in the attempts to define and achieve justice in an international setting were the representatives of organized states. In the long run, that made all the difference.

PART ONE

CONDITIONS OF STRUGGLE

CHAPTER ONE

The Bright Chain of Reason

In the ongoing search for international justice there is one constant. Running through all the efforts to define and achieve that elusive goal is a belief in the power of reason. Like a bright chain, this belief winds through the years of violence and death and offers a handhold to those who might otherwise despair. The belief is born anew in each generation and offers a standing invitation for people to turn from their violent ways. The message is the same as in the divine invitation to the wayward children of Israel: "Come now, let us reason together."[1] As was the case with that ancient invitation, the modern one is frequently ignored.

But the belief persists, and in international affairs it finds expression in a hundred unobtrusive ways: conflicts resolved, boundaries drawn, compensation paid, prisoners released, elections held, wars brought swiftly to a halt before fighting can escalate to the point of no return. The belief finds expression also in international undertakings to have recourse to reason before having recourse to force, or—ideally—*instead* of having recourse to force. Some of these undertakings are well known, such as those in the Covenant of the League of Nations in which, among other things, the member states pledged themselves not to resort to war and always to maintain justice in international relations. There are similar pledges and invocations of justice in the United Nations Charter.

Far from being empty phrases, such declarations are a necessary public expression of the belief in reason in international affairs. They help keep the chain bright. They function as a ceremony of proclamation and dedication.

The flag of good intentions is run up, and pledges of allegiance are made. Then the grubby phase begins. After articulation comes the hard work of definition and application. Much of that work is, and has been, little known. It is not dramatic in the obvious sense. But defining a goal such as justice and applying it in specific situations—sometimes successfully, sometimes not—has a drama of its own. Each instance is one more link in the chain, a standing affirmation of the possibilities in human endeavor. Taken that way, the report of a commission that has determined the facts in a situation of confusion and recrimination, or an arbitral award that has defused a situation of violence, may stand out like a trumpet blast—a fanfare to the power of reason.

To take an example: one such fanfare was sounded in November 1933 in a telegram dispatched to the chair of a League of Nations committee dealing with a serious problem. International peace was threatened by an incipient all-out war between Colombia and Peru. The telegram came from two delegates to an international conference in Rio de Janeiro, Brazil. One delegate was from Colombia, the other from Peru. The telegram read in part: "We have the honour to inform Your Excellency that, in accordance with the Geneva Agreement of May 25th, 1933, the Colombo-Peruvian Conference opened in this city."[2]

From such dull prose trumpet fanfares may arise. The telegram meant, among other things, that Colombia and Peru were honoring their earlier commitment to stop fighting. For eight months they had threatened each other and fought sporadic battles for possession of Leticia, a district in the Colombian interior with a port on the Amazon River. The initial willingness to stop fighting could be attributed to a change of government in Peru, but the successful outcome of subsequent negotiations was the result of sheer slogging through the swamps of overweening national pride. The date of the telegram provides a clue. The agreement to have recourse to reason rather than to force was signed in Geneva in May 1933. The peace conference got under way five full months later after national pride had run through its repertoire of maneuvers for advantage, tactical delays, and the mounting of numerous high horses.

Tucked into the bland and formal phrasing of the telegram is the admission that it took the efforts of a third party to get the delegates to sit down together at all, and even then there was a question about the subjects they were willing to discuss: "The delegations got into touch through the friendly intervention of the Brazilian Chancellery. On the opening of the Conference, the two delegations decided to select as President His Excellency M.

Afranio de Mello Franco, Brazilian Minister for Foreign Affairs. The delegates are at present discussing the method and scope of negotiations."[3]

Flat and unmemorable as the message is, touchy and reluctant as the delegates were, the whole affair still represents a dramatic triumph of reason over force. For months, the governments and citizens of Colombia and Peru had been whipping themselves into a wartime frenzy. Now their representatives were sitting down together to discuss their differences. The naval vessels of the two countries had been withdrawn from their forward positions. Bombers were on the ground. The conscript armies that had been called up remained in their camps. Since both countries belonged to the League of Nations, they had, thereby, made a pledge to the principle of justice set out in the League Covenant. Now the way had been opened to take that pledge and give it life and breath in a working arrangement on the ground. By such means was international justice sought in the period between the two world wars. By such means it is still sought in negotiations that are, for the most part, conducted far from the glare and clamor of publicity. These negotiations are conducted quietly by people with the ability to stay the course—people akin to the Brazilian foreign minister who in 1933 oversaw the talks that eventually returned the disputed territory of Letitia to Colombia and cemented the shaky peace between that country and Peru.

The fact that Mello Franco did stay the course, did help bring the negotiations to a successful conclusion, attests to his belief in the power of reason. It attests also to his possession of the qualities without which reason is helpless and his skill in their use. Of all those qualities, patience is foremost. After that: tact and civility, persistence and good will. An awareness of context helps with perspective, and an eye for the long term keeps daily irritants in proper proportion. Beyond that are other necessary aids: humor, on occasion; a fund of good stories; an impervious ego; a knowledge of the combatants as well as of the conflict; and, finally, a strong sense of timing that says, "Now is the time to suggest a compromise solution" or "Now is the time to let chauvinism have play."

All these qualities Mello Franco had in good measure. By his deployment of them in the service of reason—and, ultimately, in the service of justice—he not only kept bright the belief in the power of reason in international affairs. He also placed himself in the long procession of those who have shared that belief and have acted on it, sometimes at the cost of their lives, often at the cost of misunderstanding. Like Hugo Grotius, who taught that reason was the very highest principle of nature,[4] these, too, have helped forge the chain of belief in reason and have kept it bright. It, in turn, has joined them all together. Winding as it does through centuries of effort, the chain binds into one faithful company all those in the past who placed their trust in reason and all those in the present and future who still believe that people *can* sit down together and work out their differences.

CHAPTER TWO

The Faithful Company

Members of the faithful company of those with trust in reason come from different countries and periods of time. They have different personalities and approaches to life and to international affairs. They differ vastly in appearance. If, through some magic, members of this company could be seen all together, it would be hard to credit that, for example, Lord Robert Cecil, with his crook neck, his squashed hat, and his habit of sinking in his chair until he was almost out of sight had anything in common with the erect and elegant Dag Hammarskjöld. Yet, different as they were, there were qualities that marked them as members of the same company. There was, above all, devotion to the international organizations that they served. For the Briton, Cecil, it was the League of Nations. For Hammarskjöld, a Swede, it was the United Nations. These organizations were, for each of them respectively, both a barrier against force as the final arbiter in international affairs and the means through which nations, working together, could achieve international justice.

Cecil never held high office at the League, but, in or out of office, he worked ceaselessly for its success, believing that only through an organization such as the League could the nations avoid destroying themselves in war. He summed up his belief at a meeting of the League Council in 1931 when Japan's invasion of Manchuria seemed a deliberate mockery of all that the League—and Cecil—hoped to achieve: "The substitution of reason for violence in the settlement of international disputes, the strict observance of international obligations, the promotion of friendship and co-operation between nations—these are the chief objects for which the League of Nations was brought into existence."[1] No matter how often the nations turned away from these goals, Cecil never lost his faith that the day would come when reason would prevail.

Cecil did his work in relative obscurity, whereas Dag Hammarskjöld, as secretary-general of the United Nations, was much in the public eye. Yet Hammarskjöld, like Cecil, faced actions that seemed to mock the purpose of the organization that he served. Twenty-five years after League member Japan invaded Manchuria, UN members Great Britain, France, and Israel invaded Egypt. Like Cecil, Hammarskjöld came quickly to the defense of the organization that was supposed to prevent such acts. In the midst of the crisis, he went before the UN Security Council to declare, "The principles of the Charter are, by far, greater than the Organization in which they are embodied, and the aims which they are to safeguard are holier than the policies of any single nation or people."[2] Like Hammarskjöld's dress, his manner of speech was more elevated than that of Cecil, but his purpose was the same: to hold nations to the pledges they had made for a peaceful resolution of their disputes.

Scores of names could be added to those of Hammarskjöld, Cecil, and Mello Franco. There was, for example, Mineichiro Adachi, an exquisitely courteous and dapper member of the Japanese elite. Headlines went to the prime ministers and foreign ministers who put in occasional appearances at meetings of the League of Nations. Adachi was one of those who, without headlines—indeed, without much notice at all—quietly made the League work in the 1920s. When a disagreement arose, he could identify the worth in each position and then work out a way around the difficulty. At one point of delay in the deliberations of the committee that wrote the statute for the Permanent Court of International Justice, he remarked that one argument being advanced was the more logical argument and the other was the more humane. What was needed was to reconcile the two.[3] No one could surpass Adachi in the reconciliation of such differences.

Adachi was involved in the League's efforts to protect minorities, to resolve the recurring differences between Germany and Poland, to devise an agreement for the security of states so that they could put aside their unceasing vigilance and suspicion. He headed the committee that brought the construction of a new League of Nations building to successful completion. All this, and yet this kind of work was so little known that, on his death in 1934, the *New York Times* managed to write an entire obituary that did not once mention his international service at the League.[4]

In 1929, when Adachi was serving as president of the League Council, he put into words the faith that had sustained him through hours of thankless work: "We have victories yet to win—for international justice, arbitration and peace, the condition of well-being for all. What we have already achieved is a guarantee of the successes that the League will gain in the future." And he concluded his remarks with a statement that might well have been emblazoned on a banner as the motto of this faithful company: "Modest as our work must sometimes seem, we must never forget the greatness of our aims."[5]

Those who did this modest work were not necessarily modest in themselves. Certainly not many were as retiring as Mineichiro Adachi. There could scarcely be a greater contrast than that between Adachi, who, along with everything else he did, served three years on the governing council of the International Labour Organization, and Albert Thomas, the ILO's first director. Adachi was delicately built and dressed with a careful attention to detail from his high wing collar to the spats that set off his polished shoes. The Frenchman Thomas was a great bear of a man, all hair and beard and enthusiasm. He usually looked as if he had had a disagreement with his clothes and had lost the argument. He was exuberant, noisy, and impatient of delay. He was also outstandingly effective in his work for the labor organization and for the workers that it set out to protect. Thomas was, said his deputy director, a man "of tremendous vision and energy." He was also an "extremely warm-hearted human person, a brilliant and witty talker, as good a companion at a dinner-table as one could wish to find."[6]

To this brief listing might be added the name of Mary Wooley, president of Mount Holyoke College for thirty-seven years and a delegate from the United States to the 1932–33 League-sponsored disarmament conference. Tall, distinguished-looking, and decisive, Wooley might have treated her appointment to the conference as the sop to women's organizations that it undoubtedly was, but she chose not to do so. She attended the disarmament sessions regularly and spent much time and energy in efforts to educate the public about the work of the conference. She had gradually lost confidence in the ability of governments to change in any profound way, no matter how obviously necessary. Her hope was in the public, but she feared that the public did not know or understand what was happening internationally. "How many millions of our countrymen are ignorant of the vital things of which you have been speaking!" she exclaimed at one of the many meetings she attended on the international situation.[7] An educated public would be able to press for necessary change, and to that education Wooley devoted her energies.

Then there was Sarah Wambaugh, a ladylike graduate of Radcliffe College. Wambaugh's rise to prominence at the international level was not a response to pressure from any women's organization. She was, quite simply, the reigning expert on plebiscites, both in the interwar period and in the years immediately following World War II. Wambaugh's father had taught at Harvard Law School, and Wambaugh herself was very much a part of the academic community in Cambridge, Massachusetts. With this background, she might have stayed safely in that haven for scholars, exchanging ideas with those of similar inclinations and training. Instead, she went straight into the field. In the mid-twenties she was in the middle of a border feud between Chile and Peru and spent ten months on a ship anchored off the Peruvian coast so that she and the Peruvian delegation she was advising could be safe while working out details of a proposed plebiscite to resolve the issue.[8]

In the mid-thirties she was in the Saar Basin, the industrial district between France and Germany that had been administered by the League since the end of World War I. With preparations being made for an election that would decide the Saar's future after the League administration had ended, Wambaugh was there to help oversee the election. She had been provided with lists of eligible voters by the Deutsche Front, a pro-German organization that stridently advocated the Saar's union with Germany. The lists were hopelessly biased, and Wambaugh discarded them and set out to compile her own. She was busy with this when she was visited by the journalists Edgar and Lilian Mowrer, who were in the Saar to cover the election. Theirs is the picture of this Cambridge scholar, calm and competent amidst the clamor of a violently contested election, making sure that the voting was free and fair: "And if anyone voted twice, or in a district other than his own, it certainly was not Miss Wambaugh's fault." [9]

Not to be forgotten in this list are those whose weapon in the cause of reason is humor. They caper along in the procession of the faithful, turning intellectual cartwheels and inviting the world to laughter—and reflection. Behind the mask of humor stands a moralist. "God made me good," remarked Emery Kelen, a caricaturist who flourished in the 1920s, "but the capsized values of our time, a world war, and a salvo of revolutions made a jester out of me."[10]

Jesters were in good supply in those years. It was a period when international ambitions were high and the gap between rhetoric and reality often very large. The jesters pointed to the gap with glee and tried to nudge the realities of the decade a little closer to the ambitions that had been expressed in such documents as the Pact of Paris and the Covenant of the League of Nations. It amused them that the mighty of the earth had in the Pact of Paris "outlawed" war and that the League of Nations, with its high hopes, was still meeting in hotel rooms in Geneva. Kelen and his partner, Alois Derso, followed the activities of the League with affection but with an eye for its absurdities and for the extravagant expectations of its devotees. Their affection and amusement found expression in *The Geneva Testament*, a folio of spirited drawings and text that declared on its opening pages:

> In the beginning, the hotels were empty, but the spirit of Wilson hovered over Lake Geneva.
> Darkness was everywhere, and the nations were separated by an abyss.
> The spirit of Wilson said: "Let there be light!"
> Secret diplomacy disappeared at once! Three thousand journalists were accredited to the League of Nations, and Cook's Travel Agency began regular tours.
> Then the Spirit created permanent delegates, visiting experts, lawyers, and international civil servants. . . .
> And the Spirit blessed them and said, "Be fruitful and multiply."[11]

Many of the hopes of the interwar period were, of course, invested in the League of Nations, that infant organization looking for a home on the shores of Lake Geneva. The city itself could be gray and gloomy, but it could also sparkle with a light that seemed to reflect the bright promise of the League's early days. Salvador de Madariaga, who came to the League in 1921, looked back lovingly at that bright Geneva: "It was still a city, not yet a garage; and the light from the blue sky brightened and freshened the scene and made it as new as if it had just come out of the hands of the Creator."[12]

Madariaga had come from his native Spain to work in the League secretariat. He and his companions were "animated with a new spirit and a new hope. No more wars. We were to organise things so that conflicts were all settled round the table. Who could doubt that we should succeed when the Lake reflected that immaculate sky and there was no shadow to be seen anywhere?"[13]

Disappointment and failure did not sour Madariaga. It propelled him into the ranks of the humorists who indefatigably pointed out the idiocies of the age. There was scarcely an aspect of the international scene that Madariaga did not turn upside down to show the absurd underside of accepted arrangements. Was it empire, with its creed of "civilizing" the darker races and teaching them to work? Madariaga praised the higher wisdom of those races. Like the Spanish, they knew that leisure was to enjoy life, and he cited a Spanish comedy in which an idler is asked, "But don't you ever feel that you want to work?" and the idler replied, "Yes, but I refrain."

Madariaga pointed out the similarity between the behavior of states and the behavior of brigands: the brigands authorized themselves to seize other people's property; the states authorized themselves to seize other people's territory. He took wicked delight in the account of the French school-teacher who, at a ceremony honoring veterans of the Great War, thought to further the cause of peace. She had her pupils sing anti-war lyrics to the tune of *La Marseillaise* and was baffled to find that the veterans were upset. In a more serious vein, Madariaga mocked the world's reliance on national borders—the borders that divided one state from another, as if to deny the obvious fact of their interdependence. The borders were, he said, a sign of the world's spiritual "insolidarity."[14]

Jesters such as Madariaga and Derso and Kelen issued an invitation to laughter, but the thrust of their jest was an appeal to reason. No less than the rest of the faithful company, humorists relied (and still rely) on reason to perceive and then correct what is wrong or ridiculous in accustomed international arrangements. When the American humorist Will Rogers remarked that diplomacy was the art of saying "nice doggie" while looking around for a rock, he was doing more than making a joke. He was inviting serious consideration of an international system in which today's friends might well be tomorrow's enemies and even friends spy on each other and spend fortunes on defense.

So the procession goes on, its members separated by time, temperament, and country of origin but joined by their common belief in the power and final triumph of reason. They would not be flattered by or even care much about the tribute that has been paid to them here. They were and are more concerned with the results of their work than with any credit they might earn. Of no one is this more true than of another Hammarskjöld, this one very little known in his own time and now completely obliterated in the public eye by the reputation of his younger brother Dag. Yet if the first world court, the Permanent Court of International Justice, got off to a solid start in 1922 and functioned effectively for the twenty or so years of its existence, it was due in large part to the quiet labors of Åke Hammarskjöld.

The court was the epitome of the belief in the power of reason. Here the states of the world were to bring their disputes to be settled in accordance with the law—that set of principles and rules that had been built up over ages of conflict and that aimed at justice. Imperfect, incomplete, bearing clear marks of its Western European origins, that law which was the hope of the faithful found its first permanent home in the court that Åke Hammarskjöld served with such devotion. As the first and most influential registrar of the court, he set up the secretariat—the staff that enabled the court to function effectively. He initiated and oversaw an impressive series of publications. He arranged quarters for the court in the Peace Palace at the Hague. He defended its budget at the League of Nations and persuaded the League to help fund the court's reference library. He helped set up the procedures of oral and written arguments that are still in use in the International Court of Justice, the successor to the Permanent Court.

All of this, plus Hammarskjöld's knowledge of the law and his devotion to its cause in international affairs, served to prepare him to step from the administrative to the judicial side of the court. In 1936 he was elected a judge of the court, but he died shortly afterward, before he could make a mark in his new position. At his memorial service in the Peace Palace the first movement of Schubert's "Unfinished Symphony" was played. The feeling was strong among those who knew him that his work was unfinished, that, if he had lived, he would have made an even greater contribution to international justice than he had already done.[15]

As it was, his contribution was great, and it continues today in the work of the International Court of Justice. Åke Hammarskjöld had in full measure the devotion to duty that, years later, was to be so marked in his younger brother at the United Nations. He had, too, the now-legendary family capacity for sustained periods of work, often staying up all night to oversee translations or publications that would be needed in court the next day, and then appearing as usual in his place in the court, robed and self-contained, to see that all went as it should with the support operations. The two brothers, Åke and Dag, shared many characteristics: penetrating intelligence, love of the arts, wide-ranging interests and knowledge, and an unquestioned commitment to public service.

There is a clear line connecting the characteristics of these remarkable brothers with their remarkable parents, Hjalmar and Agnes Hammarskjöld. Their father was a man of formidable uprightness, a public figure with a devotion to principle that often made him unpopular; their mother, an open, warm, deeply religious woman—the fire at the heart of this somewhat forbidding family structure. Here was the source of much in the lives of the two brothers, a rich and complex heritage which they then took in hand to shape and reform, each in his different and individual way.

There is a clear line also that connects the careers of the three male Hammarskjölds with efforts to achieve international justice from the beginning of the twentieth century to the present day. The line runs from the Hague Conferences of 1899 and 1907, through the construction and dedication of the Peace Palace in 1913, through World War I and the establishment of the League of Nations and the Permanent Court of International

Justice in 1919, and on through another world war and the establishment
of the United Nations in 1945. It would be tedious to list all the Hammarskjöld connections along the way. To put the case in general terms, when
efforts were made to substitute reason for force in international affairs in
the twentieth century, a Hammarskjöld could frequently be found somewhere in the wings, if not actually center stage.

Briefly, Hjalmar was a delegate to the second peace conference at the
Hague, was a member of the Permanent Court of Arbitration, and served as
an arbiter in several important international cases. Åke was at the peace conference in Paris at the end of World War I, served for a short time in the
secretariat of the League of Nations, and helped write the statute for the
Permanent Court of International Justice, to which he then devoted the rest
of his life. His father continued to be active internationally, especially in efforts to codify existing international law. And young Dag, after completing
his education, rose swiftly to high rank in the Swedish Foreign Service, took
part in the Marshall Plan negotiations, and served as a delegate to the UN
General Assembly before becoming its best-known secretary-general.

This family saga is of interest in itself, but its chief interest here is that it
neatly mirrors the international saga of efforts to bring reason to bear in international affairs and so to achieve some measure of justice there. Through
Hjalmar Hammarskjöld we can touch the hopeful beginnings early in the
century when arbitration seemed an adequate answer to international conflicts. Following World War I there is Åke Hammarskjöld and his passionate belief—shared by many—that justice required that peace be preserved
and, moreover, that it *could* be preserved through the institutions that had
been set up after the war. Following another world war we have the United
Nations and the conviction of Dag Hammarskjöld that the charter of that
organization adds up to something greater than the political compromises
that brought it into being—that it is, in fact, a constitution for what he
called a "new community of nations."[16] He strongly believed that such a
community was coming into being, however slow and hesitant the pace.

One way of understanding this international saga is through an exploration of some of the ways in which justice has been conceived throughout
its course. It was Åke Hammarskjöld who described the idea of justice that
prevailed in the years following World War I. In 1930 in a speech at the
Royal Institute of International Affairs in London, Hammarskjöld characterized the postwar setting as a dynamic one in which the goals of peace and
justice had been combined into one. "Peace *is* justice," was the postwar
theme, said Hammarskjöld, "meaning that the ideal was the maintenance of
peace really at any cost—of course, if possible, with all due respect for legal

rights, but if necessary by conciliation, by adjustment, even if it entailed the sacrifice of such rights. It was considered, in other words, that respect for legal rights might in certain circumstances, have to yield before other considerations, of a historical, or, if you like, of a political nature."[17]

Hammarskjöld contrasted this with the period before World War I, a period in which the prevailing idea was peace *through* justice, even though that meant that war might ensue: "This was, to my mind, at that time held to be so true that, in order to vindicate legal rights, one was, if necessary, prepared to accept international unrest; the maintenance of such rights was, in principle, preferred to their violation, even should the maintenance entail armed conflicts."[18]

The pre-war attitude that justice must be upheld even at the cost of war was well expressed, in simpler and less convoluted fashion, by Alfred Thayer Mahan in 1899. Mahan, a U.S. Navy veteran and a theorist of the importance of sea power, was worried by the publicity surrounding the 1899 conference at The Hague and by what he saw as an undue emphasis on obligatory arbitration for the settlement of international disputes. Quite simply, there were times when a nation needed to fight: "The great danger of undiscriminating advocacy of arbitration, which threatens even the cause it seeks to maintain, is that it may lead men to tamper with equity, to compromise with unrighteousness, soothing their conscience with the belief that war is so entirely wrong that beside it no other tolerated evil is wrong."[19]

The wars of the early twentieth century had made this attitude, and the concomitant idea that peace could be achieved through the forcible defense of justice, a far less attractive ideal in practice than it was in theory. The Russo-Japanese War of 1904–5, in which mass armies had fought to exhaustion, the Balkan Wars of 1912–13, with their shocking and well-reported atrocities, and World War I, which had bled white its European participants and played havoc with long-established political and economic institutions—all these helped discredit the idea that peace would be the outcome of the forcible defense of justice. With each group attaching the label of justice to its own cause, however flagrantly self-serving, perpetual unrest, not peace, was the outcome of this approach.

If, however, as Åke Hammarskjöld had observed, peace was the necessary condition for justice, the ideas and the actions that flowed from that belief created an entirely different situation. "Peace *is* justice" was his way of describing the postwar approach to justice in international affairs. Another way of putting it would be to reverse the pre-war phraseology and say that in the postwar setting the prevailing idea could be expressed in the phrase "justice *through* peace." The appeal of this can only be understood against the background of the wars of the early twentieth century and, in particular, of World War I. With the horrors of that war fresh in mind, people were motivated to act on the idea of "justice through peace" by giving it institutional and practical expression.

As Hammarskjöld pointed out, this approach was not passive. If necessary, economic sanctions and collective military action could be called for under the League Covenant. The deepest hopes, though, lay elsewhere. The League could take notice of treaties that were out of date or that threatened world peace and could urge reformative action. The plan was for ongoing observation and assessment of the needs and stresses in the international system so that timely adjustments could be made and peace preserved. Here, in this provision, said Hammarskjöld, "I find a notion of justice which is not the narrow notion of legal rights, but rather of a sort of immanent justice, the tangible expression of which is the maintenance of peace."[20]

The words were Åke Hammarskjöld's, but the idea was general among those people in the interwar period who looked beyond individual nation-states to the international system of which the states were a part. Acting on the idea that peace was an expression of justice, and with some notable successes to support their faith, Hammarskjöld and others like him entered the 1930s ready to put their beliefs into action even in that charged and increasingly violent decade. The encounters of those years brought into sharp focus the struggle between this conception of international affairs and other, quite different ideas on which nations had long been accustomed to act. The struggle was not simply between the old and the new, although it was partly that. The struggle was also between perceptions, new and old, that took the world of sovereign states as a starting point and then diverged in significant ways. The one characteristic they retained in common was their creedlike quality. These were not just statements of opinion. They were articles of faith, with all that that implies about level of commitment and certainty of truth.

CHAPTER THREE

A Contest of Concepts

The world of the late nineteenth and early twentieth centuries was not a world of mindless assertions of power. When power was used, it was used for a purpose, and that purpose was defined by sets of ideas about the world and goals to be pursued there. That the pursuit often involved the use of force only shows how highly the goals were valued. They were felt to be worth fighting for. Policymakers followed a well-developed, if informal, line of moral reasoning that can be schematized in simple terms: from any set of goods and values (A), there followed a number of guides to behavior that might be formalized as rules or policy statements (B), and this, in turn, helped determine any actions taken (C), in an uncertain and dangerous world. The progression of A to B to C was direct and simple enough to allow for innumerable variations and almost any degree of explicitness and formality, a flexibility that policymakers had exploited to the full. By the early 1930s there were at least three well-established conceptual frameworks from which policymakers could draw besides the one that was slowly developing out of the Hammarskjöldian notion that peace was an expression of justice.

The Balance of Power framework is the best known and the most-studied of the three. The term is inadequate for the complexities involved, but it will serve to identify, if not to explain, a whole array of assumptions about international affairs and the need to prevent any single state or group of states from obtaining a preponderance of power. This framework provided the rationale and purpose for much diplomatic and military action in Eu-

29

rope throughout the nineteenth century, the so-called Century of Peace. It had not been discredited by its occasional failures to keep the peace in that century, nor by its glaring failure to prevent World War I. In the postwar world the ideas associated with the Balance of Power still had compelling force, a force that was morally grounded in love of country and the desire to defend that country and see it prosper.

The second framework was related to but separate from that of the Balance of Power. The complexities of its values and goals can be summed up in the term the Primacy of Order. In the recurring struggle between justice and order in international affairs, there was no doubt where the arguments of this framework led. Order was the essential good. Without order, commerce would be crippled, crops and animals destroyed, and the lives of ordinary people made intolerable through uncertainty and violence. Not incidentally, disorder was also a threat to the interests of the great powers, at home and abroad. The logic of the Primacy of Order helps explain the suppression of revolutionary movements in Europe in the mid-nineteenth century and the actions of the great powers, including Japan, in staking out islands of order and privilege in weak and turbulent China. In the New World, the United States, having erected the Monroe Doctrine as a shield against European intervention, appointed itself the guardian of order there. Time and again it intervened in Latin America, particularly in the Central American and Caribbean states, to assure the maintenance of that order which was, in this framework, the highest moral good. From the high moral good of order other goods such as peace, prosperity, and justice would surely flow.

The third framework was more recent than the other two, but by the time of World War I it had gained wide acceptance despite its obvious threat to the Balance of Power and the Primacy of Order. Its basic values and ideas about the world can be expressed as the Right to Independence. The arguments and justifications for action that grew out of this framework had kept Eastern Europe in turmoil for years as submerged nationalities in the Ottoman Empire sought freedom from Turkish rule. So long as the arguments were not advanced against themselves, the great powers of Europe could cheer on the various independence movements in Eastern Europe while still attempting to control and direct them to their own individual advantage. The contradictions in this "cooperative competition" were eventually too much, and the efforts at control broke down.

The result was the chaotic and bloody welter of the Balkan Wars of 1912 and 1913 and the swift descent into World War I. Ideas associated with the

Right to Independence were not weakened by that war. They were, if any-thing, strengthened by the assertion that self-determination would be one of the principles of the war's settlement. Liberty. Freedom of conscience. The right to self-government. These principles acted as powerful magnets for the desires of restless and discontented peoples and provided the justifi-cation and motivation for struggles against tyranny, however defined. Here also was a repertoire of ideas that could be attached to less noble causes, as people were to discover in the fierce conceptual struggles of the 1930s.

Finally, there was the framework to which Åke Hammarskjöld, Lord Robert Cecil, Mineichiro Adachi, Sarah Wambaugh, Albert Thomas, and others had pledged their lives and talents. Their views of the possibilities in this framework were heavily influenced by their views of the past. To them it was obvious that something different was required if the nations were to survive long enough to have any relations at all. The deficiencies of old ways of trying to manage international affairs had been made manifest by World War I. Not only did that war come despite the efforts of seasoned diplomats and policymakers to contain tensions as they always had. Once the war had started, those same seasoned professionals could not control or end it.

All this was to change. In the just world that was to come there would be no need for states to be suspicious of each other and to maneuver for advan-tage. Each nation would receive its due and have no cause for dissatisfaction or threat. Order would not have to be imposed. It would be the unforced outcome of agreement on peaceful means of change. Independence, too, would be a matter for agreement, not strife, and it would proceed along nat-ural and obvious lines of division.

This was the overarching vision that was contained in the term *justice through peace*. Here was a different conceptual framework for international affairs, a framework of thought and action that Hammarskjöld and others consciously opposed to that of the Balance of Power. The disastrous out-come of the balancing approach to international affairs was fresh in their minds, and they could see no compromise with the goal of balance. It was different with the goals of order and independence. They could see the need for order, and they held independence to be an obvious and unarguable good. Their quarrel was with the methods used to attain those goals. Those methods might be effective locally, but they were often damaging to the in-ternational system as a whole. The international system was one of their points of reference, and they knew—no one better—how fragile were the ties of common purpose that knit the system together. The 1920s had given hope that the ties were strengthening. Then came the 1930s.

The Balance of Power. The Primacy of Order. The Right to Independence. Justice through Peace. These were the dominant frameworks of
ideas and values that people brought to the international crises of the '30s.
To an observer standing outside the struggles of that decade, one of the
most obvious things about all four is their similarity. They all began with the
nation-state as the primary actor in international affairs. They all accepted
national interest as a legitimating concept for actions taken, whether to correct a power imbalance, restore order, support independence, or resolve a
dispute peacefully. They all faced recurring problems of definition. This
would seem to be more true of a concept such as justice than of interest, order, balance or independence, with their claim to reflect bounded and solid
realities. These are, however, highly contested terms, and they, no less than
justice, have to be defined and redefined and defined again through argument and experiment in the constantly changing circumstances of international life.

An observer would notice another striking characteristic of these four
frameworks of thought and values: their fluidity. They flowed into one another. They borrowed each other's vocabularies in order to appropriate the
largest possible amount of moral force and attractiveness to their own
cause. *Justice* as a good that no one questioned was particularly vulnerable to
these raids on vocabulary. Yet in the hands of Åke Hammarskjöld and others, both inside and outside of the international institutions of the time, this
conceptual framework maintained a distinct and separate identity. They, no
less than others of their generation, were wedded to the idea of the state as
the individual, sovereign, autonomous actor in international affairs. Yet
they also went beyond that to consider the international system as a whole,
a fact attested to by their emphasis on peace. No matter how much an individual state might benefit from the use of force, the system of which that
state was a part benefited most from the use of peaceful means to achieve
state ends. Peace was a collective good.

Those who were committed to this particular good differed in another
way from those whose commitment was elsewhere. They made persistent
attempts to separate out the "internationalness" of any question from its local and national aspects so that matters might be dealt with and judged by
new standards, less parochial than the old. There was little historical precedent for this, and the people trying it were feeling their way. The ten or so
years since the end of World War I and the beginning of the thirties did not
add up to a large block of time. Set against nearly three centuries of state-
centered thought and action it was insignificant. The idea that the ways of

thinking and acting developed during those ten years could have any effect internationally appeared almost ludicrous. Yet in the 1920s those ways had had an effect beyond any reasonable expectation. People had gained experience with an international point of view, the limitations of which were not yet obvious, and they had tools with which they could work: an international court, commissions of inquiry, arbitration panels, administrative tribunals, petitioning procedures, investigative committees, debates in the League Assembly, where the actions of states were subjected to public scrutiny, League Council proceedings, where—with the utmost tact and delicacy—states might be called on to justify their behavior. And, as a last resort, collective action.

Nor were these concerns and actions confined, as in the past, to Europe and the West. Tentatively, hesitantly, a worldwide international system was coming into being, a fact that contributed to the well-documented failures of the 1930s. Events that in the past might have had only a limited, local effect could now send shock waves around the world. The economic contraction that began in the United States in 1929 spread inexorably throughout the entire international system, and there existed neither the ideas nor the institutions to stop its spread. It was the same with many events in the decade of the thirties. The events were not only a test for the ideas of those who, like Åke Hammarskjöld, believed that international justice could be secured through peace. They were a test for *all* ideas about the international system. Rooted as those ideas were in the loosely knit states system of the nineteenth century, they proved to be inadequate to deal with the tightly meshed world that the thirties began to reveal.

Of the four frameworks discussed here, the one that emphasized justice through peace was perhaps the best suited conceptually to deal with this tightly meshed world. It was the most inclined to see beyond Europe to the international system as a whole. Institutionally it was weak, however, and its tools relied heavily on civility and reason. Those qualities were in increasingly short supply as the decade wore on and fearful or aggressive states pursued their own ends, heedless of the rest. In this changed atmosphere, the procedures of arbitration, conciliation, and the like could not function to restrain or even greatly affect the actions of the great powers. Failure in one area did not mean failure in all areas, however, and the procedures did not fall into disuse. They continued to function quietly and successfully in the more obscure corners of the world. Even in the thirties, people continued to gain experience in coping with the conflicts of that world. And from those experiences they began to complicate and enrich their ideas about international justice and about what might be required to make justice a reality in the world.

The framework of ideas and institutions that clustered around the concept of justice through peace was in no sense a winner in the conceptual contest of the times, but it did not disappear, either. Its lasting legacy, beyond the methods of dispute settlement that were pioneered under its influence, was the link between peace and justice that was forged by its adherents. The link was a strong one, and it persists to this day.[1]

CHAPTER FOUR

Invisible Barriers

Ideas about international affairs were not all that had been changed by the experiences of the first part of the twentieth century and, in particular, by the experience of World War I. The international system as it had existed throughout much of the nineteenth century had also been changed. A relatively stable system centered in Europe under the watchful care of a few great powers had been transformed into a diffuse and dynamic system beyond the capacities of the postwar world to direct or contain. The League of Nations was too weak to pressure and chastise as the great powers had done, and the former great powers were themselves weakened by the war and divided in council. Germany was defeated. The Austro-Hungarian Empire was dismembered. The formal courtesies between Great Britain and France barely served to cover their mutual suspicions. China was convulsed by inner struggles, and Russia was a battleground as its new Bolshevik leaders fought to secure control within and repel forces from without.

This left Japan and the United States as potential stabilizers of the international system, and neither wanted the job. Japan's outlook, interests, and power were directed to Asia, and the United States, which alone had the power to restrain adventurous states anywhere in the world, was restrained by its own ideology. Not only was the task of stabilization a risky one, it smacked too obviously of the "entanglements" that policymakers and public alike were anxious to avoid. George Washington's cautions still echoed down the years: "Why quit our own to stand upon foreign ground?" There were few in the United States to argue that among the changes wrought in

the twentieth century none was more profound than the erosion of that "detached and distant situation" on which Washington had placed his reliance
for the country's protection.[1]

Among those who did sense the shift was Georges Clemenceau, French
premier at the end of World War I and stubborn antagonist of Woodrow
Wilson at the Paris Peace Conference—that meeting of the victorious Allied powers where the fresh new world envisioned by the U.S. president was
to come into being. Clemenceau, bowed down as he was by the weight of his
years and his long experience in the battles of Europe, yet knew how to concentrate his strength. Tenacity was his motto and repetition his weapon in
the subtle battles at the negotiating tables. As would happen with Soviet negotiators during the Cold War, Clemenceau simply held on long after
everyone else was exhausted. He would then repeat, without change, the
hard-line position he had taken at the start of the negotiations, long hours
ago. He never tired of this tactic in his campaign to get Wilson, his upright
and fine-strung antagonist from America, to adjust the Wilsonian vision of
a new world to fit the realities of the old.

"We Europeans are a tough bunch," he would tell the weary Wilson. And
then, with a confiding air that seemed to bridge their differences: "Please do
not misunderstand me. We too came into the world with the noble instincts
and the lofty aspirations which you express so often and so eloquently." The
European experience had, however, been quite different from that of America: "Had our life lines been cast in the pleasant places across the Atlantic,
we too, I believe, would have developed and clung to the noble qualities
which you, Mr. President, assume are the universal heritage of man." And
then, gently, came the note of warning, the prophetic view of changes that
were occurring even as they contended with each other in Paris: "Yours has
been the best of all possible worlds, but there are signs and portents, and it
should be clear that your happy, your privileged position, will not endure
forever."[2]

The peoples of Europe who were newly freed from the bonds of empire
would have shared some of Clemenceau's bitter-fruit analysis of the situation at war's end, but they would not have swallowed it whole. They, too,
had been shaped by what the old warrior called "the rough hand of the
world in which we have had to live," and they were indeed "a tough bunch."
Like Clemenceau, they knew better than to rely on a "detached and distant
situation" for protection, since they had never been so fortunate as to have
one. Unlike Clemenceau, however, many of them still had dreams of a better world to come, and it was to these dreams that the Wilsonian vision
spoke. Buoyed by hope, the newly freed came rushing to Paris from their

war-ravaged lands, bringing with them searing memories of the past and extravagant expectations of the future. Both hope and experience drove them to seek the political haven of statehood with its promise of sovereignty and its sacrosanct status in international affairs. For people who had known repression and suffering in the grip of empire, statehood was more than just a goal. It was their longed-for salvation, the place where they could be secure at last behind inviolable borders and there, in safety, work out what was sure to be a glorious destiny in Wilson's new world.

Gone was the measured cadence of late nineteenth-century deliberations on the admittance of this or that candidate to the club of nations. Postwar Paris was overrun with applicants who buttonholed delegates to the peace conference, bombarded conference committees with their petitions, held public meetings, churned out pamphlets and manifestos, and generally filled the air with their clamorous demands for immediate, unconditional recognition that their own particular group deserved independent, sovereign statehood. They had reasons galore. They had grievances going back six hundred years and hatreds nourished through all the centuries since. They had promises real and imaginary. They had memories of Allied solicitation of their help in the war just past. Above all, they had Woodrow Wilson's words about self-determination and the establishment of boundaries along lines of nationality.[3] To the peacemakers in Paris it must have seemed that no village, farm, or herdsman's camp in all the world was beyond the reach of Wilson's vision or untouched by dreams of glory.

The situation at war's end raised in a new and pressing way a question that had long been a staple of debate among theorists of international law and political philosophy. The question itself was simple enough: What exactly was a state? Answers to the question, even among philosophers, revealed unexpected difficulties in defining what, at first glance, might seem obvious. Here was France. There were Great Britain, the United States, Italy, Japan, and all the rest of the Allied and Associated powers. Everyone knew that they were states. As states they were full actors in the international system, qualified to send delegates to Paris to sit in solemn and official judgment on the past and take part in shaping the future.

So far, so good. No one questioned the status of those powers or denied their right to the functions and prerogatives of statehood. But what of Czechoslovakia and Poland? Why were their delegates among the representatives at the conference and not those of the Ukraine, Armenia, or Azerbaijan? None of these five had existed as an independent state before the war, yet two were included in official proceedings and three (along with many others) were not. Why was India represented there? Why Canada,

Australia, New Zealand, and South Africa? Could portions of an empire be considered as states? If so, why not Ireland? For that matter, why not Korea? Koreans in general did not accept the legitimacy of Japanese imperial rule, and their representatives in Paris looked on this gathering of the great and powerful as a wonderful opportunity for redress. Throughout a long history of conflict between China and Japan for dominance in their country, the Koreans had maintained their own language and their own sense of self and of nationhood. Surely, then, if there were any justice in this new world of self-determination for nationalities, their claims would be heard and judged valid.[4]

But the Koreans, like dozens of fellow aspirants for statehood, never received the official blessing that would elevate them from private individuals to the status of recognized representatives of an existing or incipient state. "What a strange world it is," remarked one of the Koreans sadly; he might well have been echoed by any one of the Zionists or Arabs, Karelians or Georgians, White Russians or Montenegrins who wore paths of frustration around the perimeter of the charmed circle of established states. "The family of nations" was a name frequently used for that circle in 1919, entirely without irony or sarcasm. Suitors, however, were looked at askance, no matter how presentable. With the family of nations, as with private families, it helped a suitor to have powerful family members who would plead the suitor's cause. Rudolf Holsti, in Paris as the representative of a de facto Finnish government, spent weeks in fruitless courting until Wilson's adviser, Herbert Hoover, and French foreign minister Stephen Pichon took up the Finnish cause. Then events moved swiftly to recognition of Finland's independence.[5]

The truth was that in Paris in 1919 the theories of statehood that had been elaborated by jurists and philosophers throughout the nineteenth century played a very small part in the rough and tumble of the politics of power. The abstractions and general statements of the theories could only point in the general direction of statehood. They could not plot a path through the tangle of competing claims and disputed boundaries. The doctrine of the three elements is a case in point. As elaborated by the German law professor Georg Jellinek and widely accepted in the pre-war world, the doctrine seemed to provide a clear set of rules for determining the legitimacy of a state. To qualify as a state, three conditions had to be met. First, there had to be a population. Second, that population had to live in a specified territory. Third, within that territory, the population had to live under an organized government.[6]

When put to the test, the clarity and simplicity of these rules quickly ramified into complexities beyond the reach of philosophy or law and aroused emotions that found no place in academic explanations. International lawyers could set out with precision the practical consequences of recognized statehood. A state could send and receive envoys and expect that those envoys would enjoy immunity from local threat or harassment. A state could conclude treaties with other states and, in general, expect those agreements to be carried out if only because it was to the advantage of every state in the system to see that agreements were kept. A state could cooperate with other states in such matters as disease control, uniform standards for shipping, and international postal regulations. Finally, a state could conduct its own domestic affairs behind borders that would not be breached except in the most extreme circumstances.

All of this was true enough and none of it sufficiently explains the passions that beat against the peacemakers in Paris. Irish representatives asserted Ireland's "indisputable right to international recognition for her independence." Egypt claimed independent status "because independence is a natural and indefeasible right of nations." The Azerbaijan delegation asked for recognition of the Democratic Republic of Azerbaijan as an "absolutely independent state" and noted that, when performing the rite of recognition, the conference was engaged in "sacred work." From Circassia-Daghestan came a delegation asserting the "complete independence" of the peoples of Circassia and Daghestan and pointing out that recognition of their independence would enable them to serve as an example of democracy in their part of the world. Arab leaders took a different approach. They did not present themselves as suppliants but as allies in the war just past. They had come to Paris to claim the independence of Syria from the lands of the former Ottoman Empire. As Emir Faisal put it: "We are not asking for a favored position but merely for justice and the fulfillment of solemn promises. . . . We demand our rights and a recognition of these facts. Our lands should not be regarded as war booty by the conquerors."[7]

"Sacred work." "Natural right." Claims for "justice." Clearly there was more at stake in Paris in 1919 than simply meeting the formal requirements for statehood. There was more, too, than Clemenceau, for all his experience, could encompass in his bleak philosophy. The passion to belong, to be a part of a recognized state and gain personal identity from that membership, extended in many cases beyond the hoped-for borders of the state to the hoped-for world in which that state would function. It was not unusual for the applicants at Paris to ask for recognition as a state and then immediately ask also for membership in the League of Nations—an organization that did not even exist when the applications were made. From lands that had been overrun and parceled out for centuries the delegations came to Paris, asking to be a part of a world where they would at last be safe. Their safety would rest on twin pillars. First, they would be a state, that political entity with unassailable prestige in the twentieth century. Second, they would be a member of the League of Nations and, as such, enjoy protection from the aggressions and cruelties of the past. As the Lithuanian delegation put it, they were convinced that "peace, liberty, and the right of peoples would never be realized except through the League of Nations."[8]

The great stirring of peoples and erasure of borders that resulted from World War I and the Russian Revolution presented the peacemakers in Paris with a tabula of sorts on which to write the future. But it was not a blank tablet. It was filled to the very edge with the marks of battles, disease, displacement, hunger, bitterness, and material destruction. Small wonder that in the process of granting recognition to aspirant states, the conference officials appeared to be improvising standards in response to the rapidly changing and often-chaotic political situation. Sitting in Paris, they took testimony, studied maps and history, and then drew lines through the midst of the turmoil and said, in effect, "Here the quarrels must stop." Their answer to disorder was the creation of states.

The creative task of the peacemakers was clear when it came to the break-up of the Austro-Hungarian Empire. As victors, they could impose terms and boundaries and recognize the new states of Austria, Czechoslovakia, Hungary, and the Serb-Croat-Slovene State (later Yugoslavia). The break-up of the Russian and Ottoman Empires, however, presented problems that defied this kind of answer. The entire Middle East seethed with resentment at continued European assertions of the right to divide up the area into spheres of influence. Within a few months this resentment would break into open warfare in Syria and Turkey. As for Russia, the complications of that situation practically paralyzed the peacemakers. They feared the effect of Communist ideology in Eastern Europe. They hesitated to make a definitive move while the outcome of the Bolshevik revolution was not clear. They backed and then backed away from support for anti-Soviet invasions of Russia. Meanwhile, they recognized some states from the wreckage of imperial Russia and held others at arm's length, neither awarding nor denying the coveted prize of statehood while they waited to see what would happen.

This wait-and-see policy turned out to be definitive so far as some aspirant states were concerned. Without early recognition and effective support, a group that had seized the postwar opportunity to draw its own borders and elect its own officials could quickly find itself erased from the history it had hoped to enter as an independent state. This happened to Armenia, the Kuban Republic, Karelia, Georgia, the Ukraine, and half a dozen other states at the edges of the former Russian Empire. Estonia, Latvia, Lithuania, Finland, and Poland managed to gain the recognition that meant the difference between existence and nonexistence in a world where statehood was the sine qua non for membership. The gods of Olympus might have envied the power of the peacemakers at Paris, sitting on their mountaintop of victory and disposing of the lives of millions.[9]

For aspirant states there was one more chance after Paris, and that was admission to the League of Nations. The organization was still in the process of formation when applicants started knocking at its door. Procedures had yet to be worked out by the secretariat, the council, and the assembly as to how and when that door would be opened. The thirty-two states that had signed the covenant of the League were assured of a place as original members, as were any of the thirteen states invited to accede to the covenant. Beyond that the question of membership entered unexplored country. No one was quite sure what the organization was or how it might develop. Was it simply a conference of independent states similar to the congresses and conferences that had met at intervals in Europe in the aftermath of the Napoleonic wars? Or was it something different, something new under the sun, a collectivity with an existence separate from and in some ways superior to that of its individual members? The question was not an academic one. How it was answered would affect the meaning of membership. Further, the answer would make a vital difference in the future of the League.

In the end, criteria for League membership were established and applied with reasonable consistency, particularly where political considerations did not preempt the ground, as was the case with Germany and the other Central Powers.[10] In the end, too, membership in the League became a sufficient warrant for recognition of a new member by all the other members of the League, even if that recognition had been withheld prior to League acceptance. This apparently minor detail was of prime importance in helping establish the League as an entity with purposes and actions that could, in limited cases, trump the separate policies of its members. The path to the primacy of this collective action over the policies of the individual states was neither easy nor clearly marked out in advance. Rather, it was the unplanned outcome of fumbling and experimenting within an institution that gradually managed to achieve an identity of its own despite the reluctance of its most powerful members to allow it the slightest modicum of independent action.

By the end of the 1920s the League of Nations had fifty-four members, including all but one of the former enemy powers. Each of the members had unquestioned status as, in the words of the covenant, a "fully self-governing State, Dominion, or Colony." The wording was an explicit recognition of the complexity of political organization in the postwar international system and was, moreover, a careful compromise between theories of statehood and the realities that had emerged from the war. It allowed full participation for the parts of the British Empire, such as Canada or India, that had achieved a measure of independent action during the war. At the same time, the stipulation of "fully self-governing" precluded the parts of other empires, such as the French, the Dutch, or the Japanese, from claiming a place that the imperial powers would not have granted them anyway.

Thus, entrance into the circle of recognized states was achieved through a complicated mixture of the legal and the political. It was not simply a matter of meeting the formal requirements. The aspirant had also to make the right moves with the right people at the right time in a political environment that changed constantly and could turn threatening at any moment. Would-be states without the benefit of leaders such as Thomas Masaryk or Eduard Benes, with their persistence in urging the Czechoslovak cause and their contacts at high levels in the West, did not fare very well. When some members of the Six Nations of the Iroquois who were resident in Canada attempted to bring their grievances to the League in the mid-1920s, they were effectively denied a hearing on the grounds that the Six Nations did not constitute a state.[11] That, of course, is exactly the status the Iroquois were seeking, but they, like many other groups, ran up against the invisible barriers of influence and power that determined who would be included in the international system and who would be left out.

The years between the two world wars were years of testing and failure, but they were also years of accomplishment. Out of this complicated mix of successes and failures came broader, more sophisticated ideas about what constituted justice in international affairs and a re-evaluation of what might be required to maintain it there. The contentions and suspicions that were endemic in the system remained throughout the period, a hardy constant in international affairs. But the experiences of the interwar years, plus the searing experience of another world war, helped, in the long run, to strengthen the foundations of the hoped-for just world of the future.

PART TWO

WEAPONS OF PEACE

CHAPTER FIVE

Virtues, Old and New

Nothing is more indicative of the interwar trend toward a more tightly connected world than the international response to the 1931 Manchurian Incident. On the face of it, a railway explosion in Manchuria and the subsequent Japanese occupation of the area should not have generated much international comment. Violence in China, especially that involving the railway lines that everyone from local warlords to high government officials wanted to control, was nothing new. There was, however, a widespread international response to the incident, followed by international initiatives that, in the end, proved futile. The whole affair has become the very symbol of international failure—failure of nerve and failure to act when action was necessary. The affair is something else as well. It is a dramatic symbol of changing attitudes toward international affairs.

So, although the Manchurian Incident has been exhaustively studied, it is worth another look for what it reveals about the world of the early 1930s and the struggle of concepts and approaches to international affairs that was set off by an explosion in the Mukden suburb of Liut'iaokou the night of September 18, 1931. The incident began like the opening of a badly written opera: conspirators and secret plots; official orders of restraint deliberately delayed; hurried movements in the night; a figure kneeling beside a railway line to place packets of blasting powder against the track. Then an explosion rips the quiet of the night. There are shouts. The sound of running feet. After that, gunfire breaks out, sporadic at first but becoming heavier as well-trained Japanese troops swing into action and carry out the next stage of the conspiracy.[1]

The railway line was in one of the three eastern provinces of China—collectively, Manchuria. Having set the explosion as an excuse for action, the Japanese moved quickly against the Peiyang barracks north of Mukden and drove out the Chinese troops quartered there—sleeping men, unprepared for attack. Within a few days, Japanese forces had secured key points throughout the southern portions of the three provinces and had perfected the story they would tell to the world. If not examined too closely, the story was reasonably plausible: A squad of Japanese soldiers on routine night patrol had heard an explosion on the South Manchurian Railway, a railway that Japan owned, operated, and policed under an agreement with the Chinese government. When the members of the patrol went to investigate, they were fired on by Chinese troops hidden in a nearby field. Thereafter the Japanese had acted purely in self-defense and out of the need to protect both the railway and Japanese citizens throughout Manchuria.

The story was not widely believed, but the canons of diplomacy required a courteous reception of the lie while states with an interest in the matter decided what to do. The key word is *interest*. Under older approaches to international affairs and in a more loosely connected world, states with an interest in the matter would be those immediately affected: China, of course, since these were Chinese provinces; the Soviet Union, because Soviet territory bordered Manchuria on two sides; and Japan, where there was widespread approval of the result of the plot, if not of the method, and where the government was scrambling to make official policy fit the facts in the field while trying to reassert some measure of control over the military. Other powers might take an interest if their privileges or trade were threatened, but beyond that, what?

Why should it matter in London or Washington who governed Manchuria? Why should representatives of Sweden, Turkey, Spain, Romania, and the rest rise up in the assembly of the League of Nations to express their concern about Japanese actions? There was scarcely a state represented in that body that had not at some point in the past helped itself to neighboring territory. It was the type of action that had led Salvador de Madariaga to compare states to brigands who authorized themselves to seize other people's property. Japan, did not, of course, characterize its actions as those of a brigand, but it did argue that this was a matter that did not—or should not—concern the rest of the world. It was a matter outside the legitimate spheres of interest of the United States and the countries of Europe, not to mention countries such as Canada, Mexico, and Uruguay, whose delegates to the League felt compelled to comment on the situation. It was, said Japan, a matter between China and Japan. From the first, it professed its willingness to enter into bilateral negotiations with that country to resolve their differences.

Assuming that the Japanese foreign office meant what it said and, further, that it could deliver on its pledge of good-faith negotiations, the argument still would not wash. Twenty years earlier that kind of reasoning might have been accepted. Now it was far too late. China had already appealed to the League of Nations for assistance. Even if it had not, the argument would have been rejected. In 1931 it went completely against the temper of the times and seemed to mock the expectations that had been raised by the League Covenant and the Pact of Paris. Besides the general obligation not to resort to war that had been undertaken by Japan as a member of the League of Nations, there was the specific obligation set out in Article 10 of the League Covenant to respect and preserve the political independence and territorial integrity of all League members, which China had been from the first. These obligations had been grandiloquently reinforced by Japan's signature on the Pact of Paris (the Kellogg-Briand Pact), which outlawed war as an instrument of national policy. It was, in fact, Japan's ratification of the pact that had completed the necessary steps to bring it into force.

Finally, if these two undertakings were dismissed as smoke from the pipe dreams of postwar visionaries, there was the Nine-Power Treaty of 1922. The treaty was a solid, traditional agreement that would not have been out of place in the eighteenth or the nineteenth century. Nine of the world's states, including Japan, agreed that they would respect China's independence and territorial and administrative integrity. The treaty was, in effect, a pledge not to take advantage of China's well-advertised weakness. The Nine-Power Treaty, the Pact of Paris, the Covenant of the League of Nations—whether judged under the new dispensation or the old, Japan stood condemned for its actions in Manchuria.

Of particular interest is the fact that the widespread international response of dismay was generated less by Japan's breach of the traditional Nine-Power Treaty than by that country's failure to keep faith with the new promise of the League of Nations and the Pact of Paris. The sweep and intensity of the reaction was a measure of how high hopes had been raised. "The question before us is fraught with the gravest consequences for the future of the whole League." So said Juan Antonio Buero, Uruguayan foreign minister and delegate to the League of Nations. Joseph Connolly of the

Irish Free State, Christian Lange of Norway, Eduard Benes of Czechoslovakia, and a host of others in the League Assembly sessions devoted to the
situation responded in a similarly somber vein.[2]

Given the past history of relations between states, the outpouring of concern in the assembly was extraordinary. Consider Uruguay. By any standard
of interest as defined in the past, this small South American country would
not be involved in a controversy between China and Japan, giants in resources and population by Uruguayan measure, and on the other side of the
world to boot. Yet here was Buero saying that he had to speak up. To remain
silent would suggest approval of Japan's actions and would deprive Uruguay
of the moral authority necessary to support an appeal to the League on its
own behalf, should the need arise.

Buero put it this way: "If, in justification of what is happening in the Far
East, the peculiar position of those distant countries of Asia is adduced as
exempting them from the strict application of treaty law, on which the
Covenant, and especially Article 10, is based, what will be the position tomorrow when countries in other continents equally distant from Europe
are compelled to ask for assistance?"[3]

As if to underline the perception of universality in the principles being
defended by Buero and others, there was the report of the commission that
the League had dispatched to investigate the situation on the spot. Moder-
ate as the report was in tone and recommendations, its authors had no doubt
whatsoever that what was at stake was a universal good. Theirs was a ringing
affirmation of universality: "The interests of peace are the same the world
over. Any loss of confidence in the application of the principles of the
Covenant and of the Pact of Paris in any part of the world diminishes the
value and efficiency of those principles everywhere."[4]

This was an aspect of the new moral framework that might give the most
confirmed internationalist pause. As a guideline for action in the 1920s, the
idea of justice through peace had been successful enough to raise hopes very
high indeed. The intransigence of the Japanese began to reveal the costs of
maintaining a world where those hopes could flourish. The other side of the
promise of this new approach to international affairs was that a conflict anywhere in the world had the potential of becoming everybody's business and,
therefore, everybody's conflict. The internationalization of principles held
the possibility of also internationalizing conflicts that would once have been
seen as purely local. In theory, this had been foreseen by the framers of the
League Covenant. But the actuality—as in the Manchurian Incident—
brought sober second thoughts. Moral connectedness, like economic con-

nectedness, posed problems beyond the capacity of existing concepts and
institutions to handle.

The result was months of diplomatic floundering, the records of which
fill national archives and studies of which fill library shelves.[5] The Japanese
alone acted decisively and with confidence. No matter how bitter the inner
struggle in Japan to gain control of policy and the military, the stance taken
for the world's benefit was that of clean hands and a pure heart: they had
acted on well-accepted principles; they had acted to protect their own citizens resident in Manchuria; they had acted to restore order in a notoriously
violent and disorderly area. To buttress their account of their own actions,
they released photographs to show the seriousness of the situation with
which they had had to deal.

One photograph showed the scene of the explosion that began the whole
affair. It might have been the photograph of any spot of open country near a
railroad track except for the letters A through G marking the sites of actions
that would for the next eighteen months fix the attention of the world on
this unremarkable spot. A second photograph displayed the evidence that
had been gathered at the scene of the explosion: some broken ties, two short
pieces of rail, two garrison hats, and a bolt-action rifle with bayonet fixed.
Behind this neatly arranged pile a row of Japanese men, in solemn mode,
stare straight into the camera or down at the little pile of objects at their
feet. The neat arrangement of the pile spoke more of art than of violence,
but since the pile was presented to the world in all seriousness as evidence of
the provocation that had sent Japanese troops into action throughout Manchuria, solemnity was appropriate to the occasion.[6]

The photographs were as unconvincing as were Japan's continuing assurances that its occupation of strategic points in Manchuria was only temporary and that it would soon be withdrawing its troops into the railway
zone. Unconvincing as the photographs were, they were an acknowledgment of a new force in international affairs: mass public opinion. In the past,
national leaders would have felt the need to gain the support of the foreign
policy elites in their own country and perhaps those abroad. They would
also have expended considerable effort to mobilize their own citizens, as Japanese leaders had done twenty-five years earlier in the Russo-Japanese
War, which became a national crusade. The general public in other countries would not have concerned them very much.

By 1931, world news agencies were boasting of the speed with which
they could transmit not only news but photographs and moving pictures
from the sites of conflict to news outlets at home. Military actions in the far

corners of the world were no longer as remote in time as they were in space. If the Japanese fought a battle in Manchuria, shot a sniper in Shanghai, or bombed a Chinese city south of the Manchurian border, pictures of those actions quickly appeared in local newspapers around the world. "Every effort is made to rush the news to the public," bragged Acme Newspictures. "When the Japanese took control last fall of the railway bridge across the Taling River near Chincha, Manchuria, the camera man was soon hovering above making photos for distant newspaper readers."[7]

In this changed international environment, even national leaders confident of the rightness of their cause felt the need to make their case to a public they would never see and might secretly despise. There was no denying that the age was one of formal deference to democratic norms. The opinions of this public, whether ignorant or not of foreign affairs, might still affect the official policy of governments dependent on public approval for continuance in office or for reelection. So Japanese officials defended their actions in Manchuria at two levels: the diplomatic and the popular. Japanese diplomats used the resources and courtesies of traditional diplomacy to gain valuable time while the rest of Manchuria came under Japanese sway, and the Japanese-sponsored "independence" movement was furbished up to look plausibly local and spontaneous.

Approaches at the popular level were more varied and emphasized different themes to gain the support of different audiences. Thus Kentaro Kaneko took a common argument of Japanese expansionists regarding their destiny in Asia and, by attributing the argument to a popular U.S. president, sought to give it legitimacy in the West. In 1932 he solemnly informed the readers of *Asia* magazine that in confidential conversations before his death President Theodore Roosevelt had recommended a Japanese "Monroe Doctrine" for Asia. As leader of the Asian nations, Japan could bring stability to that troubled area. Since Japan was being criticized for its actions in Manchuria, Kaneko felt compelled to make TR's views known: "As his old friend and lifelong admirer, I cannot withhold his far-sighted views, and I now give it to the world as my tribute to the memory of one of the greatest statesmen of our time."[8]

Kikujiro Ishii took a different tack in a series of speeches in the United States before such groups as the San Francisco Chamber of Commerce, the Japan Society of Boston, and the Lawyers Club of New York. This highly respected former Japanese minister for foreign affairs dwelt on the longtime friendship between Japan and the United States. In speeches that were broadcast coast to coast he emphasized Japan's desire to cooperate with other nations in the cause of international peace and prosperity. In more private sessions, Ishii urged understanding of Japan's position in regard to the Chinese boycott of Japanese goods that had long exacerbated relations between the two nations. Was this boycott not a form of aggression? What recourse did the League Covenant provide for nations who were the victims of this kind of aggression? None, was Ishii's answer. None at all. And, in the absence of any means of redress through the League, Japan "took the only available alternative, namely force."[9]

Parallels with Western experiences were a favorite Japanese argument in this contest for the support of the public at large, particularly the U.S. public. So aloof a figure as Shigeru Honjo, commander of the Japanese forces in Manchuria, took time from his military duties to give radio and press interviews. Speaking to a reporter from the *New York Times*, General Honjo played on his personal experience in Washington and linked his memory of that city to present Japanese goals. From the window of military headquarters in Mukden, Manchuria, the reporter could see the large monolith that had been erected as a memorial to the Japanese soldiers who had died in the Russo-Japanese War. The general likened the memorial to the Washington Monument—smaller, of course, and in much different surroundings: "a bleak landscape surrounded by a snow-covered, frozen land in which millions of common people are suffering poverty and the results of long and merciless exploitation." The Japanese aim was to help Manchuria become a fruitful land so that the memorial would stand, as Honjo had seen the Washington Monument, among blossoming cherry trees in a fertile and prosperous country.

As for the Manchurian "independence" movement that was growing in strength every day, the general took the official Japanese line and tailored it for his American audience: "These aspirations compare with those of the forefathers of Americans today, who fought for lofty ideals, independence, freedom and opportunity. I am satisfied that the citizens of America, who love righteousness and justice, maintain a predominantly fair and understanding attitude toward the difficult position of the imperial Japanese Army which fundamentally strives for real peace and a just and lasting adjustment of the Manchurian situation."[10]

Thus the Japanese blended ideas about justice, order, and independence into one argument designed to vindicate their occupation of Manchuria and their establishment there of the "independent" state of Manchukuo. Arguments from ideas about the balance of power in the area were not forgotten either, since the Soviet Union loomed large on Manchurian borders and in the minds of foreign policy elites uncertain what the militant leaders of the Soviet state might do. It was altogether an impressive marshaling of argu-

ments that had a respectable history in international affairs and that many of
the states condemning Japanese actions had used to justify their own actions
in the past.

For supporters of the League and of the Pact of Paris, the whole point of
the controversy could be summed up in those three words: *in the past.* For
them, the ways of the past had disappeared with the days of the past. The establishment of the League and the promulgation of the Pact of Paris had
ushered in a new era in which force was to be replaced by reason and nations
were to settle their conflicts by peaceful means. Those looking to a more
just and peaceful future for the world at large had been filled with hope that
the foundation for such a future was being laid on a much more solid basis
than in the past. As the Dutch scholar J. H. W. Verzijl put it in 1930, "*this*
new foundation would seem to offer better prospects that it will gradually
grow strong enough to uphold in the future the authority of international
law and a peaceful community of states." There had been, said Verzijl, a fundamental change in the relations of states.[11]

It was that fundamental change that Japanese actions threatened and that
their arguments seemed to mock. They spoke of justice, but they defined
justice to their own advantage, as nations had persistently defined it in the
past. The weight of the past hung heavily over attempts to give justice a different meaning, one with an international as well as a national reference
point. In their attempts to do so, supporters of the League and of the Pact of
Paris had settled on the collective good, peace, as the way to achieve that
different, more equitable definition of justice. When they were confronted
by the use of force in Manchuria, they fell back on procedures they had used
before when force had threatened the structures of peace they were building
with such care. The council of the League asked for explanations and assurances. The explanations were lengthy and assurances were forthcoming but
the rhetoric in Geneva never seemed to match the reality in the field. Finally, the council dispatched a commission of neutral observers and experts
to bring back a report of the facts and to make recommendations for resolving a conflict that kept spreading no matter what was said or done by the
League or by the United States, its temporary ally in this cause.

The commission's report was almost universally praised as a model of
fairness and restraint, with suggestions for settlement that could be accepted
by all parties without loss of pride or national standing. George H. Blakeslee, a technical adviser who accompanied the commission on its investigative travels, spoke feelingly of the spirit that had animated the members and
staff after they had visited Japan, China, and Manchuria and had gathered in
Peking (Peiping/Beijing) to write their report:

I wish you might have been in Peking and sensed the feeling which pervaded the Commission and the whole staff. There was an earnest determination to write the fairest possible history of events, well-balanced, just and clear. . . . I thought at the time, and remarked to some of my friends, that the way to make a diplomat or distinguished official almost a religious person is to appoint him a member of a commission of inquiry, because then his duty, his business, that which he thinks about all day long, is how he can bring together two countries whose controversy he is studying, and help them to cooperate and develop a measure of good will.[12]

The occasion for Blakeslee's remarks was a Foreign Policy Association luncheon and discussion in New York city shortly after the commission's report was made public. Blakeslee, a Clark University professor who was frequently called on for advice and consultation at government levels, was joined in the New York discussion by Nathaniel Peffer, a Columbia University professor with much experience in eastern Asia. Peffer was convinced that the world was indeed changing, but not as Blakeslee and League supporters hoped. Asian powers were on the rise. Europe's day was past, and the power and privilege that Westerners had once enjoyed in Asia was gone, disappearing along with the old order in China, where "a white skin has ceased to be a *laissez passer* and guarantee of safe conduct. I have felt the steel of a pirate leader's gun prodding my throat as his followers ransacked my cabin in the foreigners' first class of a British ship on the Yangtze quite as turbulently as they did the coolie quarters below deck."[13]

In such a world, talk of justice, peace, and reason was futile. Peffer was polite in his response to Blakeslee's enthusiasm and optimism, but he rejected his conclusions completely. Yes, as Blakeslee had said, the report of the League commission was fair to all parties: fair to China because its recommendations preserved Chinese sovereignty in Manchuria; fair to Japan because that country's special interest and investments in Manchuria were preserved; fair to the Manchurian people because when these recommendations were carried out, peace and good government would follow; fair to the commercial interests of the world because the principle of free trade was upheld. Above all, the report was fair to the promise of the League and of the Pact of Paris. Through it a troubling conflict could be resolved and work could continue toward the more just and peaceful world envisioned in those international undertakings.

And all this, said Peffer, did not matter one bit in the world as it was. The commission's report was fair, accurate, and sound. If it were to come up for consideration in a vacuum, it would be an admirable document. Lacking that vacuum, it was an exercise in futility. The Manchurian Incident was a closed incident. It was closed before the commission arrived in Asia to begin its investigation. It would stay closed until the issue was finally settled by, as Peffer said, a "test of strength between China and Japan militarily, or by the intervention of a third power, or by, as I say, the advent of a civilized international society, which cannot yet be foreseen."[14]

The basic point of difference between Blakeslee and Peffer, and between those who supported League principles and those who were skeptical of them, concerned the degree of change that had taken place in the world since the end of World War I. For Blakeslee, Verzijl, Åke Hammarsköld, and others, there had been a fundamental change in the relations between states. The change had been brought about by the states' agreeing to certain principles that had been set out in the League Covenant and the Pact of Paris and to courses of action based on those principles. Much of this action was directed toward the peaceful settlement of disputes, and through the peace that would ensue, toward the achievement of international justice.

For Peffer, the important change was the decline of European power and prestige. Beyond that, the world was as it had always been: a place where power was sovereign and force was the judge in conflicts. For him, as for those who argued the Japanese case, the past was the present writ plain. Seeing how states had acted in the past, one could predict how they would act in the present. The League had changed nothing. The Pact of Paris had changed nothing. Peffer put his case succinctly: "Everything that has happened in the last year has happened as if there had been no League of Nations. You must be aware of that. Japan has proceeded exactly as it would have proceeded in 1913."[15]

Peffer's comment went straight to the heart of the controversy that swirled around the Manchurian Incident and subsequent events. Internationally speaking, *had* anything changed since 1913? A look at one of the League's favorite approaches to peaceful settlement may help answer the question. The commission that was sent to investigate the incident and recommend ways to resolve the conflict gained some of its prestige from precedent. Such commissions had been used by the League in the past, and they had a good record of success. In using them, the League itself had relied on precedent. Investigative commissions were not new in international affairs. That being so, they provide a basis for comparison across time and a way to answer the question, *Had* anything changed, internationally speaking, from 1913 to 1931?

CHAPTER SIX

The Transforming Years

The three international commissions of inquiry that are compared here had the same basic purposes. Whether sent in 1913, 1925, or 1932, their primary job was to determine the facts of the crisis that had prompted their appointment. This was to be done through inquiries on the spot: interviews with the immediate protagonists and with eyewitnesses and government officials, the collection and study of documents, both current and historic, and personal surveys of the actual sites of conflict. Next, the commissioners were to make recommendations of ways to resolve matters and transmit them to the appropriate authorities.

The commission findings might or might not be made public, depending on the temper of the times and the nature of the problems. In the case of the 1913 commission, dispatched to the Balkans by the Carnegie Endowment for International Peace in the midst of one of the Balkan wars, publicity was the chief weapon with which to pressure the antagonists toward settlement. The 1925 commission of inquiry sent by the League of Nations to the site of a conflict between Greece and Bulgaria had to be more careful about publicity lest these two proud and independent states take offense and refuse to cooperate. And finally, the Lytton Commission, dispatched by the League in 1932 to investigate the differences between China and Japan, had to take pains to keep its report secret until the League Council had had a chance to see and act on it. In the highly charged atmosphere of the East, premature disclosure could wreck what hope there was for a resolution of the conflict.

There were other differences, of course, between the three commissions of inquiry. There were differences in personnel, in competence, in the facilities available for their use. These, however, are not the point. Of interest here is what, if anything, these three missions can reveal about changes over time in the international system in which they functioned.

1913

It may have been chance that Nathaniel Peffer picked 1913 as the date to make his point about the unchanging role of force in the international system but, whether chance or not, he could hardly have picked a better date for the purpose of comparing investigative commissions across time. On August 2, 1913, just such a commission set out from Paris to inquire into the causes and conduct of two wars in the Balkans. The first began in October 1912 and continued, now hot, now lukewarm, until brought to a close by a peace treaty in May 1913. The war was conducted by the Balkan League, a loose alliance of Greece, Bulgaria, Serbia, and Montenegro on one hand and Turkey on the other. The outcome was an effective end to Turkish possessions in the Balkans. The second war, still under way when the commission set out, was a battle among the victors for the land taken from the Turks, and it pitted Bulgaria against Greece and Serbia. Romania and Turkey soon jumped into the fray to see what spoils could be snatched from the general upset of territorial arrangements. Bulgaria was defeated in this round of fighting, a fact that shaped the new territorial arrangements spelled out in two peace treaties, one in mid-August and one in late September, between the former combatants.[1]

All this was for the most part business as usual in the Balkans, where the rise of national feeling against Turkish rule had combined with the intrigues of interested European powers to keep the area in incipient or outright turmoil for many years. What was not usual was the press coverage given to this particular outbreak of Balkan violence. Instead of rumors about the conduct of the two wars there were eyewitness reports of its savagery and interviews with those who claimed to have been present and seen the horrors that were described in detail by news correspondents from western Europe and the United States. Some of these dispatches appeared in the *New York Times* and were the immediate cause of the investigative commission's being formed. Horrified by the situation described in the *Times*, Nicholas Murray Butler set about to organize and send to the area an impartial body "to ascertain facts and to fix responsibility for prolonging hostilities and committing outrages."[2]

As president of Columbia University and director of the Division of Intercourse and Education of the Carnegie Endowment for International Peace, Butler was in a position to make the contacts and the moves to get such an undertaking organized and under way. The Endowment was new as an organization but it had personnel with experience in the peace movements of the time, and it had the money Andrew Carnegie had given at its founding three years earlier. These made it possible to secure the assent of prominent internationalists with an interest in peace to serve on the commission. After much correspondence between the New World and the Old, the commission's roster was complete.

Eight men agreed to serve, but only four of them made the trip to the Balkans. The rest helped with the planning and organization and, after the return of the subcommittee, took part in the writing and editing of the final report. Butler's optimistic initial deadline for publication of the report was September 1913, when public interest would still be high. Obstacles of one sort or another delayed publication until 1914. The report received limited attention before being swept out of the news by the outbreak of World War I.[3]

Memory of the two wars that the commission went to investigate has also been swept aside by the impact of World War I. At the time they occurred, the Balkan wars were seen as highly significant. Leon Trotsky saw them as a sign of the decadence of the old social and political order in Europe. The young Joyce Cary hurried out from England to experience these "last" wars before the burgeoning peace movement did away with war altogether.[4] And the wars became an unwelcome epiphany for Paul Scott Mowrer of the *Chicago Daily News*, a sudden glimpse into the depths of human nature. At first this was just another assignment for him, and Mowrer filed local color stories from Belgrade, the capital of Serbia. Then the color shifted to reveal a different city, no longer just a place of peasants and oxcarts and little orange streetcars but one of potential savagery that shocked Mowrer's very soul, experienced journalist though he was:

> What is that group at the window of that store, gazing in with such fascination? Horrible! They are viewing a picture, but, what a picture! It represents in large dimensions a party of business-like Turks of the old times, setting stakes with sharpened tops into the snowy street of a village and then impaling writhing Serbians on the stakes—right straight up through the center of their bodies! There is plenty of blood—a hound is licking at a pool of it. If even this feeble description is revolting, you can imagine what the original must be. Yet the people

seem to like it. With a sudden shock one realizes that one is really in the Balkans.[5]

Or simply in the midst of the horrors of unbridled war. This kind of slaughter was neither a product of the artist's warped imagination nor specific to the Balkans. A hundred years earlier Francisco de Goya had sketched a similar scene in his collection of etchings titled "The Disasters of War"—different time period, different protagonists, identical savagery. The enormous cruelties of the Peninsular campaign, which filled Goya with such fierce revulsion, were faithfully reenacted in the two Balkan wars a hundred years later, and Paul Scott Mowrer was not the only one to be filled with horror. The horror was compounded by distress at the failure of hopes that this kind of conduct was a thing of the past. What of the Hague Conventions of 1899 and 1907, which set out rules to govern the conduct of war on land? All of the combatants had signed at least one of these international agreements. Yet rape, robbery, massacre, and torture were practiced by all sides, and all sides believed the worst of one another—with good reason.

Many prisoners were summarily killed. Others were kept under conditions that contravened every regulation of the Hague Conventions on the treatment of prisoners of war: no shelter of any kind; for beds, the bare ground; no blankets or medicines even for those who were ill. Villagers were forced out of their homes to join the bands of refugees fleeing from the devastation that spread across the land behind them. Houses, schools, mosques, and churches were burned. Livestock was killed or driven off by hungry troops. Crops were destroyed. Refugee camps were often little more than seas of mud with here and there a tent or a wagon box for shelter. For lack of oxen or horses, the dead on the battlefields sometimes lay unburied for days, and the vultures grew fat in the land. One of the members of the Carnegie commission investigating the causes and conduct of these Balkan wars found the situation almost beyond his powers to describe or comprehend: "I sometimes feel as though I had been standing on the brink of Hell."[6]

For Samuel T. Dutton this was more than just a figure of speech. It was a place in his personal universe of meaning. His evocation of the image is a measure of his distress at what he saw in the Balkans. A committed Christian lay leader, an organizer of peace movements, a professor in Teacher's College at Columbia University, Dutton found himself in the late summer and fall of 1913 far from the committee meetings and classrooms where he usually functioned. He was in the Balkans more by accident than by design. He had not been Nicholas Murray Butler's first choice for the investigative commission, but, said Butler—after failing to get two other Americans to accept the assignment—although not qualified as a Balkanist, Dutton was wise and experienced, and his reputation would insure wide coverage of the report.[7]

As it turned out, Dutton carried much of the burden of the investigation. His very ignorance of Balkan affairs proved to be an advantage. Not having publicly expressed opinions on the subject, he did not have to fight the suspicion that he was prejudiced either in favor of or against one side or another. The Serbian government objected to the presence on the commission of the Russian scholar Paul Milyukov, a Balkan expert whose views did not always match those of Serbia, and the Greek government objected to the English journalist Henry N. Brailsford, who, although a friend of Greece, had been known to criticize some Greek activities. The fourth member of the subcommittee was Justin Godart, a member of the French Chamber of Deputies and, like Dutton, a neophyte in Balkan affairs who functioned effectively within the limitations of the circumstances.[8]

And the circumstances were extremely limiting. Consider the situation of this oddly assorted little group of men, one French, one Russian, one English, one American, traveling together through the war zones of the Balkans to investigate the causes of the wars and the conduct of all participants. Before they had set out from Paris, the president of the commission, Paul Estournelles de Constant, had notified the Turkish ambassador and the ministers of Bulgaria, Greece, and Serbia of the subcommittee's plans and mission. If the news caused much of a stir in Constantinople, Sophia, Athens, or Belgrade, that was not apparent when members of the subcommittee arrived in those capital cities. They were not received at the official level by the Serbian and the Greek governments, and their requests for documents that would set out those two governments' version of events were denied. Both governments claimed to welcome an impartial investigation of atrocities but said that this was not the group to do it.

What pressure could members of the commission bring to bear, either in the Balkans or through their governments at home? What standing did the commission have in the international system of the time? The answer to both questions is, none. None whatsoever. By what authority did the members of the subcommittee ask for documents or for transport to sites of battles or places of reported atrocities? Again the answer is, none. The reputation of the individual members of the commission was their only means of gaining the attention of government officials busy with a war and with war's aftermath, and the reputation of two of the members proved to be more of a barrier than a means of entry.

Estournelles de Constant, who remained in Paris, was probably the best known of the eight members of the commission for his work in the peace movements of the time, but this was not saying much once the field of recognition is extended beyond those interested in such efforts. Beyond that, there was the very young and relatively unknown sponsoring organization, the Carnegie Endowment for International Peace. It was hardly a by-word even in the United States where it was founded, much less in the far reaches of the Balkan countryside. Endowment officials felt that they spoke for the conscience of the civilized world, but they were self-appointed for this role. Governments were polite, but they were not impressed.

There was a place for international investigative commissions in 1913, but that place was carefully marked out and even more carefully limited by governments that might one day find themselves involved. The procedures for these commissions of inquiry had been set out in the two conventions on the pacific settlement of disputes that emerged from the Hague Conferences of 1899 and 1907. The rules were slightly different in the two conventions, but the purpose was the same: to resolve international disputes peacefully through investigation and, usually, recommendations for settlement. The commissions were not standing bodies. Each was appointed to ascertain the facts in a particular dispute. To ensure that the disputants' views would be heard, each was allowed appointments to the commission. Their predictable partisanship was then balanced by the appointment of commissioners from neutral powers.[9]

The 1913 Balkan Commission of Inquiry departed from this accepted pattern in a significant way. By appointing people who were not officially connected to any of the combatants in the Balkan wars, Endowment officials attempted to give a truly international, nonpartisan flavor to the inquiry. The report of the commission could be issued as an objective account of events in the Balkans—one that could be relied on for its accuracy and impartiality. The hope, as Dutton expressed it, was that this report could set in motion all available means "for reaching human minds and human hearts." If that happened, "it might almost seem that such a reaction would result as to make another war impossible."[10]

The very advantages that Endowment officials saw in their approach to this investigation was, of course, its undoing. Nonofficial members meant nonofficial standing in the international system, and that meant no standing at all. Some nonofficial groups, such as the International Red Cross, and various ad hoc relief organizations were beginning to be accepted there, or tolerated if their actions did not intrude too much on state activities. The day had not come when the international community as such had the authority or the organization to make its voice heard in international affairs. "Must we allow these two Balkan wars to pass, without at least trying to draw some lesson from them?" asked Estournelles de Constant, in anguish at the indifference he encountered or the outright hostility toward the commission's work.[11]

And the answer is that the wars themselves have passed into oblivion, along with the lessons to be drawn from them. Even the report was forgotten for eighty years until reissued by the Endowment in response to later conflicts in the Balkans.[12] But the report stands as a monument to faith in the power of reason and to the belief that, through the knowledge that fact-finding can bring, ways can be found to settle disputes peacefully with justice to the participants and to the international community as a whole. The institutions that could give effective expression to these beliefs did not exist in 1913, nor were the states of the international system ready to acknowledge the claims of what one of the Hague Conventions called "the laws of humanity, and the requirements of the public conscience."[13] This meant that at the end of its mission, the Balkan Commission of Inquiry remained exactly what it had been at the beginning: an isolated, private undertaking without international standing, without even the power to mobilize the public opinion it claimed to represent. It was also an early, noble attempt to make international standards of behavior something more than promises on paper and to act on behalf of a community of nations that in 1913 existed mostly in imagination and wishful dreams.

1925

The boundaries between states in the Balkans have for many years expressed what Salvador de Madariaga called the world's insolidarity. They rest uneasily on memories of victory or defeat, with the victors determined to hold on to what the defeated hope to regain. In the meantime, the losers engage in efforts to destabilize society in the "lost" areas and to keep territorial and ethnic claims fresh in everyone's mind. It was this that led to a fresh outbreak of fighting in the Balkans in the mid-twenties, and to the dispatch of an investigative commission that retraced some of the steps of the Balkan Commission of 1913, but with completely different results.

Fighting between Greece and Bulgaria began with a border incident. The boundary between the two states had been redrawn following the first Balkan war. It was redrawn again after the second Balkan war, and then again after World War I. The changes provided a field day for map publishers, but the new lines translated into catastrophe for many of the people on the ground. If they took their chances with the new regime, they found in many cases that they were forbidden to speak their own language or attend their own church and were under constant pressure to deny what they had formerly been. If they left their homes and crossed to the other side of the new border, they more often encountered resentment than welcome, and they discovered that ethnic identification was no substitute for having a place to live. The commission investigating the outbreak of fighting between Greece and Bulgaria identified this scrambling of people's identities and locations as a basic cause for unrest along the countries' shared border.[14]

The border might have been designed by de Madariaga himself to demonstrate the effect of national pride and suspicion. On the maps the boundary looked like nothing so much as a line between a double row of bared teeth, flanked as it was on either side by symbols representing Greek and Bulgarian frontier posts. There was a symmetry of suspicion in the placement of the posts. Bulgarian Post Number One, where the trouble began, was immediately opposite Greek Post Sixty-nine, Bulgarian Two opposite Greek Seventy, Bulgarian Three opposite Greek Seventy-one, and so on across the rugged countryside. On the afternoon of October 19, 1925, firing began at Posts One/Sixty-Nine. No one knew or would say what had started it. Before it was finished, a Greek soldier was dead, and his body was in Bulgarian territory—dragged there by the Bulgarians, said the Greeks; shot there while trying to infiltrate Bulgarian territory, said the Bulgarians.

The situation, although serious, was not in itself a cause for war. There had been similar incidents in the past, and the resulting tensions had been resolved by officers on the spot. The October incident quickly escalated out of local control, however. It became a *cause célèbre* throughout Greece, and the name of one Greek officer, Captain Vassiliadis, became a rallying cry for patriotic fervor and demands for revenge. Vassiliadis was the officer in charge of Post Sixty-Nine on the Greek side of the border. He had been trying to arrange a parley with the Bulgarians when he was shot and killed. Adding fuel to the flames of Greek fury was the fact that Vassiliadis had been killed while bearing a flag of truce.

From then on, the two sides acted in ways that confirmed each other's worst suspicions. Messages of alarm were transmitted to their respective headquarters. Reserve forces were moved into position, followed by air surveillance, artillery fire, wild estimates of the size of opposing forces, and a sweep of Greek troops into Bulgarian territory. Within a few days, the Greeks had occupied ten Bulgarian villages and were threatening the town of Petric. The forces involved were small when compared to those in recent wars, but they were large enough to cause numerous deaths and serious destruction. On the morning of the day the Greeks were set to shell Petric and send their troops forward, an unexpected message came from Greek head-quarters. The troops were ordered not to attack. They were to await further commands. When those commands came, they were for an orderly with-drawal to the Greek side of the Greek-Bulgarian border. The unimaginable had happened. A war had been stopped.

The immediate cause for the no-attack order was a telegram from Aris-tide Briand, the French foreign minister, then serving as president of the council of the League of Nations. Council members had been called into emergency session in Paris to meet with Bulgarian and Greek representa-tives in a joint effort to defuse the explosive situation. In the telegram Briand reminded the governments of Greece and Bulgaria of their obliga-tions as members of the League not to resort to force: "I therefore exhort the two Governments to give immediate instructions that, pending consid-eration [of this] dispute by Council, not only no further military movements shall be undertaken but that troops shall at once retire behind their respec-tive frontiers."[15]

Such a message would have been impossible in 1913. Who would have sent it? Another difference from that earlier period lay in the make-up of the body exhorting the combatants to break off fighting. There were ten states represented on the League Council in 1925. Of the ten, only Italy might be accused of self-interest in the matter, and Italy had shown no sign of coveting Greek or Bulgarian territory. The investigative commission that the council dispatched was equally unthreatening. The five-member com-mission was composed of individuals from France, Great Britain, Italy, The Netherlands, and Sweden. The propagandists who had made so much of the presence of Milyukov and Brailsford on the 1913 Balkan Commission could do little with the likes of Droogkever Fortuyn, the Dutch representa-tive, or with Sir Horace Rumbold, the Briton who headed the commission. Fortuyn was a member of the Netherlands parliament, a body and a gov-ernment with no record of interference in the Balkans. Rumbold was then British ambassador to Spain, a post he had been given after serving with dis-tinction as high commissioner and ambassador to Turkey. Upright, taci-turn, and monocled, he was, in appearance and character, a model of the perfect diplomat described in the diplomatic manuals of the time.[16]

In theory, it did not matter which states were represented on the council or the commission. In theory, their delegates were not acting in their capac-ity as Dutch or Swedish or Italian citizens but as temporary representatives of the international community. In retrospect, it is clear that League as-sumptions about the extent and cohesion of that community often outran reality. Successful League actions masked that fact, however, and this was a successful action. The first shots were exchanged on October 19. Three weeks later the League Commission of Inquiry entered Belgrade to begin its work. The contrast with the dragged-out proceedings following the Manchurian Incident could hardly be greater.

Once in Belgrade, commission members met with the British, French, and Italian military attachés who, at the request of the League Council, had been monitoring the ceasefire until the commission's arrival. Three men could, of course, do next to nothing in the event of any hostile move, but that was not the point. The point was what they represented. There, in the uniformed flesh of three military attachés, was a living symbol of international attention and concern. Small-scale as this symbol was, and only briefly in place, the attachés nevertheless functioned as an observer group under international auspices, a peacekeeping tool that was increasingly used in the years to come.

Like the Balkan Commission of 1913, the 1925 Commission of Inquiry took its task seriously. To help in the performance of that task, the 1925 commissioners had what the earlier commissioners had never had: some semblance of international authority. The authority of the League of Nations was relatively untried, and it was shaky at best, resting as it did on the willingness of states to cooperate. Some authority the League did have, however, and that was enough to let the 1925 commission speak for a world collective, not just for a few self-interested states, nor for self-appointed guardians of peace and morality. The League's emphasis on securing justice through peace was reflected in the council's instructions. Commission members were to go beyond investigation of the incident that had led to the outbreak of fighting. They were to examine as well the whole situation that lay behind the outbreak and make recommendations to reduce or eliminate persistent points of conflict. Through such actions, justice might be done to both sides.

The commissioners took these instructions as far as the times would permit. They did not say that an inflated notion of state sovereignty encouraged the very behavior they were sent to investigate, nor that the Balkan turmoil was partly the result of great power meddling in the past. Neither did they recommend demilitarization of the border that snaked along between the bared teeth of opposing frontier posts—a recommendation that would never have been accepted by either unstable government. Instead, they concentrated on the small and the possible. Their report is a model of ways to give practical effect to an abstract principle such as justice within the limits imposed by intractable circumstance. There was nothing the commissioners could do about the past wars that had uprooted thousands of Bulgarians and Greeks, stripped them of their lands and possessions, and dumped them into "homelands" that had neither the resources nor the experience to take care of them. The report simply noted that these resettled peoples were a constant source of tension in the area and provided fertile ground for the seeds of violence.

The report then went on to recommend the small steps by which justice might be brought down to the level where fighting starts and people live: faster processing of the refugees' claims for compensation; better training for the frontier guards; more reliable communication between the front lines and the command posts in the rear to avoid the confusion that had helped precipitate an incident into an invasion. These were for the future. More immediate was the question of reparations for the damage done in the invasion, including Bulgarian property losses: "The Commission found long trails of tobacco, cotton and cereals along the roads leading to Greece."[17] Taking this into account, and allowing Greece compensation for the death of Captain Vassiliadis, the commissioners recommended that Greece pay to Bulgaria an indemnity of thirty million Bulgarian *leva* (approximately $225,000).

The report was accepted by the League Council without dissent and by the two combatants with only pro forma protests about some of the details. Where full-scale war had threatened, the situation now was calm. The fighting had been stopped. Greek troops had withdrawn. The body of the Greek soldier from Post Sixty-Nine had been recovered without incident. The Greeks agreed to pay for the damage caused by their invasion, and, within two months of the acceptance of the commission's report, they did so. The aftermath of all this was notable for its bold expansion of the idea of a symbolic international presence. The commissioners suggested, and the council and the combatants agreed, that army officers from a neutral state be stationed for two years with the frontier guards on both sides of the border to act as advisers and impartial observers. The idea of a continuing international watch on the sites of potential conflicts was thus given concrete expression, and two Swedish Army officers, Lieutenant-Colonel Sigurd Siefvert and Lieutenant-Colonel Axel Lindh, were detailed to this task.[18]

It was a moment of unadulterated triumph for the new ways of the League. Council president Aristide Briand found the words to express both the triumph and the vindication of the League's long-term goals: "I hope that tomorrow the example set in this affair will become contagious and enable us to anticipate an epoch, which I hope is near at hand, when conflict between nations, like conflicts between individuals will be settled not by force but by justice, to which all parties will have recourse."[19]

By December 1925, when Briand spoke these words, he had become the voice of the League of Nations. Two of the founding fathers of the institution, Léon Bourgeois and Woodrow Wilson, were dead. Lord Robert Cecil's positions in successive British governments were never high enough to allow him to speak with authority, nor did he have Briand's dramatic flair in manner and speech. No one who had heard Briand speak in the council or the assembly ever forgot it. One friend likened him to a great cellist: "his cello was his voice, which he was able to use and control superbly."[20]

Within a few years, illness and age would still that voice, and there would be no one to take Briand's place. It is only fitting, then, that his words sum up what was accomplished by the 1925 League Commission of Inquiry when it carried out its task, as Briand said, "with full impartiality and justice"—and this in an area where the rarity of those qualities has brought so much grief to the inhabitants and to the rest of the world. The report could be accepted by the two combatants because, in Briand's words, "there is neither victor nor vanquished. There are two nations which, forming part of the same great family of peace, have shown their desire for conciliation by agreeing immediately to accede to reason and justice in the dispute in which they were engaged."

Reason and justice, Briand continued, were the very qualities that the two states could expect to find at the League:

> In this lies the great strength of the institution which has been so often criticized and so often ridiculed, the League of Nations. Herein lies the family character of this organization. It is composed of nations great and small, all equal and all sure of finding within the League the same justice for every member. When two nations like Bulgaria and Greece are at issue in one of those disputes which, alas! it is very difficult to avoid between peoples, they can at once take shelter within the shelter of this family and be sure of finding justice. In this case you have been able to see that the League of Nations has not failed to fulfil either the spirit which inspired its foundation or the purpose for which it was intended.[21]

It was a moment of triumph for Briand and for the League. For neither was it a resting place. Briand went on to further successes before political defeat in Paris and suspicion in Geneva sapped his spirit. His cherished plan of European economic union was considered by some to be little more than a flimsy cover for the furtherance of French economic interests. Despite his reputation as an advocate of international well-being, Briand's most forward-looking and innovative idea was sidelined to a study committee and then quietly buried.

Suspicion and quiet burial was the fate of many ideas in the 1920s for new ways of conducting international affairs. And there were plenty of people who would have been happy to see the League of Nations follow those ideas into the grave. Instead, the League reached the end of its first decade with a growing reputation for usefulness and even for effective action, as in the Greco-Bulgarian conflict. Despite setbacks, failures, and the persistence of old ways of thought and action, the outlook at the close of the decade of the twenties was encouraging.

1932

Prior to the Manchurian Incident, the League of Nations had appointed five commissions of inquiry to investigate disputes between states: Sweden and Finland (1920), Yugoslavia and Albania (1921), the Allied Powers and Lithuania (1923), Great Britain and Turkey (1923), and Greece and Bulgaria (1925).[22] All had performed useful work, and the inquiry into the conflict between Greece and Bulgaria had been a spectacular success. It was with a degree of optimism, therefore, that the council of the League, after finally obtaining the consent of Japan and China, dispatched a commission to Asia to investigate the Manchurian situation on the spot and suggest ways to resolve the conflict. Since the conflict eventually led to full-scale war— just as Nathaniel Peffer had predicted—the effort is usually accounted a failure. The commission could only make recommendations, however. It could not initiate action. If actions were to be taken, they had to be taken by the states. Given the economic stresses of the times and the confusion of great power purposes, the outcome of the commission's journey to the East is not surprising. What is surprising is that the journey took place at all.

Because it did, it is easy to assume inevitability. There was nothing inevitable about it. No one could be sure that the Japanese government could carry through on the agreement made by its representatives in Geneva. Behind the façade of government as usual in Japan was a witches' brew of plots and maneuvers for control of that government—maneuvers that did not stop at violence. When the League commission of inquiry arrived in Tokyo at the end of February 1932, the mood in the capital was one of nervous tension. Twice in the preceding year plots had been uncovered among radical army officers who were willing to overthrow the government if necessary to achieve their ideas of national reconstruction. Government officials were deeply divided about the lenient treatment of the conspirators in the most recent plot, discovered just four months before the arrival of the commission. The officials were also divided about the best way to satisfy and at the same time control the disaffected officers in the military and about the wisdom of allowing the League investigation at all. And they were apprehensive about the future.

Into this tense national atmosphere came the representatives of the League on behalf of that nebulous body, the international community. Officially, commission members were welcomed. They were received by the emperor, granted interviews by high officials, and allowed to talk to private citizens and to members of nongovernmental organizations. On the surface, all was well, but superficial courtesies could neither calm nor control the troubled depths. The commissioners were received and entertained. They were also lied to, spied on, and deliberately exposed to deadly cholera.[23] Their coming was a catalyst for opposing forces within the Japanese government, just as it was for opposing views of the international system and what was acceptable there. In that lies its interest for today—that, and the fact that this group of League representatives made a truly remarkable journey.

In their pursuit of the facts behind the Manchurian Incident, commission members traveled more than seven thousand miles in Asia alone. They traveled by train, ship, car, and plane. They went to Shanghai, where fierce fighting between Chinese and Japanese troops ended only a few days before their arrival. They traveled through the flood-ravaged, disease-ridden Yangtze valley. They spent six weeks in Manchuria, where raw military power was the arbiter of events. Despite the Japanese-backed declaration of independence from China that had been made in February and the establishment of the putative state of Manchukuo, the area was in violent turmoil. It was a sprawling battlefield of contending egos, both collective and personal, that would have justified Thomas Hobbes in his grimmest reading of the human condition. "Yet in all times," Hobbes wrote in 1651, "kings, and persons of sovereign authority, because of their independency, are in continual jealousies, and in the state and posture of gladiators."[24]

Conditions in Manchuria in the spring and summer of 1932 would have been no surprise to Hobbes, nor would conditions in the rest of China. The Nationalist government at Nanking, the Communists in Kiangsi, and powerful leaders in the southern provinces were in "continual jealousies," and, when they were not actually fighting each other, were "in the state and posture of gladiators." It could, in fact, be argued that this was the condition of the whole international system before World War I and that it was precisely this condition that the League of Nations was seeking to change through fact-finding inquiries and proposals for the peaceful settlement of disputes.

The League commission in Asia in 1932 consisted of five members, one each from France, Germany, Great Britain, Italy, and the United States. It was headed by the British representative, Lord Lytton, whose position as governor of Bengal in British India and then as head of the Indian delegation to the League of Nations had given him some experience of the world beyond England. His experience was complemented by that of the American, Major-General Frank R. McCoy, a career officer, who had headed the American relief mission to Japan after the disastrous earthquake of 1923. His was a position and a personality that had made many friends in Japan, a fact that gave hope to those who believed that personal friendship was the key to international understanding. Lytton and McCoy were the dominant members of the commission, but they had always to take into account the views of Heinrich Schnee, the German member, and Count Aldrovani and General Henri Claudel, the Italian and French members, respectively.

For support these core members had a large and competent staff: three personal aides, five members of the League secretariat on a full-time basis and two others part-time, seven technical experts drawn chiefly from the academic community, and a Japanese national to act as translator. In addition, Isaburo Yoshida for Japan and Wellington Koo for China served as assessors, or legal representatives of their governments' respective positions, and provided the commission with information and documents to support those positions.[25] With this impressive assemblage of talent, experience, and expertise, the Lytton Commission set out on its six months' journey to bring to East Asia the concept of justice through peace. Their methods were those of civility and reason, and their only weapon was persuasion. With these they traveled straight into the heart of a Hobbesian universe of violence, cunning, betrayal, and greed.

If the kind of world that the members of the Lytton Commission were trying to build ever comes into being, theirs will be seen as an epic journey. On one of the maps that accompanied their report to the League, their travels are laid out in lines that cover southern Japan, cross the East China Sea, make looping circuits through central and northern China, go north into Manchuria as far as the fighting there would allow, swing down through the Korean Peninsula, and move back to Japan across the Korean Strait. After consultation in Japan, they took another swing through China and then settled down in Peking to write their report.[26]

If there was discomfort, strain, or fatigue in any of these journeyings

through a violent land, one would never know it from the commissioners'
report. They succeeded admirably in their goal, which was to make their report an impartial, factual account of the points of conflict between China
and Japan and to set out their recommendations for ways in which these
conflicts might be resolved. They were like scientists reporting their obser-
vations of a hurricane: wind velocity, forward movement, probable course,
width of the storm path, assessment of damage. In these detached observa-
tions, the effects of the winds of violence all but disappear. The result has
been that the commission itself has all but disappeared from the written history of the period with no tribute paid to their bravery, their stamina, and
their sheer determination to persuade the Hobbesian sovereigns at war all
around them that the best hope for justice lay in reason and in peace.

One approach is of special interest for what it reveals about the League's
operations. The future governance of Manchuria was a particularly tricky
problem that Lord Lytton attempted to solve by suggesting privately to Japanese officials that the area might temporarily be put under international
administration. This would give other tension-easing arrangements time to
work. Lytton's suggestion was rejected out of hand, and the recommendation actually made in the commissioners' report was for a joint administrative body that would allow input from interested parties and at the same
time preserve China's sovereignty.[27]

Lytton's suggestion of an international administration was not as far-
fetched as it might seem, however. The League was quietly experimenting
with this procedure with some success in the Saar, where French and German passions had threatened a renewal of war. The League was also administering the industrial and mining area of Upper Silesia, disputed between
Germany and Poland. The very obscurity of the League mission there is a
testimony to its success in containing the provocative actions of both parties
for fifteen years. And, less than a year after Lytton made his suggestion, the
League was to take on the task of administering another disputed territory,
this one in South America. The task was small-scale, short-lived, and highly
successful.[28]

Whether international administration under the direction of the League
would have worked in Manchuria in the early thirties is a question that cannot be answered today. What is of interest is that this was one of the tools at
the League's command. By 1932 the commissioners had a repertoire of procedures they could offer, procedures that had worked and were working
elsewhere. For the commissioners and for many in Geneva, these were the
preferred ways out of the frightening situation that had been created by Japanese actions. They felt strongly that there was no need to invoke Article 16

of the League Covenant, which would have mandated the imposition of economic sanctions against Japan. Those familiar with Japan's record of international cooperation in the 1920s could not but feel that Japan's present behavior was an aberration, and one that government leaders would soon regret. What was necessary was to provide a way for Japan to retreat with dignity and for China to see that appeal to the League was an effective recourse. It was important, too, to demonstrate that through procedures of arbitration, conciliation, adjudication, and the like there might be justice for all—including the international community that was awaiting the report of the Lytton Commission with a mixture of hope and anxiety.

Knowing as we do that Japan dismissed the report as completely unacceptable, it is difficult to recapture the sheer excitement that had built up in anticipation of its findings. The excitement reflects the belief that somehow things *had* changed internationally, that the League of Nations and the Pact of Paris *had* made a difference, and that the Lytton Report and its reception would somehow reflect those changes. Japan's rejection killed that hope. Had it also killed the notion of change, and was Nathaniel Peffer right? Was Japan's behavior exactly what it would have been in 1913 as though the League of Nations and the attendant efforts to achieve justice through peace had never existed?

Certainly, much of the Japanese military was not friendly toward the League or of the policy of international cooperation that had been pursued by their government in the 1920s. Many officers felt that that policy had shamefully weakened the nation and tarnished their professional reputation as well. News correspondents, interviewing General Jiro Tamon after he had led the successful Japanese campaign into North Manchuria, asked him his attitude toward the League of Nations. Tamon smiled. "The League? What do those talkative gentlemen in Europe know of conditions here? It is absurd for them to attempt to regulate the movement of Japanese troops while we are establishing peace and order in Manchuria. Their activities are very tiresome."[29]

General Shigeru Honjo, commander of Japanese forces in Manchuria, was more tactful but equally sure of Japan's right to carry out its own policy in Manchuria without interference from the rest of the world: "You know, it is too bad about the League. It has a history of ten years during which it has worked for peace. We don't wish to obstruct it nor to lower its prestige. We would like to cooperate with it. But if it does not recognize Japanese rights and interests in Manchuria there exists no basis for cooperation."[30]

Recognition of Japanese rights and interests was not, of course, all that Japan wanted. It also wanted a free hand to protect those rights, and if that meant bringing all of Manchuria under Japanese control, so be it. In fact, given the temper of the military and the confusion and tension in Tokyo, no other way of protecting those rights was given serious consideration. The Lytton Commission's painstaking efforts to acknowledge Japanese claims and suggest alternative means of protection while preserving China's sovereignty was never a matter of policy debate. Too much had happened by the time the report was made public in early October 1932. By then Japan had given official recognition to the "state" of Manchukuo and was publicly committed to the fiction of its independence. Since Japanese "advisers" were the effective government of the area, there was no problem at all in securing protection for Japanese rights and interests.

All of this is on the "1913" side of the balance sheet. Japan had acted unilaterally, overrun Chinese territory, used stalling tactics at Geneva, rejected the substantive findings of the League's commission of inquiry, and, as a dramatic gesture of repudiation, withdrawn from the League entirely. What then of the argument that there had been a fundamental change in the relations between states? Were Aristide Briand, Lord Robert Cecil, Åke Hammarskjöld, and others in their company the soft-headed wishful thinkers they are sometimes made out to be? Briand and Cecil, along with U.S. secretary of state Henry Stimson, had been ridiculed as "idealists" on posters throughout the city of Mukden as part of a carefully orchestrated protest against League "interference." The Lytton Commission had arrived in Hankow to be greeted by handbills that proclaimed, "The Commission are not messengers of peace as they are called. They are merely the spies of the International bandit organization, the League of Nations."[31]

When all of this has been taken into account, it is still possible to argue that there had indeed been a change in international affairs since 1913. It was not so fundamental a change as was believed and hoped by many in the relative calm of the 1920s, but it was still a change. A comparison of the three international commissions of inquiry helps bring this change into focus. The commission dispatched to the Balkans in 1913 by the Carnegie Endowment for International Peace had no official standing, was not received at the highest level by the Greek and Serbian governments, could not get from those governments the documents it needed for a full exploration of the conflict, and claimed to represent the opinion of a public that scarcely knew it existed. The contrast between this and the 1925 commission of inquiry dispatched to the Balkans by the League of Nations is a stark one. The 1925 commissioners had the authority of their League appointments to ask questions of the combatants and to request transportation, food, and lodging so that they could carry out their official tasks. They could also request and, if necessary, demand that they be given the documents they needed to carry out their investigation. The situation did not arise. The combatants had agreed to the dispatch of the commission and cooperated fully with its investigation, as they did in carrying out its recommendations for resolving the issues and preventing further conflicts.

The reception of the Lytton Commission falls somewhere between these two extremes. The commissioners received what might be called semicooperation. It was less than that extended to the 1925 Balkan Commission and a great deal more than that accorded to the 1913 commission. Members of the Lytton Commission were received at the highest levels of government. There *were* instances when the diplomatic courtesies extended to them barely served to cover resentment and a fierce national pride that rejected the very idea of an international investigation. Nevertheless, the commissioners were received. Transportation was provided. Documents were produced. Interviews were granted. In the commissioners' list of more than 150 interviews are the names of prime ministers, presidents, and ministers of war, navy, finance, and foreign affairs, as well as army officers in the field.[32]

It cannot have been easy for Japanese war minister Sadao Araki, for example, to receive men whose opinions, under pre-war circumstances, would not have mattered to him in the slightest. Yet he did grant the commissioners interviews on two separate occasions. In Tokyo in 1932 this was no small matter. The very reception of Lytton and his companions implied, first, that the situation in Manchuria was of international concern and, second, that Japan needed to explain its actions. These were dangerous implications even for so powerful a minister as Araki, but he nonetheless felt constrained to grant the interviews. An intensely moralistic man, his principles of right and wrong were based on his devotion to the state and the emperor. From this flowed his conviction that Japan was divinely appointed to be the leader in Asia. Others might urge economic necessity as the stimulus behind Japanese actions and speak of Manchuria as the "lifeline" of Japan. Araki's argument was much simpler: Japan was destined for greatness, and greatness was defined in terms long familiar in the West. The terms could be encapsulated in one word: empire.[33]

Here was a crusading faith for which men such as Araki in Japan and Honjo and Tamon in Manchuria were prepared to take risks. If, to achieve their goals, they had to overturn the whole framework of international relations exemplified by the League of Nations and the Lytton Commission, they were prepared to do so. Yet they could tell themselves, as they did tell the commissioners on a number of occasions, that they, like the League, desired only peace. They, like the League, were in pursuit of justice.

Two totally different concepts of justice, of peace, and of the international system itself thus met head-on in Asia in 1932. The encounter can be symbolized in the meetings between Victor Alexander George Robert Bulwer Lytton, the second earl of Lytton, and Lieutenant-General Sadao Araki, minister of war in the Inukai and Saito cabinets and one of the leaders of the army's Imperial Way faction. They differed in almost every way it is possible for two men to differ—in appearance, temperament, background, training—but they shared a superb self-confidence. Lytton had the massive, somewhat dense poise of a British peer whose position in life had never been in question and whose approach to international affairs was grounded in a gentleman's code of conduct. Araki's poise was equal to this. Short in stature, he could still stand tall in his own eyes and in those of his fellows, secure in the knowledge that Europeans were not invincible—witness Japan's victory in the Russo-Japanese War—and, further, that no Western power had the political will to stop Japan's destined march to greatness.

Two men. Two faiths. Two kinds of world to be shaped by belief and action. And that was the nub of the matter. Each man could feel justified, even self-righteous, in upholding certain actions in the international sphere. Their justifying points of reference were, however, to different worlds of meaning. Lytton's references were to the League Covenant and the Pact of Paris and the rules of behavior derived from those agreements. These were *international* points of reference. For Lytton, a term such as *justice* took its meaning from this international context. Araki's references, like those of other Japanese spokesmen, were to bilateral agreements with China that, in their view, China was not fulfilling. In this nationalist context, *justice* took on a totally different meaning while losing none of its emotional appeal.

The world that the League of Nations had been shaping since the early 1920s went up against a far older, more powerful world in Asia in the early 1930s and suffered the defeat that looms so large in the accounts of the period. It was not destroyed, however, but continued to exist and to function successfully in areas marginal to great power interests. In this way the hope of securing justice through peace was kept alive for a few more years until World War II overwhelmed the idea entirely and forced a rethinking of the whole concept of justice among nations.

But that was in the future. The question here is the extent, if any, of change in the international system since 1913 when the Balkan commission of inquiry traveled along the edges of officialdom while investigating the conduct of the two Balkan wars. One change is obvious. All the governments involved in 1932, no matter how hostile or resentful, felt obliged to give at least the appearance of cooperation with the League commission of inquiry. Government officials might try to restrict the commission's contacts, as happened most obviously in Manchuria, but heed was paid to this international presence. Officials took care to present the best possible case for their actions and so to influence the report that the commissioners would make. Even so militant a nationalist as Sadao Araki joined the chorus of explanations that poured forth from Tokyo, Mukden, Changchun, and Geneva. This was not a response to great power threats, as it might have been in 1913. Great power policymakers were too distracted by domestic problems to make threats credible, had they been inclined to make any. Japanese explanations were a response to expectations that had been created in the preceding ten years, expectations that reason could prevail, that conflicts could be settled peacefully, and that this was the path to justice. Japanese expansionists might despise these ideas, as they despised the League and its representatives, but in the early 1930s the expectations based on them were too strong to ignore.

So the Japanese were at pains to defend their actions and to nudge them rhetorically into the legitimating sphere of justice and peace that had such a powerful appeal. They defended them in the press and on the radio. They defended them to the Lytton Commission. They defended them in Geneva before the League Council and then, at length, before a special session of the League Assembly. This is the most telling example of the changes that had taken place in the international system since 1913. Japan stayed the course until the final judgment of the assembly, and Japanese spokesmen listened carefully to the parade of speakers and offered counterarguments to the points being made. It is hard to imagine this happening at an earlier period. Can anyone visualize the United States of the late nineteenth century standing before an international assembly to explain its conduct in the Spanish American War or Great Britain answering an international summons to justify its policies in the Boer War? The very idea is ludicrous. But in 1931, 1932, and 1933, the Japanese appeared in Geneva knowing that they would be called on to explain and justify. This was small comfort to the Chinese nation and to residents of Manchuria fleeing before Japanese troops. But it was indeed a measure of change, and a small hope for the future.

CHAPTER SEVEN

The Fruits of Defiance

The special session of the League of Nations Assembly that considered the Lytton Report was more like a trial than anyone intended. In the session, which took place in late 1932 and early 1933, strict formalities were observed. Evidence was presented. Arguments were made. A jurylike body withdrew to consider the evidence and brought in a verdict that was then formally accepted by representatives of forty-two countries.

The obvious defendant before this multinational bar was Japan, and the obvious issue was Manchuria. A close reading of the proceedings, however, makes it clear that Japan's actions in Manchuria were simply the point of attack for accusations against the real defendant: a way of thinking and acting that had, so the prosecution charged, been put aside forever. To a remarkable degree, the accusations came as references to principles of behavior that had been breached or damaged by Japan. This was extremely exasperating to those who were conducting the Japanese defense at Geneva. Kenkichi Yoshizawa, soon to become Japan's foreign minister, was stung to an uncharacteristic outburst: "The League is dealing with ideals while Japan has to deal with facts."[1]

In Yoshizawa's reading of what constituted a fact, Japan's adherence to the League Covenant and the Pact of Paris apparently did not qualify. *Facts* were Japan's interests in Manchuria and the situation of unrest and boycott in China. Added to these was concern for the attitude of those non-League powers, the Soviet Union and the United States. Japanese representatives, whether in Manchuria, Tokyo, or Geneva, never tired of reciting this litany of "facts," and the chief spokesman sent to Geneva to carry the burden of the defense after Yoshizawa had left was no exception to this rule. Yosuke Matsuoka hammered them home again and again and unblushingly cast Japan in the role of savior of peace in Asia: "In a word, Japan is today faced with an appalling situation throughout Eastern Asia, and is fighting single-handed to save the Far East—not to start war in the Far East; far from it. And we are confronting that situation with Soviet Russia still outside the League of Nations."

Given this situation, Matsuoka continued, surely there was room for a looser interpretation of the covenant than other speakers had allowed: "Now, having these cold facts before you, gentlemen, would it not only be common sense to suggest to yourselves that Japan cannot be judged under the Covenant of the League without any elasticity or flexibility being allowed to it—as though the League of Nations included Soviet Russia, the United States of America and all other Powers among its Members, and as though the League of Nations were perfect today?"[2]

But facts, of course, were precisely what the Lytton Commission had been sent to Asia to ascertain, and the League had delayed any substantive action while it waited for those facts to be gathered and brought back to Geneva. The effect of this, as pointed out by W. W. Yen, chief Chinese spokesman at Geneva, had been harder on China than on Japan. After using the interim to occupy China's three eastern provinces, Japan was even now moving against the neighboring province of Jehol—Japanese interests apparently being an infinitely expandable "fact." Yen was courteous but firm: "It is far from the intention of the Chinese government to make any complaint against the slowness of the peace machinery of the League. But the fact remains that delay does not work evenly on both parties to a dispute, and that, so far as the Manchurian case is concerned, the delay has told disastrously upon China."[3] The unequal impact of delay was exactly the point German delegates had made at the Hague Conference in 1899 when objecting to arbitration.

In this case the delay arose from the concern of League officials and delegates to abide strictly by the rules of procedure. The preliminary hearings before the council of the League in the fall of 1931 had been postponed several times at Japan's request. When it finally became clear that, no matter what reassurances were given in Tokyo and Geneva, Japanese troops were not going to be withdrawn into the railway zone, there was further delay while the scope and competence of the commission of inquiry was argued out. These tedious proceedings did not come to a close until December 10, 1931, almost three full months after the explosion on the South Manchurian

Railway. Twelve more months were to pass before Matsuoka and Yen faced
each other in the assembly to present their arguments before their peers and
the public.

Such a meeting would have been inconceivable in 1913, as would the
backgrounds of these two men. They were both products of a general Asian
reaction to penetration by the West in the nineteenth and early twentieth
centuries. The reaction was a complicated mixture of admiration and hostility that often found expression in a determination to take what the West
had to offer and apply that knowledge to a furtherance of Asian goals. In this
case, both men had come to the United States. Wen had left China to seek
his knowledge at the University of Virginia, and Matsuoka had gone from
Japan to the University of Oregon. They were well matched. One reporter
who followed the proceedings in the assembly noted that Matsuoka, besides
having "a winning smile and a friend-making manner," also had the ability
to plead Japan's case in the colloquial English he had learned at Oregon. As
for Wen—he was, said the reporter, "certainly one of the most eloquent and
hard-reasoning debaters the University of Virginia has ever graduated."[4]

The sense that the assembly meetings were, in effect, a trial before peers
and public was reinforced by the setting. A new building for the League was
then under construction, but it would be five years before the assembly
could occupy the new quarters. Meanwhile the assembly, like the council
and the secretariat, made do with makeshift, a fact that seemed to reflect the
ambivalent attitude, particularly of the great powers, toward this new actor
on the international scene. The situation that the caricaturists Derso and
Kelen had found so amusing in the early 1920s still obtained in the early
1930s. The high hopes for justice in the world were crammed into rooms in
the Hotel National and the Hotel Victoria, venerable institutions still redo-
lent of the potted-palm atmosphere of their tourist days.

The assembly met wherever it could, first in the dark and narrow Hall of
the Reformation, then in the more spacious Electoral Building. For the special session that considered the Lytton Report the delegates moved yet
again. In early December 1932 they gathered in a room in the building that
had been constructed for a disarmament conference, then in temporary ad-
journment. The room had the appearance of a courtroom. As one reporter
noted, "It gets this aspect mostly from its long bench. In the center of that
bench sits, on December 6, Paul Hymans, the Belgian Foreign Minister,
who, thirteen years ago, presided over the first Assembly of the League of
Nations."[5]

In this setting, where the highly respected Hymans presided with judicial
impartiality, Wen condemned Japan's actions in Manchuria and Matsuoka

defended them. The other delegates had more general concerns, triggered by Japan's actions but going beyond the specifics of battles and bombings to the effect these might have on the world of justice through peace that the League was trying to bring into being. It was obvious that the web of agreements that was to contain such aggressive actions was being badly torn. The deepest fear was that the very existence of the League was in question. For Joseph Connolly of the Irish Free State (Ireland), the League had no choice. It had to rise to the challenge presented by Japan's actions. If it did not, if it failed to uphold the principles of the covenant, then "it will not survive and, in my opinion, will not deserve to survive."[6]

What were the principles in the Covenant of the League of Nations, principles that speaker after speaker referred to with concern? In 1932 the code of principles that was designed to guide state behavior was not articulated in the detail and precision it later attained in such documents as the United Nations Charter and the Charter of the Organization of American States. The covenant's reference is brief but clear, particularly in the preamble, where the maintenance of international justice was linked to "a scrupulous respect for treaty obligations." Relations between states were to be conducted in the open, not in secret as was common in the past. Members of the League also obligated themselves not to resort to war and to take international law "as the actual rule of conduct among Governments." One important principle was embodied in the tenth article of the covenant, which dealt with preservation of the territorial integrity and political independence of the member states. These were the explicit principles but they were not all, nor the most important. Implied throughout the document was the principle of the peaceful settlement of disputes. Indeed, the whole structure of the organization, particularly the procedures set out in the tenth through the seventeenth articles, was an expression of the principle of peaceful settlement, the necessary, underlying condition for international justice, as then conceived.[7]

Missing from this list is any mention of human rights, the environment, or the international economy—subjects that figured prominently after World War II. In 1932 the concern was almost entirely for the state and its relations with other states. In the special assembly session, the critics of Japan felt comfortable relying wholly on state-centered principles for their arguments. Principle One: disputes were to be settled peacefully. Japan had couched her arguments in bullets and bombs. Principle Two: war was not to be resorted to except in self defense and then only until League procedures could be brought into play. Japan had claimed self-defense in Manchuria but the claim was stretched to the point of absurdity as Japanese troops continued to expand their areas of operations. Principle Three: treaty agreements were to be kept and treaty obligations carried out. This was a modern expression of the very ancient virtue of promise-keeping, an indispensable condition for any lasting relationship. Here, too, Japan had notably failed to uphold an international principle, and in this case it was one on which all the states relied.

Whatever the grievances of either China or Japan, the sanctity of treaties had to remain inviolable or every state was threatened. As Panamanian delegate Narciso Garay observed: "Today, as in the past, my main interest is in the fundamental principles of the Covenant, the safeguarding of the legal guarantees upon which depend the existence and future of all States which do not trust to arms." And again, regarding the League Covenant and the Pact of Paris, "Our one concern is for the fundamental principles and the inviolability of the agreements to which we have loyally adhered."[8]

If there was tension in the assembly it was not because the delegates were unsure which principles needed to be upheld. Tension arose from the fact that the preferred solution to the problem before them was an impossible solution. The delegates wanted to uphold the principles of their corporate existence and at the same time keep Japan in the League. They were certain that defending the principles was the right thing to do. It was also the expected thing. As never before, the attention of those who looked beyond their own national boundaries was fixed on Geneva, and there were not many who, like the American George Bronson Rea, were ready to argue Japan's case. If the delegates failed to uphold the clearly stated principles that Japan had breached, they would be, in effect, cutting off the roots that sustained them all and provided a reason for their existence.[9]

And yet . . . And yet . . . The delegates did not want to force Japan out of the League, and Matsuoka had made it clear that that was the likely consequence of unfavorable assembly action. When a resolution mildly condemnatory of Japan's actions was offered to that body, Matsuoka's reaction was immediate and vehement. He protested against the "one-sided" presentation of the situation in the resolution and asked its sponsors to withdraw it. If they did not, he would ask Hymans to put the resolution to a vote, "so that we may know the sense of the assembly. I am afraid, let me add, that the handling of this resolution may, I even think will, entail consequences not intended or anticipated by the authors of the resolution."[10]

The past lay heavily over the "courtroom" where the delegates to the special session struggled to close one breach—that in the treaty barriers against force—and at the same time avoid opening another—that in the relationship with Japan. The burden of the past was twofold. There was the weight of old ways of thinking and acting that had from the first coexisted with efforts to displace them and were now, seemingly, more powerful than ever. There was also the past record of Japan in the League, which made many delegates reluctant to indulge in open recrimination. Personal friendships were involved, and memories of shared endeavors in which Asians and Europeans had labored together to avert some crisis and preserve the always-precarious peace. As Madariaga observed in a somber vein:

> We all have friends in Japan, dear friends who have taken their part from the first hour in the organization of the League, and the memory of whom has so often tempered our judgments and sealed our lips; friends and colleagues, some of them of long standing on successive Japanese delegations, whose exquisite courtesy has at all times enabled the thorniest problems to be discussed.[11]

Such memories stood like silent and constraining witnesses to the struggle being enacted in Geneva in December 1932. There was Nobuaki Makino, Japanese representative at the Paris Peace Conference of 1919, a quiet, unassuming man of wide sophistication who had helped draft the covenant of the League. Makino, like many in the 1920s and 1930s, saw cooperative action in the League as the way to reconcile the claims of country with the needs of the world at large. So, too, Inazo Nitobe, Yotaro Sugimura, Kikujiro Ishii, Naotake Sato, Mineichiro Adachi. Their faces were familiar and welcome in Geneva; their names and accomplishments were respected there. Nitobe and Sugimura in the League secretariat, Ishii, Sato, and Adachi on numerous League committees, had all spent freely of their patience, talents, and objectivity in furthering the goal of justice through peace.[12]

It was hard to fit these men and their accomplishments into the picture that was emerging as day after day Japanese troops pushed deeper into the province of Jehol. Which was the real Japan? War Minister Sadao Araki with his bellicose statements about Japan's imperial destiny? Or Mineichiro Adachi, a perfect fit for the role of judge on the court that symbolized hope for the rule of law in international affairs? As if in answer, the large delegation that Japan dispatched to Geneva for the special session of the League Assembly was not made up of men like Mineichiro Adachi.

There were six military officers among the group, including Colonel Kanji Ishiwara, one of the chief conspirators in the plot to set the explosion on the railway line in Manchuria. Even Matsuoka, smooth and capable as he was, seemed to have no link to Adachi and other members of past Japanese delegations other than the accident of birth. Matsuoka's tireless defense of Japan's actions, his skillful navigation from point to point in the Lytton Report while ignoring the unfavorable seas between, had one purpose only: to justify Japan in the eyes of the world. Matsuoka did not, like some of the army officers in his own delegation, despise the League. He simply wanted League approval and he worked hard to get it. In effect, he sought an international blessing for Japan's purely national venture.[13]

And that, said Madariaga, was the very heart of the tragedy being played out at Geneva. Two ways of thought and action, two systems of belief were in collision there. The opposing systems were "the national attitude, which sees everything from the angle of national interest, understood in the widest sense and felt with the utmost acuteness, and the international attitude, that newcomer in history, the new moral force which before our eyes is toiling to create a better world." The tragedy was that Japan, while "acting under the influence of a high sense of duty," drew inspiration and strength from a belief system that was antithetical to that of the League. For Madariaga, there was nothing to do but speak plainly, difficult as that might be: "We believe that the permanent interests of Japan are at one with the permanent interests of the League, and that therefore anything that runs counter to the true interest of the League runs counter to the true interests of Japan; and consequently that Japan, the permanent and historic Japan, has a right to learn from us that we are not in agreement with, at all events, the methods of present-day Japan." In response to the insistent Japanese claim that military action was needed to restore order in Manchuria, he added: "The world needs order: but order does not mean uniforms or soldiers. Order is rule, order is right. Let us affirm the right. Let us believe in it. Let us proclaim it."[14]

And so at length the testimony ended, and a committee was handed the task of sifting through and evaluating the mountain of material that had been generated by this controversy: the report of the commission of inquiry, supplementary documents to that report, Chinese and Japanese responses to the report, annexes to those responses, the records of council and assembly proceedings, and the documents that had been provided to the commission by Chinese and Japanese authorities in support of their respective claims. In addition, there were the materials that the commissioners had collected on their own initiative while on their tour of investigation: the handbills that had been posted and circulated and the handwritten petitions and printed statements that had showered in on them from non-official sources. If volume of evidence alone could have solved the ideological dilemma, everyone could have gone home satisfied that justice had been done.

The committee withdrew, but not only to consider the evidence that had been provided in such abundance. For the next two and a half months committee members tried to work out arrangements that would satisfy Japan's stated concerns for its citizens and investments in Manchuria and at the same time restore Chinese territory to China. It was a task undertaken without much hope but with a grim determination to explore every possibility, no matter how slim. Their failure is well known. On February 24, 1933, the assembly adopted the report of its committee. This was, in effect, the Lytton Report, complete with its evaluation of the situation, its careful listing of the grievances of both parties to the dispute, and its recommendations for moving forward. That done, everyone waited for Matsuoka to drop the rhetorical bomb he had been threatening all along.

He did so. "The Japanese Government now finds itself compelled to conclude that Japan and the other Members of the League entertain different views on the manner of achieving peace in the Far East, and the Japanese Government is obliged to feel that it has now reached the limit of its endeavors to cooperate with the League of Nations in regard to the Sino-Japanese differences."[15]

A few more words about peace, a few words of thanks, and that was all. The journal of the assembly session says simply, "(The Japanese delegation withdrew)." It was a muted, courteous defiance, but it was defiance all the same, defiance of everything the League was trying to do. Following the bleak note about Japanese withdrawal, the journal makes the customary notation about the end of formal business: "The Assembly rose at 1:50 P.M."[16] So the events triggered by a minor explosion on a railway near Mukden, Manchuria, at 10:20 P.M. on September 18, 1931, came to a climax in a crowded room in Geneva, Switzerland, at 1:50 P.M. on February 24, 1933. In the annals of international history, these had been an extraordinary seventeen months. They were extraordinary not for the conflict involved—conflict, after all, antedated the states system itself—but for the efforts that had been made to resolve the conflict on lines other than those of sheer power and the usual horse-trading among special interests. The proceedings in Geneva give striking evidence of these different lines of settlement and of what was widely felt to be their utility in the Sino-Japanese conflict.

For many of those who spoke at the special session of the League Assembly, the word *utility*, although accurate, would scarcely be strong enough to convey their feelings. *Necessity* would be closer to the message that emerged as speaker after speaker took the podium to state his government's policy on the issues before them. All declared that the issues were momentous. Not one failed to mention the principles of the covenant and of the Pact of Paris that must be upheld. Delegates from twenty-five countries other than China and Japan spoke on December 6 and 8, the two days when there were public hearings in this exceptional session. They were Australia, Canada,

Chile, Colombia, Czechoslovakia, Denmark, France, Germany, Greece, Guatemala, Hungary, the Irish Free State, Italy, Mexico, The Netherlands, Norway, Panama, Poland, Romania, Spain, Sweden, Switzerland, Turkey, the United Kingdom, and Uruguay.

There was a remarkable degree of unanimity among these speakers. They came from countries that differed widely in size, location, history, resources, population, and forms of government, but they were agreed on one thing: the principles of the League Covenant and the Pact of Paris had to be upheld. Even Sir John Simon of the United Kingdom, whose lukewarm attitude toward the League was well known in the assembly, stepped out of character on this occasion: "For all of us alike the Covenant of the League of Nations is our constitutional law. It is the reason why we are here; it is the fundamental law. . . . We are not at liberty to disregard it. We are bound to sustain it."[17]

Some of the delegates spoke, as did Simon, of the covenant in general; some referred in broad terms to the covenant's principles and to those of the Pact of Paris; some mentioned specific principles on which the well-being and safety of all states depended. Regarding treaties and their obligations Carlos Saavedra Lamas of Argentina stated: "Of these principles we attach particular importance to the one which has so often been proclaimed and must inspire every international organization—namely strict respect for treaties." Equally concerned was Osten Undén of Sweden: "The weakening of confidence in the interpretation and application of the international treaties concluded with a view to organizing peace, and, in particular, of that on which the League is based, is being felt everywhere and is disturbing the relations between all countries."

Regarding the obligation not to resort to force, except in self-defense, Eduard Benes of Czechoslovakia stated: "When examining similar cases in the past, we have solemnly affirmed one of the essential principles of the Covenant—namely, that, when a dispute arises between a Member of the League and a neighboring State, that Member shall never have the right to take the law into its hands by resorting to force." The point was emphasized by the Swiss delegate, Giuseppe Motta: "If the States Members of the League ceased to admit the maxim that none may take the law into his own hands, or that the very justification of our institution is its categorical condemnation of violence in international relations, then it would be better to say quite frankly that our hopes of achieving a new international order are vain!"

Regarding the Japanese claim of self-defense, Nicholas Politis of Greece commented: "This question of self defense, which is so difficult of exact definition, has already been subjected to rules drawn up by our organization. . . . The first rule is that every act of violence does not necessarily justify its victim in resorting to war and does not release it from the specific obligations [for peaceful settlement] laid down in Articles 12 and following of the Covenant. . . . The second rule is that legitimate defence implies the adoption of measures proportionate to the seriousness of the attack and the use of which is justified by the imminence of the danger."[18]

And so it went, as twenty-five speakers in turn affirmed their government's support of international principles that, if observed, would have reduced the Manchurian Incident to the minor affair it actually was on the night of September 18. In the short run, these affirmations had little effect. The Japanese military did not care what "the talkative gentlemen" in Geneva were saying. They saw themselves as warriors of destiny with an empire to win. Matsuoka, keen as ever, saw clearly that the weakness of the League lay in its inability to follow through on the brave words being spoken in Geneva. As he said, even if every recommendation of the Lytton Commission were adopted, who would see them through to completion? "In case any plan for settlement is found by the League, this organization must take upon itself the responsibilities for its execution. Considering the actual condition in China, the execution is one that is likely to be costly, and the League should have both the will and the means to make the necessary sacrifices. Is any Member of the League ready to participate with others in such an undertaking?"[19]

In 1925, on the small scale of the Greco-Bulgarian dispute, the answer might have been yes. In fact, there *was* meaningful follow-through on that conflict, with the League helping to arrange loans for both countries for the purposes of reconstruction and then handling the distribution of seed, livestock, and farming equipment, and the rebuilding of houses for the dispossessed.[20] In 1932, both the scale and the context of events were completely different. In the midst of widespread economic distress, no member of the League, and certainly not the United States or the Soviet Union, was willing to go beyond the methods of investigation, persuasion, and moral pressure that had been tried for seventeen months and had failed. The victory of Japanese expansionists appeared to be complete, and Matsuoka's skepticism about the political will of Japan's critics and their readiness to sacrifice was fully justified.

But this outcome was not the only fruit of Japanese defiance. The effort to define what justice might be in an international context registered a clear victory in the special assembly session. The international principles of the League of Nations Covenant were overwhelmingly affirmed. Here was a public debate about standards of international behavior, a debate that did not take place in the abstract or in the academy but in the very center of a political arena of clashing interests and national passions. Here were political veterans—shrewd, experienced, knowledgeable—giving serious attention to matters that had hitherto been the concerns of those with little power to influence events: peace organizations, study groups, law and arbitration societies. Constrained as they were by the domestic and foreign policies of the countries they represented, the delegates yet rose to heights of philosophy as they struggled to bring principles and practice into some kind of working relationship. "We sincerely wish to act in this matter as practical men," said Sir John Simon with the self-satisfaction of one who is convinced that he himself is eminently practical. And again: "We must concern ourselves with the realities."[21]

But even for Simon and other "practical" men, the realities included the principles on which the League was based and which, if they were to have any meaning at all, needed to govern relations among the member states. For an example they had the Lytton Report, that supremely practical document. Its authors had not hesitated to speak of the principles on which a settlement of the Sino-Japanese dispute should be based, and one of those principles was conformity with the provisions of the covenant. So Simon was driven back to the same ground where other delegates had taken their stand and could only call for good will in application of the principles they all supported: "If we are going to act as practical people, we must have a basis, and I can see no basis except that which this report provides. We must stand by the principles of the League, and stand by them not for the purpose of reproaching others in language of superiority, which is so easy, but in a spirit of friendliness and comradeship we must promote conciliation."[22]

Although he prided himself on his practical approach to international affairs, Simon's words spoke more of hope than of practicality. The League principles that informed the Lytton Report's recommendations had been rejected by Japan. It was hard to see what friendliness and comradeship could accomplish unless the giving was to be all on one side while Japan continued on the way it had chosen in 1931. It was a way that would, within fifteen years, lead to a trial in Tokyo, where some of the Japanese who had been involved in the Manchurian Incident would stand charged as war criminals.[23] In the early thirties, even the most rabid supporter of Japan's expansionist policies could scarcely have foreseen that outcome.

The arguments in the Tokyo trial were a continuation of the debates that had taken place in the League Assembly in Geneva in late 1932 and early 1933. They were also a continuation and elaboration of the arguments that

Hugo Grotius had made three hundred years earlier. When was war justified? How should it be fought? What about promises? How made? To whom? How kept? What *were* international standards of behavior? How were they to be enforced? Was the Grotian approach the last word or just the beginning of the long and complicated task of giving justice an international meaning? Even in 1932 there were some who wanted to push beyond Grotius: "The nations must become imbued with the idea that war is a crime," said Dutch foreign minister Beelaerts van Blokland, "that it must be abandoned as a means of national policy, and that the settlement of disputes must never be sought except by pacific means."[24]

The Greek delegate, Nicholas Politis, agreed. On his election as president of the assembly in the fall of 1932, he took the occasion to list the gains that had been made in international affairs: the Permanent Court of International Justice, the General Act of Arbitration, the Paris Pact with its rejection of war as an instrument of national policy. Politis then offered this somber observation: "These guarantees, I well know, are not yet enough to give the peoples the certainty that—admitting the possibility of sheer madness—they may not find themselves once again exposed to the horrors, the mourning, the ruin of war—war which they have stigmatized as the most odious of crimes, which they have outlawed, to which they have solemnly vowed never again to have recourse."[25]

When Politis spoke, this "most odious of crimes" lay just a few years ahead. Among the many effects of this renewal of war was a change in the whole interwar concept of international justice. The idea of peace as the vehicle of justice was not abandoned. Instead, added to that idea was the realization that, under certain circumstances, more might be required.

CHAPTER EIGHT

An Era Unknown

All was not gloom and doom in international affairs in the early 1930s. There was also a little-known period of optimism and success that buoyed hopes even in the midst of struggles with Japan. Many people, both in the League of Nations and outside of it, kept faith with the interwar dream of international justice through international peace. Using the concepts and institutions at their command, they continued to build up barriers to the unilateral use of force—procedures of adjudication, administration, and conciliation. These barriers could not withstand the concerted attacks of the mid-1930s, but until then they made it possible to believe that justice through peace might still be achieved in relations between nations.

ADJUDICATION AND A CIVIL QUARREL

Any account of the early 1930s must recognize the importance of empire and its influence on the international actions and attitudes of powers great and small. These would include the major powers, France, Great Britain, and the Soviet Union, but also The Netherlands, Portugal, Belgium, Italy, and Denmark. The United States, too, is on this list even though by the early thirties it was making various moves toward independence for the Philippines, one of its possessions. Interventions in the Caribbean and acquisitions in the Pacific as a result of the Spanish-American War at the end of the nineteenth century qualified the United States as an imperial power. And empire was central in the international history of this period. No move was made or vote cast without a consideration of the possible effect on the colonies, those outlying hostages to uncontrollable fortune. This was the club from which Germany had been ousted after World War I, when the country was stripped of its colonies. And latecomer Japan sought increased standing there.

Even as Japan was reaching for greater empire in eastern Asia, cracks were appearing in the structure of European empires. A portent of things to come arrived in London in 1931 in the person of a small brown-skinned man wrapped in layers of homespun. As sole representative of the Indian National Congress, Mohandas K. Gandhi (Mahatma) had come to London to present India's demands to its imperial masters. He was not then seen as a portent, however, but more as an oddly dressed nuisance who had to be dealt with because of his support back in India. The official attitude toward empire that was common then can be seen in the elaborate colonial exposition that opened near Paris in the spring of 1931. The Exposition Coloniale Internationale was designed to impress but also to inform and, not least, to strengthen the emotional ties of empire. Visitors could shop in an Algerian marketplace, stroll through a French West African village, or gaze at a replica of the temple of Angkor Wat, all the while absorbing the glories of empire. Despite domestic difficulties and persistent economic woes, it was, in many respects, a confident time.[1]

Japan's actions in Manchuria in 1931 had shaken international confidence somewhat, but these aggressive moves were balanced by actions elsewhere that seemed to point in a different, more positive direction. For a while in 1931 the leaders of several European states seemed willing to give serious consideration to the plan of European union that was the pet—and last—project of the French leader, Aristide Briand. There was a brief wave of optimism that the states of Europe would at last recognize their common interests in the free exchange of goods and would put aside the economic rivalries that had in the past led to fratricidal wars. Optimism was given another boost by the entry of a new and vibrantly hopeful state government on the international scene. Nineteen thirty-one was the year of the Spanish Spring, when a republic was proclaimed in that old and violent land and a constitution adopted that announced, "Spain renounces war as an instrument of national policy. The Spanish state will respect the universal rules of international law and will incorporate them in its positive law."[2]

In the early 1930s the word *law* was an unbroken vessel, still strong enough to carry the hopes that had been expressed in the preamble to the Covenant of the League of Nations. There the member states had agreed to "the firm establishment of the understandings of international law as the actual rule of conduct among Governments."[3] So 1931 was notable also for an incident of potential violence between two states in which it was agreed from the first that the understandings of international law would indeed be their actual rule of conduct. In the midst of public passion and reckless accusations in the press of both countries, the foreign ministries of Denmark and Norway took their conflicting territorial claims to the Permanent Court of International Justice at The Hague and let the outcome of their conflict be decided by law.

The incident that set off this train of events was a minor one. In any other context it might well have passed unnoticed or been settled on the spot by the parties directly involved. In an international context where national pride and pressure from opposition parties have to be figured in as part of the proceedings, the smallest of incidents has explosive potential. So it was in the early summer of 1931 when some Norwegian hunters led by Hallvord Devold proclaimed Norway's possession of a portion of Greenland's east coast, despite Danish claims to sole title and possession of the whole island.[4] In a bid for historical legitimacy the hunters called their claim Erik Raudes Land, suggesting a title that dated from the discovery of Greenland by the Norse explorer Eric the Red. In a bid for current support they called on that most potent of modern symbols, the national flag. There on Greenland's rocky and windswept coast they raised the Norwegian flag. This flag, with its white-bordered blue cross on a red ground, evoked Norwegian pride with unusual force. During Norway's stormy and difficult union with Sweden, which had ended only in 1907, Swedish restrictions on the use of the Norwegian flag had been a constant irritant. Now Norwegians were free to display their flag as they chose, and if those in the homeland would not have chosen the east coast of Greenland for that display, still, there it was. Something would have to be done about the situation.

After some hesitation, the Norwegian government accepted the fait accompli, and on July 10, 1931, issued a proclamation declaring sovereignty over and possession of Greenland's east coast between 71° 30′ and 75° 40′N. Denmark immediately asked the international court at The Hague to find Norway's actions to be a breach of the legal order and as such to be illegal and invalid. The Danish application to the court asserted strongly that "Denmark, for a long time, has had complete sovereignty over all of Greenland, a fact that has found expression in legislative and administrative arrangements as well as in a series of treaties both old and recent."[5] The die was cast. It was now up to the court.

Clearly, a dispute at this level had not flared up overnight. The hunters' coup and the subsequent proclamation by the Norwegian government brought to a climax more than a decade of diplomatic exchanges and disagreements. These were rehearsed in great detail in the written and oral arguments presented to the court. The two states did not simply have their day in court. They had many days. The court sat in public session on thirty-one days to hear the disputants' oral arguments, and on most of those days there were sessions both morning and afternoon. This was after hundreds of pages of written arguments had already been filed with the court, along with supporting maps and documents—247 for Denmark, 269 for Norway.[6] If all that had been involved was possession of a strip of coast that was ice-bound for much of the year, these efforts would have been ridiculously out of proportion. But that was not all that was involved.

In a system of territorially based states, boundaries are of primary importance. They separate ways of life and systems of government and taxation. They can make a difference not only in quality of life but in life itself. The question of where a border is drawn is significant not only for the disputants but for the system as a whole, since the arguments that are found compelling in one case may well become the determining factor in future cases. Even outside the law, precedent is a powerful support.

In justifying the movement of Japanese troops out of the railway zone in Manchuria, for example, Japan relied heavily on precedent. Japanese spokesmen pointed out again and again that this action was not unprecedented, that an international force had been sent into China during the Boxer Rebellion to rescue diplomatic personnel, that the United States had sent troops into Haiti and Nicaragua to restore order, and that as recently as 1927 Great Britain had sent troops into Shanghai and had all but told the League of Nations to stay out of the affair.[7] So it mattered what arguments the international court accepted in the case of East Greenland. Nobody but the disputants cared much who got the narrow strip of land on the eastern border of Greenland's central ice shield, but it made a difference to others how the question was decided.

Both sides in the case relied on three types of argument. They argued from history, from principles of international law, and from present circumstance. The history that Norway brought to its case was one of bold early exploration and settlement of Greenland. They did not dispute Denmark's sovereignty over the *west* coast, but they argued that the east coast was *terra nullius*, a land without a sovereign. According to all legal authorities—which the Norwegian agents quoted at length—Norway had a right to proclaim its sovereignty over this area where there were neither settlements nor natives and where there *were* Norwegian hunters. Hard as conditions were, those men wrung a living from the land through their bravery and endurance. They deserved to be protected by Norwegian, not Danish, law.[8]

For their part, the Danes saw the historical record as a clear confirmation of the Danish claim. The record showed that at least since the eighteenth century there had been a continuous Danish occupation and administration of the whole island. The Danish trade monopoly, of which Norway and others complained, was simply part of the protective administrative mantle that Denmark had thrown over Greenland and maintained at considerable cost to itself. The removal of that mantle, even if partial, would not only open the way to depletion of the natural resources there, it would also injure the natives who depended on hunting and fishing for their subsistence.[9]

The welfare of the natives was a recurrent theme in Danish arguments before the court and in Danish efforts outside the court to mobilize public opinion on their behalf as well. To this end, the Danish government sponsored a Greenland Pavilion at the 1931 Exposition Coloniale in Paris that featured views of the island's rugged scenery and examples of native art and accomplishments under Danish administration. According to the Danish Ministry of Foreign Affairs, their exhibit at the colonial exhibition, where they were cheek by jowl with the heavyweights in empire, had "attracted great attention." The ministry did not add that by its very presence the exhibit had also asserted Denmark's claim to this Arctic land in the ongoing dispute with Norway.[10]

Through perception or luck, the Danish government had retained one of the best legal minds of the time to help present its case at The Hague. When at the end of November 1932 Charles De Visscher rose to address the court, those familiar with this Belgian's work knew that the argument was in a master's hands. Within five years, De Visscher would be elected to the bench that he faced as an advocate in the quarrel between Norway and Denmark.[11] His task in 1932 was to sum up the Danish case. But for De Visscher, the immediate and short-term were always linked to longer-term considerations. It is this that gives his arguments relevance beyond a 1930s courtroom and lifts this dispute over a rocky strip of coastland out of its limiting and somewhat trivial circumstances.

De Visscher's opening was brief and to the point. He noted Denmark's request that the court find Norway's actions illegal. He referred to Norway's contention that the land in dispute was terra nullius, hence legally open to occupation. He then swung into action. It may be useful, he said, to look in a general way at this idea of terra nullius. The question "by its very nature is of interest to all states."[12] Thus, within a few minutes of starting,

De Visscher had moved the argument to the higher ground of general considerations that alone could keep a mind such as his engaged in international law. Since World War I the field had been growing rapidly, but its development could not keep pace with its pretensions. Throughout his life De Visscher was aware of this. Surveying the field twenty years after his 1932 appearance at The Hague, he could still say of the rules of international law, "Too often an atmosphere of unreality surrounds their ritualistic exposition."[13] In 1932 he was concerned to avoid this and yet show how such rules developed in relation to the political realities with which states of the international system were faced.

Take the question of sovereignty over eastern Greenland. Until the early 1920s, no one had questioned Denmark's sovereignty, which had been expressed in many Danish administrative and legislative acts. Quickly De Visscher moved to his larger point: When, over a long period of time, the community of states has affirmed the sovereignty of a state over a particular place, that, in itself, is a form of international recognition. So the problem before the court is not simply a problem between two states. It is a question that concerns "the general international order."[14]

Thus did De Visscher link the quarrel between Norway and Denmark to one of the fundamentals of the international system: recognition. The validity of any territorial claim—indeed, the very legitimacy of a state—depended then and still depends on recognition by the other states in the system. This need for collective endorsement leads quickly to questions that cluster around the whole concept of independent states in relation with each other. What constitutes recognition? Who is to decide? If, as De Visscher asserted, there is a "general international order," what kind of order is that? How established? How maintained? These questions were of immediate, short-term interest to those in the courtroom that November day, but their importance extends beyond that day and the case that was being argued. The lawyers who stood to plead, the judges who sat to listen, had given their careers to the consideration of such questions and to other seemingly trivial disputes as well. In the past, such disputes had most often been resolved by force of arms. Now the hope was that that would change. The very courtroom in which the case was being heard was a concrete expression of that hope.

The room was designed to impress, to convey a sense of the grandeur of the effort to bring force within the reach and rule of law. It was called the Great Court, or sometimes the Great Hall of Justice, and its dimensions and design lived up to the adjectives. Its crystal chandeliers hung from a vaulted and elaborately decorated ceiling thirty feet above the floor. Oak-paneled

walls, a painting of Peace and Justice, and large stained glass windows contributed to the general sense that here was the abode of majesty, and if the
majesty lay more in concept than in execution, the splendor of the surroundings yet served as an ever-present reminder of the goal. There was
room on the floor for three hundred spectators, and there was a small
gallery to hold any overflow. A railing separated the spectators from the
agents and counsel who sat at tables to either side of the lawyer's stand. Before them, four broad steps led up to the focal point of the room, the long
curved bench where sat the judges. They faced the courtroom, slightly removed by elevation and distance from the disputants in the case but deeply
involved in the most minute details of argument.

The panel of judges, which was elected by the council and the assembly
of the League of Nations, had recently been enlarged from eleven to fifteen
to obtain wider representation on the bench. The make-up of the first panel
(1921–1930) had been heavily weighted toward the West. The enlarged
panel before which De Visscher argued was about evenly divided between
the developed states of the West and the less-developed states of eastern
Europe, Asia, and Latin America.[15] It was a small start, but it was a start
toward including more of the world in this first world court of international law.

The court's supporters were at all times aware that there was opposition
to the whole idea of an institution that could in any respect be thought of as
a world court. The image of an international body sitting in judgment on
the actions of sovereign, independent states was enough to push some national patriots into spasms of fear. The fact that the court could operate only
in the extremely cramped and limited space allowed it by those same states
had little effect on the opposition. The hope of the court's supporters was to
win over its opponents by compiling a record of such careful and judicious
behavior that the most rabid patriot could not take alarm. To this end, if the
regular panel of judges did not include judges from the countries that were
parties to a dispute before the court, each of those countries had a right to
appoint one of its nationals to the bench. These ad hoc judges sat with the
rest, were equal partners in the deliberations, and voted on the judgments.
There were two ad hoc judges on the panel considering the case of eastern
Greenland, one from Norway and one from Denmark.[16]

In a further effort to allay any fears of railroading or carelessness in details of the law, the court's procedures were designed to allow the parties in
the disputes before it their full and complete say. One consequence of this
was that events could easily outstrip the deliberations of the court. This had
happened when the court was asked for an advisory opinion on the legality

of a customs union between Germany and Austria and did not manage to issue its opinion until after the union had already been canceled by the two states in response to heavy political pressure from France.[17] In the Greenland case, the Norwegian hunters in East Greenland were patient and the two disputants were cooperative, and the case followed a stately and deliberate course through the procedures of the court to the very end. The end came in the spring of 1933 with the final judgment in the case. The judges upheld Denmark's claim to sovereignty over all of Greenland and found that the Norwegian occupation of East Greenland was "a violation of the existing legal situation"[18] and was, therefore, unlawful and invalid. There were two dissenting opinions. The Italian judge disagreed with the grounds of the judgment. The Norwegian judge simply disagreed. Not surprisingly, he thought that Norway had a valid claim

When the judgment was read on April 5, 1933, almost twenty-one months had passed since the Norwegian declaration of sovereignty over Erik Raudes Land on the east coast of Greenland. As foreign correspondent Clair Price had noted earlier in the *New York Times*, the world of the Permanent Court was far removed from the volatility of international politics. At The Hague one would not find "the quick compromise, the exhilarating expediencies, the lively sense of reality which make international politics the most fascinating game in the world." Instead one would find "a solemn and academic atmosphere in which the most full-blooded of international disputes pales away into legal formulae."[19]

That was not the final word, however, for anyone following the work of the Permanent Court with sympathy and an understanding of the conditions under which the court worked. Price went on: "Politics pass, but law endures, and the fact that every judgment of the court adds to the still incomplete structure of international law has a significance which far outruns the passing moment."[20]

Tedious and slow as the process of adding to that structure was (and is), there were advantages in the "solemn and academic atmosphere" that Price had noted. The "legal formulae" to which nationalistic passions were reduced in such an atmosphere provided grounds for discussion and argument, rather than the head-to-head confrontation of conflict outside the courtroom. Even as the judgment in the Greenland case was being read at The Hague, other methods of dispute resolution were being tried in the "fascinating game" of international politics. In South America, Peruvian planes were bombing Colombian boats on the Amazon River, and Bolivian forces were launching attacks against the Paraguayan fort of Nanawa.[21] In eastern Asia, Japanese troops continued to campaign outside the three east-

ern provinces of Manchuria. They had taken the neighboring province of
Jehol and were even then pushing south of the Great Wall, where they were
engaged in battle with Chinese troops.

In the midst of these conflicts it was easy to overlook the quiet reading of
a legal judgment at The Hague and its prompt acceptance by the losing
party in the case. Norway immediately withdrew its proclamation of sovereignty over Erik Raudes Land. The judges in the case, the lawyers, the
agents, and—not least—the governments of the two disputing countries
had achieved a signal triumph. Under severe pressure for bold and forceful
action, the two governments had kept the peace. Because they had done so
they were able to go to court and ask for justice under the law. As might be
expected, in their arguments before the court each relied on a different definition of justice. The important point, though, is that each was willing to
let the court weigh these conflicting claims in the scales of the law. The unspoken assumption was that the disputants would abide by the result of that
weighing on the grounds that, imperfect as it might be, it was still the best
approach to a just solution in an imperfect world.

The deliberations of the judges of the international court are conducted
in private, so it is not known what arguments might have gone on behind
the scenes before the judges filed into the courtroom on April 5, 1933, for
the reading of the final judgment. What can be known from an examination
of the judgment is that the judges had not addressed the case as national advocates but as advocates of the law. Clearly they had been mindful of the
oath they had taken when sworn into office: "I solemnly declare that I will
exercise all my powers and duties as a judge honourably and faithfully, im-
partially and conscientiously."[22]

A perfect exemplification of the virtues set out in the oath of office was
Mineichiro Adachi, president of the court when the East Greenland case
was heard. His was a special relationship to the newly fledged institution.
Not only had he served in 1920 on the committee that had written the
court's statute, he had, even as a law student in Japan, dreamed of the day
when an international court might be created and on which he might serve.
The first part of the dream came true when the Permanent Court of International Justice was inaugurated in the Peace Palace at The Hague on February 15, 1922. The second part began to come true when Adachi was
elected to the bench by the unanimous vote of the members of the League
Council and an overwhelmingly favorable vote in the assembly.

His inaugural address as president of the court put into words the strong
sense of duty and responsibility that he felt toward this institution "which
was to be the living embodiment of the conception of peace based on law."

Adachi put great faith in institutions, both as stabilizers and as creators of international order. People would come and go, making their contribution in the brief span of their activity, but the institution would remain. As Adachi noted, "The conception endures, and the institution remains, but men change." It was important, then, for the judges "who at any given moment have the great responsibility and honour of composing the Court" to be mindful that, although their tenure was but "an instant" in the life of the institution, they had a sacred duty to pass on to their successors "the heritage of confidence and authority which their predecessors, to their lasting merit, have succeeded in winning for the Court in public opinion."[23]

Åke Hammarskjöld, who, besides being registrar of the court was also Adachi's longtime friend, recalled that Adachi's delicate appearance and refusal to argue deceived those who did not know him well. Behind this apparent fragility and willingness to yield were strong convictions that upheld him even in the days of his final illness. One of the strongest of Adachi's convictions concerned the moral obligation of a judge. This obligation was twofold, extending, on one hand, to the court as an institution and, on the other, to the law that was both interpreted and developed by that court. For this moral obligation, said Hammarskjöld, Adachi had found a happy phrase, "a phrase which is worthy of recalling: He said that it was a judge's duty to robe himself with divinity—*de se diviniser.*"

Hammarskjöld went on, "To fulfil this duty to the end, even beyond the limits imposed by his physical strength, that was for him the goal, that was his aim every day and every moment of each day which he spent in the Court. It was striking and inspiring to see that great diplomat transforming himself by the power of his will into a judge in the lofty sense in which he understood the word."[24]

It was perhaps asking too much of the human beings who composed the panel of judges that heard the East Greenland case to clothe themselves with divinity for their judicial roles. It was enough that they worked hard to be impartial and thorough, to find according to the law as they understood it, and to contribute to the development of that law through which—as they believed—the prideful, quarrelsome states of the international system would find justice, and—as a result—that long-sought prize, security.

There is one last picture to hold in mind of these mostly forgotten judges of a mostly forgotten court: a row of black-robed men, a froth of white lace at their throats, enthroned behind the curved bench at the front of the Great Hall of Justice in the Peace Palace at The Hague. As they sat in solemn attendance on the law, they were themselves a symbol of the world they wanted to bring into being. Japanese troops were battling Chinese troops south of the Great Wall in China, but the Japanese judge, Mineichiro Adachi, and the Chinese judge, Ch'ung-hui Wang, were colleagues and co-workers at The Hague. The Belgian, Charles De Visscher, was not afraid to entrust his client's cause to the German judge, Walter Schücking, despite German-Belgian enmity in World War I. Schücking, in turn, was a valued member of a bench that included three judges from countries his country had fought less than twenty years earlier: Henri Fromageot from France, Sir Cecil Hurst from Great Britain, and Henri Rolin-Jaequemyns from Belgium. This is not the full panel, but it is enough to make the point that these fifteen men, proud and devoted servants of their countries as they were, took on a different role at The Hague. They were first and foremost servants of the law and of the idea that through the law the linked goals of justice and peace could be attained.

Before the court was formed, Léon Bourgeois had found the words to express the concept behind the judges who sat on the bench that April day in 1933 to give judgment in the case before them. Bourgeois was a veteran of the battles that had finally brought the court into being—battles with indifference, with skepticism, with the "realism" that placed its reliance on armed might. Shakily, emotionally, the ailing and battle-scarred Bourgeois addressed the committee that was drafting the statute for the court:

> You are about, Gentlemen, to give life to the judicial power of humanity. Philosophers and historians have told us of the laws of the growth and decadence of Empires. We look to you, Gentlemen, for laws which will assure the perpetuity of the only empire which can show no decadence, the empire of justice, which is the expression of eternal truth.[25]

SUPERVISION AND A TEACUP WAR

In the period between the two world wars, no institution had the power to force contending states to take their dispute to the Permanent Court of International Justice, as Denmark and Norway had done. If adjudication was refused—and it frequently was—other means of resolution had to be found. One means that was used with some success in the early 1930s was that of international supervision. The term covers a range of activities from the oversight of elections to the administration of a disputed territory on a day-to-day basis. International supervision was never the preferred option, but when agreement could not be reached on the disposition or governance of an area, the problem was sometimes placed in the hands of an international body. In theory this was a kind of holding action to allow tempers to cool and satisfactory arrangements to be made. In practice, rather more was achieved. In Upper Silesia, the Saar Basin, and the Letitia Trapezium, invaluable experience was gained in the art of maneuvering between contending forces while carrying out essential civic functions that the disputants were unable or unwilling to perform for themselves.

The people performing these civic functions represented the international community at large, rather than any single state, even their own. They compiled lists of eligible voters, observed the voting process, served on standing arbitral commissions, acted on petitions, ruled on conflicting claims, and consulted endlessly with the aggrieved. The tasks of the international representatives varied with the circumstances with which they were confronted. There was, however, one common element. Their very presence in the disputed areas helped deter the violence that lay always near the surface of ancient animosities or unbridled ambition. They were a reminder of a world beyond local rancor and national pride, and their activities served daily notice that that larger world now had a stake in the outcome of events.

Without the internationally headed Mixed Commission and the Arbitral Tribunal in Upper Silesia, there would have been open battle between Germans and Poles long before the end of the 1930s—when those mediating bodies no longer existed. Without the international Saar Governing Commission, conflict between Germany and France could never have been contained long enough for the 1935 plebiscite to be held—as it successfully was. Without the international Letitia Commission, Colombia and Peru would have laid the foundation for generations of bitter reprisals as they fought for possession of the small Amazonian port of Letitia and its hinterland (roughly trapezoidal, hence called the Trapezium).[26]

When the members of the commission stepped outside their temporary headquarters in Letitia the morning of June 25, 1933, and raised a flag bearing the legend "League of Nations Letitia Commission" in dark blue letters on a white ground, they symbolically proclaimed an international presence and interest in this remote trouble spot in the Amazonian basin. But this flag, which for some internationalists might serve as a symbol of the future, was joined by another, more evocative of the past. On a separate flagstaff, the commissioners raised the Colombian flag, and the two flags flew side by side, an apt declaration of the contradictory mix of ideas and authorities that characterized the international system in the 1930s and that still characterizes international relations today.

The events that led to the presence of a League of Nations commission two thousand miles up the Amazon River began in 1932. These events, like those in Greenland and in Manchuria a year earlier, were set in motion by people acting without the authorization of their respective governments. In Greenland, when Norwegian hunters seized a portion of the eastern coast, they forced the hand of the Norwegian government in its ongoing dispute with Denmark. The Japanese government was put in a similar position when conspirators in the Japanese army stationed in the South Manchurian Railway Zone forced open combat with Chinese troops outside the zone. So in Letitia in the early morning hours of September 1, 1932.

The port of Letitia and the whole of the Trapezium belonged by treaty to Colombia, but the treaty was recent (1922) and much disputed by those who felt that the area belonged by right to Peru. This "right" was forcibly asserted by a band of armed Peruvians early on September 1. They drove out the Colombian officials stationed in Letitia and took possession of the town and the government buildings. They thus forced the hand of the Peruvian government. Like Norwegian and Japanese officials before them, Peruvian officials felt constrained to support actions taken without authorization. Diplomatic negotiations could not but seem tedious and fruitless compared to these bold moves on the ground. Norway's diplomatic engagement with Denmark, Japan's with China, and Peru's with Colombia had produced little that could compel public support, much less the public enthusiasm that greeted these sudden strikes to seize the sought-for prize and thus to change the terms of the argument. Besides, in all three countries, there was an opposition party in the wings, eager to take advantage of any sign of government weakness. After a show of reluctance, the Peruvian government backed the armed men in Letitia and sent government troops to their support.

While diplomatic moves by the United States and by members of the League attempted to contain the conflict before blood was shed, the two countries alternated between professing peace and preparing for war. Conscripts were called up. Arms purchases were increased. Colombia sent troops up the Amazon. Peru sent airplanes to bomb the troops. A small force of Peruvian ships was hurried through the Panama Canal and down the coast to enter the Amazon and proceed to the scene of action, a journey of five thousand miles to the mouth of the Amazon alone.

As these maneuvers suggest, the ability of the two countries to inflict damage on each other was limited by their mutual unreadiness for battle and by the fact that the scene of conflict was awkwardly far from their centers of population. Nonetheless, in February 1933, Colombian forces managed to take a Peruvian fort in the northeast corner of the Trapezium. This victory, remote and minuscule as it might seem, sent jubilant Colombian crowds into the streets and raised war fever in that country to such a pitch that the government's room for diplomatic maneuvering was severely limited.

Crowds poured into the streets in Lima, Peru, as well, but they were furious, not jubilant, and they directed their fury against the Colombian embassy. The Colombian minister barely escaped with his life, and the crowd looted and burned the embassy building. This ugly turn in what until then could scarcely be called a war was followed by several skirmishes in the Trapezium that inflicted casualties on both sides. Suddenly the bizarre aspects of the affair were overshadowed by the fact that people were being killed. There were renewed peace efforts by the League, by Brazil (uneasy neighbor to the conflict), and by the United States. Most interestingly, there were also admonitory notes to Peru from Great Britain, France, Germany, and Italy.

Traditionally, a border dispute between two South American countries would be of interest only to themselves, their immediate neighbors, and the United States. In this case, Ecuador and Brazil, as neighbors to Peru and Colombia, were concerned for obvious reasons. United States interest is also easy to explain. Early in the nineteenth century the United States had, in the Monroe Doctrine, warned other powers not to interfere in hemispheric struggles. Since it was by far the most powerful state in the Western Hemisphere, the practical effect of this prohibition was to give the United States sole claim on the right of interference, a right it has exercised on more than one occasion. So, for traditional reasons of national interest, the United States was concerned about the struggle between Colombia and Peru. Why then the diplomatic intervention of European powers?

The same principle was involved in South America in 1932 as in Manchuria in 1931. The Lytton Commission report had stated the principle clearly and forcefully in words that bear repeating: "The interests of peace are the same the world over. Any loss of confidence in the application of the principles of the Covenant and of the Pact of Paris in any part of the world diminishes the value and efficiency of those principles everywhere." Colombia and Peru were both members of the League of Nations, and both had signed and ratified the Pact of Paris (the Kellogg-Briand Peace Pact). In it they had not only renounced recourse to war as an instrument of national policy but had also made a definite promise that the settlement of any disputes that might arise "shall never be sought except by pacific means."[27] The notes sent by France, Great Britain, Germany, and Italy were reminders to Peru of that country's obligations under the Pact of Paris.

There is, of course, something slightly anomalous in the concern of states such as Germany and Italy—given their actions later in the decade—

that the provisions of the Pact of Paris be faithfully carried out in South
America. It cost them nothing, however, and it made some points with the
United States. In his eagerness to make the pact more than just a high-
sounding declaration of good intent, U.S. secretary of state Henry Stimson
had urged its signers to put diplomatic pressure on Peru. He had emphasized the importance he attached to this request by holding a special meeting in Washington with the ambassadors of Great Britain, Italy, Germany,
and France.[28] Thus it was that European "interference" was invited into the
hemisphere by no less an official than the U.S. secretary of state. International interest in peace everywhere in the world, including the Western
Hemisphere, was thus acknowledged as a valid concern at a very high level
in the U.S. government. The difficulty that this acknowledgment might
pose for traditional foreign policy was quickly made manifest, however, and
Stimson backed down from his attempt to hold together two concepts that
were at odds with each other in their basic orientation, one national, the
other international. When Great Britain went further than a note to Peru
and came up with a peace plan of its own that did not follow the U.S. line,
Stimson saw what complications might come through the door he had
opened, and he shut it as firmly and swiftly as diplomatic protocol would
allow.

Through a combination of circumstances, including a change of government in Peru, the combatants finally accepted a League-sponsored plan
that put the fighting on hold while attempts were made to work out their
conflicting claims to the Letitia Trapezium. The plan consisted of two basic
parts. Negotiators from Colombia and Peru were to meet in Rio de Janeiro,
capital of neutral (but very-much-concerned) Brazil, under the leadership
of that patient and wily Brazilian, Afranio de Mello Franco, who was mentioned earlier in this study. While these negotiations were going on, Peruvian troops would be withdrawn from the Trapezium, and the area would be
administered for one year by a League of Nations commission.

So there the commissioners were in late June 1933, the half-ruined town
of Letitia around them, the Amazon in front and the jungle behind, with
their plain makeshift flag flying next to the Colombian flag of brilliant red,
blue, and yellow. Colombia's striking banner had the power to evoke and
symbolize national pride—pride in Colombia's struggle for independence
from Spain in the early nineteenth century and pride in its close association
with Simon Bolívar, hero of South American independence movements.
The powerful feelings evoked by the Colombian flag could send crowds
into the streets in Bogotá, pull young men in from fields and villages and
launch them into battle, bring down governments, and beggar the country

through purchases of arms and munitions, planes and ships of war. What could the commission flag evoke? And from whom?

As yet there was little history and less glory to cluster around any League symbol. The League's accomplishments were not of the dramatic and swash-buckling kind, being devoted more to picking up the pieces in the swash-bucklers' wake or persuading those bent on war to put down their swords and bucklers before much damage was done. Yet the League commissioners in Letitia understood the value of symbols and did their best to invest their flag with meaning. It received full honors along with the Colombian flag, and when at the end of the year the commission flag was lowered for the last time, the Colombian troops taking over Letitia presented arms in a formal salute. This much at least the commission was able to extract from jealous national pride—recognition of the value of an international presence when opposing national prides had closed off every option except slaughter.

Critics have often pointed out that international administration of dis-puted areas, as in Tangier and Shanghai, was little more than an agreement among the great powers for a division of spheres of influence and activities. Those administrative arrangements had been made before there was a League of Nations, however. Slowly, subtly, the context of international af-fairs was being changed as the powers had to make at least a show of living up to their own public statements about the importance of collective action through the League. So in Letitia, where there was no coal or oil and little great power interest, the League commission was free to operate in a truly impartial manner—which it did. Where houses had been damaged, they were rebuilt, no matter the nationality of the owner. Streets were repaired in every quarter. Swamps were drained. Schools were opened. A building that had housed a colonization office was converted into a hospital where anyone could be treated. Materials to construct a generating plant were assembled, and work was begun with the goal of providing electricity to the residents. The commissioners even addressed the problem of venereal diseases among the prostitutes—diseases that also showed no national partiality.

A census of the population taken at the end of the commissioners' term of office showed the mix of nationalities that might be expected in a frontier community: Brazilians, Colombians and Peruvians, for the most part, with a sprinkling of Spaniards and Portuguese, plus the far-from-home expatri-ates that are a staple of exotic fiction. In this case a Briton, a Frenchman, an Italian, and a Syrian brought a cosmopolitan flavor to the little jungle com-munity, as well as providing a test of community tolerance in the days before Peru seized the area and turned a diplomatic dispute into a battleground. There is nothing to suggest that this mix of nationalities prevented the people of Letitia from living peaceably together before the dispute, as they were able to do again once international representatives had arrived on the scene. The Colombians who had been driven out in the Peruvian incursion returned to their homes. Under the direction of the commission, they joined their neighbors, Peruvians and others alike, in the rebuilding process.

The commission's work was not conducted to the accompaniment of sustained applause but rather in the midst of a community with its full share of malcontents and troublemakers. The commissioners received enough cooperation, however, that they rarely had to call on the very small force of Colombian troops at their disposal. Mostly the soldiers performed the police functions needed in any community, and through their regular patrols discouraged patriots of various persuasions from any attempt to seize and possess the disputed area. The troops were supplied with special armbands that they wore to indicate that they were temporarily an international rather than a national force—a distinction that carried more weight in Geneva than in Letitia.

As with much else in a system of sovereign states, the line between *national* and *international* was hard to draw and even harder to maintain. When, in their international role, the soldiers ordered some Peruvians to lower a Peruvian flag that had been raised in a burst of drunken defiance, the Peruvians refused to be ordered about by a bunch of Colombians. The arrival on the scene of the League commissioners helped focus the fuddled minds of the defiant Peruvians. The little fracas became not just a quarrel between two groups of nationals but an affair with possible international complications that, at this point, neither government would welcome. Part of the power of the commissioners lay in the fact that, in their present role, they could shed their countries of origin, so to speak, and simply serve as a reminder that at least part of the wider world that they represented was watching events in Letitia. The reminder brought a measure of sobriety to the Peruvians and they lowered the flag without further incident.[29]

Six months of hard negotiations in Rio de Janeiro finally produced an agreement that the delegates of Colombia and Peru felt able to sign on behalf of their respective governments. There is evidence that this was possible because Peruvian officials were beginning to be worried about their international reputation, as well as by the possibility that Ecuador might ally itself with Colombia should the war resume. However that may be, part of the successful outcome in Rio was surely due to the patience and skill of the Brazilian chairman, Mello Franco, who sailed through the storms and tantrums of the negotiations with unruffled calm. As the chairman of the Colombian delegation noted, Mello Franco's "contagious optimism and imperturbable serenity always shone above the sometimes stormy vehe-mence of the debates." He was able "to find points of contact for every ap-parently irreconcilable difference between negotiators."[30]

But Mello Franco had something else that kept him at a task that often seemed hopeless. He fully shared the new international vision of justice through peace. Although concerned as a Brazilian about this quarrel on his country's borders, he was also concerned about its international impact. He was, as the Colombian delegate said, "a notable citizen of the world."[31] As such, he had an extra incentive to bring Colombia and Peru to agreement. The agreement would demonstrate to Japan and the rest of the world that the peaceful resolution of a dispute could, in fact, bring justice to the dis-puting parties. His efforts came to fruition on May 24, 1934, at a ceremony in Rio de Janeiro when delegates from the two countries signed a protocol of peace and friendship.

The provisions of the agreement were simple. Peru regretted that the friendly relations between the two countries had been disrupted. Colombia was to resume possession of the Letitia Trapezium. The validity of the treaty of 1922, through which Colombia had acquired the Trapezium, was affirmed. Commercial matters were dealt with at some length, and a com-mission was established to monitor the arrangements that had been worked out for customs-free trade on the Amazon and Putamayo Rivers. It was all very practical and low-key. No one reading the terms of the agreement would guess at the passions that had been aroused by this quarrel. Nor would anyone reading the agreement ever guess that the League of Nations had been involved at all, much less to the extent of actually administering the disputed territory while the two countries worked out their differences. From beginning to end of the agreement, there was not one mention of the League.

So the quarrel between Colombia and Peru came to a conclusion that up-held the sanctity of treaties—of cardinal importance in a system of sover-eign states—and affirmed the emerging international principle of the nonrecognition of a territorial change that had been brought about by force. The conclusion was not reached without bloodshed, which, although small by the standards of other South American conflicts, still meant that some lives were cut off in fighting for the possession of a territory where most people in the contending nations would not want to live anyway. To national pride, the point is irrelevant. For pride, what is relevant is posses-sion and sovereignty.

In a final assertion of pride, the Colombian Ministry of Foreign Affairs rejected any reference to a "re-establishment" of full Colombian sovereignty in Letitia, since that would imply that its sovereignty had been less than full during the period of League administration. The rejection was of some concern to the commissioners, who wanted to make sure that the transfer back to Colombian control met all legal requirements. As they pointed out in their final report to the League Council, "Colombia had *de facto* voluntarily renounced certain attributes of sovereignty" in the Trapezium[32] while the commissioners carried out the functions of government. An informal renunciation was one thing, however. A reference in an official document was something else again. That would be an acknowledgment of international authority that Colombia was not prepared to make.

The question of authority is, of course, at the heart of international disputes, as it is at the heart of relations between national states and an international body such as the League of Nations or, at a later period, the United Nations. For Colombia and Peru, sovereignty over the Letitia Trapezium meant, in practical terms, the authority to tax, to colonize, to dispose of what resources there were, to extend to the people living there a national system of law that would, among other things, compel them to pay their taxes and, when summoned, perform military service. So national pride had a practical underpinning. This underpinning was, however, somewhat shaky in the Trapezium, where resources were negligible and the population thin—only twelve hundred after the League commission had stabilized the situation enough for the Colombian refugees to return.

The commission's authority was of a different kind than that of a sovereign state and was always subject to challenge. The formal authority of the commission derived solely from the consent of the parties to the dispute. Its informal authority rested on what reputation the League had been able to achieve by the early 1930s and on its own competence and impartiality. Unlike the arrangements in Upper Silesia and the Saar Basin, where interesting experiments in international supervision were also taking place, the arrangement in Letitia had not been imposed by the victors in a war. It had been arrived at through a series of long and tedious negotiations in Geneva under the sponsorship of the League, and it had the hard-won consent of both Colombia and Peru.

These facts suggest the reasons for looking with care at this successful venture in international administration, small though it was, and in an area remote from the high politics of the day. As the American minister to Switzerland remarked, Letitia might as well have been on Mars so far as many diplomats were concerned.[33] For them, the sun rose and set in Europe, with perhaps a few stray rays lighting up Asia now and then. But if Letitia was remote from great power interests, it was, at the same time, remote from great power intrigues. For this reason, the idea of a temporary, impartial international administration of a disputed area could be tested on its merits, free from outside meddling. There were few models. The international aspects of administration in Tangier and Shanghai, as has been noted, were little more than truces in great power rivalry. The international commission that regulated commercial activities on the Danube River might have served as a model, but there is no evidence that the Letitia commissioners drew any lessons from the Danube commission's ten-year experience in international administration.

The commissioners were on their own for the most part, and they succeeded in their task. They coped with the obstacles thrown up by national pride. They kept order, heard grievances, resolved disputes, received and evaluated claims, repaired damaged buildings, attended to matters of health and education, and made and enforced regulations that allowed people to live together, no matter their differences in opinions or background. When it is considered that these are exactly the kinds of tasks faced elsewhere by people representing the international community, it can be seen that the Letitia experiment has more to offer in the way of example than its small scale would suggest.

Above all, the League of Nations Letitia Commission kept the peace between Colombia and Peru. The point bears repeating. It kept the peace. Later generations might quarrel with much that happened under international supervision in Letitia, or the Saar, or Upper Silesia, but to a war-scarred generation the important thing about these international ventures was that they kept the peace. In so doing, they helped keep alive the idea that justice in the international system was not an unobtainable goal, that if peace could only be maintained, then justice would surely follow.

MEDIATION AND A WAR TOO FURIOUS

A number of events in the spring of 1933 inspired hope in those concerned for justice through peace in international affairs. In April the Permanent Court of International Justice handed down its decision in the conflict between Norway and Denmark, and Norway withdrew its claim to the eastern coast of Greenland. In May the fighting between Colombia and Peru was brought to a halt, and arrangements were made for international administration of the disputed territory of Letitia while negotiators sought a settlement of the issue. There remained the problem of Japanese aggression, but the Japanese appeared to be slowing their advance into China. By the end of May they had stopped altogether, and a truce had formalized an end to the fighting that had generated international concern since its outbreak in 1931.

Among those who followed these matters, the view of the cessation of fighting in China seemed to be "Better a bad peace than no peace at all." From the first, the Japanese had insisted that the safety of their citizens and investments in Manchuria was their only concern. Manchuria in the guise of Manchukuo was now under firm Japanese control, and to it had been added the buffer province of Jehol and a security zone in northern China. The May 31 truce at T'ang-ku suggested that the Japanese might be satisfied with these gains, which more than fulfilled their stated purpose. Optimists held on to the possibility that Japan might even return to the League and to its earlier role of international cooperation.

These developments in the spring of 1933 left one ongoing conflict as a challenge to the idea that peace was both an essential condition for justice in the international sphere and a means by which that justice could be achieved. For almost a year the South American states of Bolivia and Paraguay had been battling each other for possession of the large alluvial plain that lay between their settled areas. Known generally as the Chaco, or the Chaco Boreal, the area had been a point of diplomatic tension between the two countries for many years. In June 1932 the tension broke into open conflict. On May 10, 1933, Paraguay declared war on Bolivia. This act made official the conflict that was already well under way, but it did more than that. It finally pushed the council of the League of Nations into taking decisive action on its own instead of passively supporting other mediation efforts, as it had done for the past year.

Within ten days of Paraguay's formal declaration of war, the council committee that had been keeping watch on the conflict while various American states attempted mediation recommended that the League now become directly involved. Bolivia was at first not receptive to the idea of a League commission of inquiry on the lines of the Lytton Commission, but after much discussion at length gave reluctant approval. In early July a five-man commission was appointed by the League Council. At exactly the same time, Bolivian forces in the disputed region launched a massive attack against the Paraguayan post of Nanawa, an attack that was met by furious resistance on the part of its defenders. Behind the public protestations of a desire for peace lay the iron determination of each antagonist to wrest the entire territory from the other before mediation could put a stop to the fighting.

Every conciliatory move was met by a countermove. Every initiative foundered in the delays caused by studies and consultations that managed to spin themselves out until the situation in the Chaco had changed to the advantage of one side or the other. First the commission of inquiry was asked by the combatants to delay its departure from Europe while several South American states made yet another try to mediate the conflict. When that effort failed and the commission finally arrived in South America, there were further delays while commissioners tried to reassure Bolivian officials that their inquiries would not in any way infringe on Bolivia's sovereignty. Paraguayan officials, on the other hand, greeted the commissioners warmly, at the same time that Paraguayan forces launched a fierce attack against the Bolivian post of Campo Via. And so it went, like some stately dance of death, a mediation proposal here followed by a battle there. More than twenty-six hundred men died in the Battle of Campo Via, and as the commissioners were making their first formal proposal to end the fighting, Paraguayan troops were rounding up five thousand survivors of the Bolivian Fourth and Ninth Divisions and sending them into captivity.[34]

There would be little point in an examination of this conflict and the efforts to end it if the situation were an unusual one in international affairs. But it is not. The maneuvers for advantage that marked the Chaco War are a fair representation of the conditions in which mediators have to operate. The swollen pride, the suspicion, the stalling that marked mediation efforts in the Chaco War could be duplicated many times over in better-known conflicts, as, for example, in efforts to end the Vietnam War forty years later. Lethal weapons and troops on the ground are matched against arguments for conciliation and attempts to find a just middle ground. It is an uneven contest. As the Paraguayan president, Eusebio Ayala, put it in his speech of welcome to the League commissioners: "When one considers the origins of wars, and especially of this war, one can hardly help thinking how frail are the means available for preventing or stopping them."[35] They are, however, the means available.

Those not directly involved in the Chaco War had no difficulty in evaluating it. Everyone on the outside agreed that this was a wholly unnecessary war. What was at stake, after all? An area of 115,000 square miles (298,000 square km) of scrub and desert, short on water, long on insects and disease, with soil that dissolved into glutinous mud at the first touch of rain. There were a few cattle ranches in the southeast, a modest export trade in quebracho wood down the Paraguay River, and, in the interior, a small colony of Mennonites from Canada and Russia whose greatest desire was to be let alone. There were rumors of oil, with rival oil companies being blamed for feeding the fires of war, but the rumors, if true, took no account of the costs of production and transport, and, in plain fact, had no effect on the length or conduct of the war.

The combatants needed neither the machinations of multinationals nor the prospect of riches to feed their wartime passions. These ran high enough without outside help, and it was this that outsiders found almost impossible to understand. Members of the commission of inquiry, sober and conscientious observers that they were, ended by characterizing the war as "senseless." All that was needed, they said, was a "little will for peace" and the combatants' opposing points of view could find a meeting place in the treaty that the commissioners had drafted (and the combatants rejected). After three months of futile effort, the commissioners decided that the best they could do was provide the League with the facts of the situation in hopes that the League Council could find a way "to put an end to this senseless war."[36]

Members of the commission came from France, Great Britain, Italy, Mexico, and Spain. Not having any particular interests or involvement in the Chaco, they could see clearly the futility of fighting over that bleak, inhospitable land. Was Bolivia advancing its military posts into the heart of the Chaco, thus alarming the people and government of Paraguay? Then Bolivia should stop. Did Paraguay control river access from the continent's heartland to the Atlantic Ocean? Then Paraguay should make it clear to land-locked Bolivia that this accident of geography would not be used against it. To outsiders the solution was simple, and it was only pig-headed pride that kept the war going. As one later commentator put it acidly, "The Chaco war may be regarded as the triumph of nationalist unreason over every sentiment of morality and common sense."[37]

If war in South America was a triumph of unreason over common sense, what was war in Europe? It would perhaps be a challenge to find an objective observer who would characterize World War I as a triumph of *reason* of any kind. Instead, the observer might point out that the Chaco War faithfully reflected the instability of a world of sovereign states, jealous of each other's possessions and fearful of each other's power. South America in 1933 was Europe on a smaller scale. Its history was quite as bloody, its suspicions quite as justified as any that Europe could show. This was what had caused the failure of the mediation efforts that had been going on for almost a year before the League of Nations became actively involved. All these earlier efforts had been by American states, and the two combatants had good reason to be cautious about the proposal of any American state, no matter how well-intentioned.

Despite the rhetoric of American solidarity that was customary on ceremonial occasions, deep rifts and long memories divided the countries of the New World from one another. With its power and interventionist tendencies the United States had managed to offend nationalist pride practically everywhere in South America. In the spring of 1933, as efforts were being made to stop the Chaco War, the more conciliatory approach of the first Franklin Roosevelt administration had not yet had time to smooth the ruffled feathers of South American states. Beyond the generalized suspicion that greeted any U.S. initiative were more specific reasons for the combatants to put any peace proposal through a very fine sieve, especially if it came from a neighboring state—as many of them did. No Paraguayan with a sense of history could forget the War of the Triple Alliance (1865–70), in which Argentina, Brazil, and Uruguay had joined forces against neighboring Paraguay in a conflict in which Paraguay had lost much of its territory and most of its male population.

As for Bolivia, it had so frequently been the odd man out in the military and diplomatic struggles of the continent that its negotiating stance was one of truculent determination not to be victimized again. Bolivian grievances were many, and there was a deep reservoir of wounded pride from which to draw. Members of the commission of inquiry got a taste of this in Bolivia's first official communication to them following their arrival in Montevideo:

> Bolivia does not and will not agree to any functions of a judicial nature which the Commission might endeavor to exercise either on its own initiative or on the instructions of the League. Such functions would affect the sovereignty and independence of the nations and would only complicate the international situation and still further embitter the present dispute.
>
> Bolivia will only be able to take part in peace discussions based on respect for the freedom of the individual peoples under the friendly guidance of the League of Nations.[38]

Here, in an exaggerated form, is the unyielding insistence on sovereignty that is a common response of a combatant state to efforts at mediation. The underlying, unspoken text goes something like this: "I welcome these mediation efforts. I approach them in good faith. I did not seek this war. It was forced upon me. Again and again I have offered honorable terms to end this conflict. They have been rejected by my opponent. Nevertheless, I am willing to try once again. I stand ready to cooperate—without, of course, compromising in any way the sovereignty and independence of the country I have the honor to represent."

To these must be added the effect of domestic politics on negotiations. In the Chaco case, as in many international negotiations, every move made by diplomats of the contending countries came under close scrutiny by opposition parties at home. Bolivian and Paraguayan diplomats in the various mediation locales were, therefore, about as flexible as rocks. Once they had taken a position, there they stayed, since any move that was to their country's disadvantage, or could be made to seem so, was a gift for the opposition. Thus domestic politics directly influenced the course of negotiations and, indirectly, the course of the war. Adolfe Costa du Rels, Bolivian delegate to the League of Nations during much of this period, put the matter elegantly and subtly in a reflection on negotiation that he made to the League Council in May 1933:

> Negotiation implies an effort on all sides to round off the angles, to endeavor to reconcile the different points of view, and to achieve that psychological state in which justice and the rights of the parties are harmonized, while, at the same time, sight is not lost of certain political imponderables which are like grains of sand in the very delicate machinery of conciliation and, consequently, of peace.[39]

There were indeed grains of sand in the negotiations to end the Chaco War, as the imponderables of the two countries' domestic politics made themselves felt at the negotiating tables. This was especially true of Bolivia, where president Daniel Salamanca was devoting more energy to a bureaucratic battle with his own military for control of the conduct of the war than he was to any efforts to end that war. It was a battle that Salamanca eventually lost when in November 1934 Bolivian military leaders removed him from office and installed a man more to their liking. The protracted battle at home did, however, distract Bolivian negotiators and make them anxious not to take a position that would put them at a disadvantage, no matter which side won the battle.

Finally, there was the nature of the war itself—the real war being fought in the Chaco, not the bureaucratic ones that accompany almost any conflict. The longer the war went on, the more bitter became the feelings of the opponents in regard to each other. By the time the League of Nations commission of inquiry arrived on the scene, the war had been going on for eighteen months and bitter feelings were as entrenched as the military posts and as resistant to assault. Each side had grievous losses to avenge. Each side had faithfully followed the tactics of World War I and had demonstrated again and again what had earlier been proved on European soil: machine guns in entrenched positions can decimate assaulting troops no matter how brave or determined.

Each side had managed to equip itself to take full advantage of the destructive power of modern weaponry. The League commission noted the use of "aeroplanes, armoured cars, flame-projectors, quick-firing guns, machine-guns and automatic rifles." In regular use also were mortars, hand grenades, and cannon of various sizes, in addition to the more traditional, and somewhat less lethal, machetes and bayonets. Paraguay had two fast, modern gun boats for use on the rivers that bordered the Chaco. This gave that country an advantage when it came to the rapid movement of troops and supplies. Bolivia, however, controlled the air with bombers and pursuit planes. The two countries were in a position to inflict a great deal of damage on each other's troops in the field, and they did so to the best of their ability.[40] In adopting this manner of warfare, they were squarely within a Western tradition of war in which each side fought to inflict the maximum of damage on the other. Hugo Grotius had known this tradition and had sought to restrain and modify it.

The members of the League commission of inquiry expressed shock at the losses incurred in the Chaco War. They spoke of it as "singularly pitiless and horrible." But they spoke from within a tradition that had for centuries nurtured those very qualities in warfare. Their own bitter war, not far in the past, had displayed those qualities to the full. It was left to outsiders to the tradition to comment most cogently on the way the heirs of the West fought both outsiders and each other. Briefly, trenchantly, the Western way of war was summed up thus: "It is too furious, and slays too many men." The comment was made three centuries earlier by the Mohegan allies of the English in the Pequot War, but it was as apt in the 1930s as in the 1630s. The Chaco War was indeed a war "too furious" and it killed too many men. Approximately ninety thousand fell in that bleak, inhospitable land and were buried there, or their bodies burned because there was no time or equipment for burial.[41]

In the end, the Chaco War proved too furious a war for mediation alone to bring to a halt. There had to be a change of circumstances before mediation could function effectively. By the end of 1934 the pace of negotiations began to pick up as each side came to the reluctant conclusion that the decisive victory it sought was beyond its power to achieve. There was also an arms embargo, imposed by most of the members of the League of Nations and by the United States as well. This was the most dramatic collective action since the end of World War I, and it sent a clear message to the combatants. Even with the reservations and exceptions to be expected from the foreign offices of so many different countries, the mere fact and extent of the embargo was a signal of collective disapproval that Bolivia and Paraguay could not completely ignore. Like other states, particularly the smaller ones, they were dependent to some extent on international good will in the day-to-day exchanges of diplomacy and trade.

So with many a misstep and hesitation, despite sharp debates and quarrels with mediators in the New World and the Old including a Paraguayan notice of withdrawal from the League of Nations, the two combatants were brought to the place where their representatives could sign a protocol of peace. This happened in Buenos Aires, June 12, 1935, under the auspices of Argentina, Brazil, Chile, Peru, the United States, and Uruguay. The triumph for mediation in this case was not that it, by itself, had brought the war to a close but that, when the two combatants were ready to talk, mediation could provide them with ways to back down from their positions of threat and recrimination while preserving their national pride.[42]

It took three more years of intense mediation before the final Treaty of Peace, Friendship and Boundaries between Bolivia and Paraguay was signed in Buenos Aires on July 21, 1938. Then there were parades and speeches and a symbolic binding up of the wounds of war. Schoolgirls carried flags of the two combatants plus those of the mediating powers to places in front of an equestrian statue of General Manuel Belgrano, hero of Argentine independence. To the cheers of the assembled crowd, the flags of Bolivia and Paraguay were crossed in front of the flag of Argentina to mark the renewal of friendly relations between the two countries that had fought each other so long and so bitterly in the Chaco. The six years of mediation efforts were at last at an end.[43]

And that is one thing to note about this mediation. It persisted throughout the three years of fighting and the additional three years of arguing over the terms of peace and friendship. Quietly, doggedly, people from many different countries worked at the job of mediation. When one effort failed, another effort would be made in Washington, or Geneva, or Buenos Aires, or Montevideo. And, despite failure after failure, persistence paid off. When the combatants were ready to listen, the mediators were ready to talk. More than that, the talks did not have to start from scratch. The mediators had plans ready to put on the table, and one was finally worked out that was acceptable all around. If wars proceeded as slowly, fewer people would be killed. But if no one was willing to mediate, wars could go on forever.

It is difficult to believe that the three years of mediation efforts during the actual fighting of the Chaco War had had no effect at all on the combatants. At the least, they had been shown again and again that there were ways out of their hostile engagement. One of the suggestions was that the whole dispute be turned over to the Permanent Court of International Justice.

This was a tribute to the reputation for fair dealing that the court was beginning to acquire. As events turned out, there was not time for this reputation to grow much beyond the time of the Chaco War. Within five years of the signing of the Protocol of Peace between Bolivia and Paraguay, Germany invaded The Netherlands and German paratroopers descended on The Hague.

It is doubtful whether anyone in those hectic days remembered a comment made by Paraguayan president Eusebio Ayala in November 1933 when he greeted the members of the League commission of inquiry. His comment is not the kind to be engraved in bronze and mounted along with the other engraved mottos that adorn the walls of the Peace Palace in The Hague, the home of the Permanent Court of International Justice at the time of the German invasion. But the comment is just as apt as those about justice, amity, and concord. Speaking of the frailty of conciliation efforts when compared to the strength of violence, President Ayala remarked, "International justice, we must confess, has still but little power."[44]

In the context of the 1930s, Eusebio Ayala spoke more truly than he knew.

PART THREE

QUESTIONS OF LAW

CHAPTER NINE

A Limited Reach

Throughout the 1920s and well into the 1930s, people with an internationalist outlook engaged in a sustained effort to make peace the vehicle of international justice. During that same period, people with a *nationalist* outlook were unwittingly preparing the ground for a major change in the whole concept of justice in the international sphere and of what might be required to achieve it there. This change was not the result of anyone's plan or policy. Rather, it was the unintended outcome of a whole series of initiatives with other ends in view, ends that were, for the most part, narrowly focused on advantage for a particular country or political party.

In theory, such efforts should have had little international impact so long as they were carried out within a strictly domestic sphere. In actuality, many of those efforts and their consequences claimed international attention right from the start. One result was a prolonged and painful scrutiny of the rules by which nations are supposed to act. Was it enough to outlaw aggressive war? Had the concentration on peaceful means of settling disputes between states meant neglect of other standards of behavior? Which standards *were* international, anyway, and which ones ought to be? The debate was both confused and deeply serious. The people engaged in the debate strained hard to stay within the limits imposed by respect for state sovereignty while they were under steady pressure to take positions and actions that would stretch those limits to breaking.

The struggle to maintain and at the same time to overcome the constraints of sovereignty was particularly acute in the League of Nations. Under ordinary conditions, the member states had no doubts about their standing in relation to the League and to each other. They stood on equal grounds within the League, no matter their size or power. They were sovereign within and without their borders, their actions outside their borders subject only to the restraints that they had voluntarily assumed. Taken altogether these restraints constituted a system of law, but in the interwar period there was general agreement that this was law of a special kind. Instead of a law of subordination, as in an individual country where a supreme authority could promulgate and enforce the law, it was a law of coordination. There was (and is) no supreme international authority. Equal and independent states agreed to limit or perform certain actions. The expectation was that the reciprocal benefits of such coordination would lead states to conform, if only out of self-interest.

This expectation of conformity was, of course, the obvious weakness in the concept of international law as a system of coordination. If a state did not conform, the other members of the system were faced with the problem of what to do about it. Much of Part Two dealt with the states' attempts to answer the question "What to do?" in the many different forms and contexts within which the question was raised. This reliance on unenforced conformity meant that the whole system of coordination rested on shaky ground, a weakness that was often lamented in the interwar period. The laments did not get beyond the discussion stage since any move toward change was blocked from the start by the fear that conformity, if enforced, would undercut sovereignty, the foundational concept on which the whole system relied. Meanwhile, another weakness in the international law of the time went almost unnoticed until events in the early 1930s brought it to the fore.

The system of rules and restraints that were supposed to govern—or at least guide—states in their relations with each other dealt with actions by a state in relation to other states. The rules had been developed through long experience of state interaction, and they covered most of the areas of potential tension in relations between states. What they did not cover, as became increasingly evident in the period between the two world wars, was actions of states within their own borders.

Where the international law of the period concerned itself with a state's *internal* actions, that concern was considered to be a special case, a departure from the general norm. Thus the several postwar treaties that made the League of Nations the guarantor of the rights of minorities in countries such as Poland and Czechoslovakia were particular to the situation in those countries. They were exceptions to the general rule that forbade interference in internal affairs. The exceptions were justified on the grounds that only through international protection of the minorities within certain countries could those countries survive the strains of disaffection and, in the extreme case, dissolution.

The outcome was a system of League-guaranteed minority protection that gradually took on a life of its own. By barely perceptible degrees it moved toward universality and, as it did so, it set up a tension between state sovereignty and international protection that still has not been resolved. The original intent of League protection, however, and its justification in the theory of the time, was to preserve certain countries as independent sovereign states, able to take their places in a system of other independent sovereign states.[1]

This mostly-hands-off system worked fairly well in the 1920s. It was to the advantage of every state to preserve a system that allowed each to work out its destiny in its own way behind its own borders even if that way did not command approval outside those borders. There was, for example, a certain disquiet outside Italy at the repressive actions of Italian authorities against opponents of the Fascist regime, but the disquiet was muted by the norms of diplomatic conduct. There was no consensus outside Italy that international action was required or even appropriate. And if a League member such as Italy could act internally without fear of being called to account, states that were not League members, such as the Soviet Union and the United States, enjoyed an even greater freedom. The consequences of their domestic policies fell quite outside the scope of legitimate international concern. Thus, Soviet collectivization policy with its attendant hardships and the exclusionary policy of the United States that denied entry to Japanese immigrants were both strictly domestic affairs. Their contribution to international tensions was felt to be unfortunate but, in the context of the times, also unaddressable from an international point of view.

The sharp line that divided the domestic from the international had profound theoretical significance. Freedom in internal affairs was inherent in the very concept of sovereignty and was a pillar of the theoretical structure that upheld the nation-state. But this sharp division had practical resonance as well. Agreement not to comment unfavorably on others' use of their internal freedom facilitated diplomatic exchanges and made it possible for countries with different political systems to maintain relations with each other. The restraint could, of course, be breached in exceptional circumstances, but this was considered to be more a matter of past record than of current concern.

Restraint was thus an understood assumption of the times as the decade of the '20s drew to a close and the '30s got under way. That assumption was promptly called into question by events in Germany. As a result of yet another political crisis in that crisis-ridden country, the National Socialists under Adolf Hitler came to power. Within four months of Hitler's assumption of the German chancellorship, the League Council found itself embroiled in a dispute that had nothing to do with threats to international peace—the League's chief concern—and everything to do with domestic policy versus international standards of behavior. There was no way council members could avoid the issue. In May 1933 it came directly to the council table in the form of a petition from one Franz Bernheim. Bernheim was a German who was also a Jew, and therein lay the point of conflict for the council.

The conflict was between the conventions of ordinary diplomatic discourse and the sense of outrage that was building outside Germany at the harsh treatment of German Jews by the new National Socialist regime. The conventions of diplomatic civility and restraint grew out of the very concept of sovereignty that underpinned the whole international system. The outrage grew out of a sense of what was fair and equitable in the treatment of human beings. The struggle at the League Council in Geneva in May and June 1933 prefigured the agonizing debates that are still going on, debates through which people have attempted to reconcile or to balance these two opposites: the perceived needs of the international system and the felt needs of humanity. It is to the credit of the men sitting around the council table in 1933 that they were willing to look beyond the specific situation of Franz Bernheim to the larger issues involved, even as they tried to maintain the civility that would allow a continued relationship with Germany—at that time still a member of the League.

THE FRANZ BERNHEIM AFFAIR

Under ordinary circumstances the proceedings of the council of the League of Nations were outstandingly boring. For the most part, the meetings were open to the public. This openness had been achieved only after much hesitation and discussion, but the public showed little interest in following the formal exchanges there. Budgetary and administrative matters, reports from the Committees of Three through which the council addressed problems in the international sphere, self-justifying speeches intended to maintain the dignity of the states represented on the council—these were not the kinds of matters to claim public attention. Yet they took up much of the council's time. Only occasionally, as when the Japanese representative appeared before the council to defend Japan's actions in Manchuria, did the proceedings emerge from obscurity into the light of public attention. Thus it was that the petition of Franz Bernheim, an obscure Jew in an area of the world little known outside central Europe, came before the council with no fanfare and was handled there in a way that did nothing to lift the fog of public indifference that blanketed most council actions. Only those who had followed the routine business of the council could perceive how the handling of the Bernheim petition, calm and low-key as it was, departed dramatically from the norm.

The secretary-general of the League, Sir Eric Drummond, must have known full well the potential for conflict that lay in the Bernheim petition. On May 19, 1933, he sent a copy to the German government for its comments and at the same time circulated copies to members of the League Council. In a note accompanying the petition, Drummond observed that he "considered that this case required the application of the urgent procedure laid down in the Council resolution of September 8th, 1928, as requested in the petition." The petitioner had indeed requested that the secretariat "treat this petition as *urgent*,"[2] and the secretariat had responded by transmitting copies to the council immediately after receiving the document, which was dated May 12. Council members who were familiar with Drummond's usual phlegmatic approach were thus put on notice that here was something out of the ordinary, an impression that was confirmed by a reading of the petition itself. Clearly, Franz Bernheim had more than an individual grievance to express. The language of the petition, stilted and formal as it was, condemned the entire system of discriminatory legislation by which German Jews were gradually being deprived of livelihood and security in their native land. Not only did Bernheim request redress of his own particular grievance. He invited League consideration of the whole thrust of National Socialist policy in Germany.

League consideration of National Socialist domestic policy was, by any of the standards of usual diplomatic discourse, entirely out of the question. The presence of Friederich von Keller, the German representative on the council, would have discouraged any such discussion even if other members had agreed to put it on the agenda. In the initial stages of the handling of the Bernheim petition they were not willing to do so and risk breaching the conventions that insulated their own countries as well as Germany from official criticism of domestic actions. There was, however, a way to approach the subject of German anti-Semitic legislation and actions that was well within the competence of the council, and it was a way that did not breach any diplomatic conventions. This stemmed from the fact that Franz Bern-

heim was not only a German and a Jew, he was also—or had been until recently—a resident of German Upper Silesia. This gave the council a way to
take hold of the matter without, it was hoped, grasping too many of the
thorns that bristled from its every surface.

Upper Silesia was one of the special cases where the League could, under
certain circumstances, be involved in affairs within national borders insofar
as those affairs pertained to the protection of minorities. The rights of minorities in Upper Silesia were numerous and specific. They were spelled out
in detail in ninety-seven different articles in the Geneva Convention of
1922, the international instrument of governance in that hotly disputed territory. Further, the specified rights, in the words of the convention, "constitute obligations of international concern,"[3] and, as such, were placed under
the guarantee of the League of Nations.

The dispute over Upper Silesia began after World War I, when Poland
was reconstituted as an independent state after more than a century of division and submersion within the borders of neighboring states. The Poles
promptly claimed as part of their national territory the entire area of Upper
Silesia with its rich coal deposits and highly developed industry. Germany
laid claim to the same area with such vehemence and determination that the
peacemakers in Paris feared a renewed outbreak of war. Through a long
process that, for the residents of the area, involved an internationally super-
vised plebiscite, and, for German and Polish leaders, a good deal of pressure
and persuasion, the area was divided into two parts, German Upper Silesia
and Polish Upper Silesia.

This division was seen as temporary (fifteen years) but necessary to preserve peace in the area and allow tempers to cool. It was also hoped that the
years of cooperation under the Geneva Convention would have a positive
effect. Every effort was made to facilitate cooperation. Elaborate procedures were drawn up to preserve the economic unity of the area. Equally
elaborate arrangements were worked out for minority protection. Nationalities were so mixed in Upper Silesia that, even with the most careful drawing of borders, a considerable number of Germans ended up in the Polish
portion, the reverse being true for a number of Poles. Two special international bodies were created to advise in the workings of this complicated system of governance and to arbitrate the disputes that were sure to arise. Beyond that, individual members of minorities were given the right to petition
the council of the League of Nations directly and ask for a redress of their
grievances. So the petition of Franz Bernheim came before the council in
May 1933 and sat there like a small bomb waiting to go off and shatter the

protocol that protected the National Socialist regime in Germany from criticism at the official level.

In May 1933 the National Socialists had not been long in power, but the thrust of their policies was already clear. They were determined, by any means including outright violence, to eliminate every trace of opposition so as to gather into their hands the entire apparatus of the state. They were also determined to drive Jews out of the political, professional, legal, and economic life of the nation. This was done in the name of the purity of the German nation, the *Volk*, a core principle of National Socialist ideology. At the highest level, much was made of the characteristics and needs of the "Folkish State," a body that did not—and by definition *could* not—include Jews, or any non-Aryans. Immediately after gaining control of the Reichstag in early March 1933, the National Socialists began to promulgate a series of legislative acts to strengthen and protect the Volk, which, in practical terms, meant driving Jews out of their jobs and practices as government officials, teachers, doctors, lawyers, judges, and others in positions of authority and responsibility.

After Germany's defeat in World War II, when the country was being governed by the Allied Control Council, these diktats were the subject of the very first law promulgated by the council: "The following laws of a political or discriminatory nature upon which the Nazi regime rested are hereby expressly repealed, together with all supplementary and explanatory laws, ordinances and decrees." Thus read the Control Council's introduction to a listing of twenty-five different discriminatory laws dating from 1933 to 1944. Among them were the laws through which Franz Bernheim lost his job in 1933 while living and working in German Upper Silesia. Nor was he alone. As he noted in his petition, at the time he was fired he had been "employed from September 30th, 1931, to April 30th, 1933, by the Deutsches Familien-Kaufhaus, Ltd., Gleiwitz branch, and then discharged for the reason that all Jewish employees had to be dismissed."[4]

With the scrupulous attention to detail that characterizes this petition, Bernheim named the discriminatory laws that were depriving Jews of their positions and livelihood and also provided the dates of their publication in the official *Reich Legal Gazette*. The names of the laws gave little hint of their intent. They appeared under such titles as "The Re-organization of the Civil Service," "Admission to Practise as a Lawyer," "Against the Overcrowding of German Schools and High Schools," and "Admission of Doctors to the Panels of Health Insurance Funds." These laws, said Bernheim, had been put into force even before their promulgation. Then, with his persistent reach beyond the specific to the general case, he noted that this had happened not only in German Upper Silesia but throughout Germany.[5]

Von Keller, the German delegate on the League Council, was by no means a passive bystander in the matter of the Bernheim petition. He was fully capable of using procedural means to delay consideration or deflect any possible criticism of German actions, even if those criticisms were limited to Upper Silesia. When the petition was listed on the council's May 22 agenda, he immediately asked for a delay on the grounds that it was not clear that Bernheim was a legitimate member of a minority in Upper Silesia. If he were not, then, of course, he would not have the right of petition to the council. Secretary-General Drummond's response was bland and conciliatory. He said that he had put the petition on the agenda under the assumption that Bernheim was indeed a member of a minority under the Geneva Convention. If there was some question of this, then it would be quite right to wait for further information before proceeding with the matter.

As it turned out, this maneuver on von Keller's part was to prolong the proceedings despite his best efforts to kill them, but at this stage it gave him time to consult with the German Foreign Office on the best approach to the whole potentially explosive matter. Four days later he was ready. He was, he said, withdrawing his objection to consideration of the Bernheim petition on the understanding that the petitioner's status would be investigated. Further to that matter, he wished to present a statement that the German government had authorized: "It is obvious that international conventions concluded by Germany cannot be affected by internal German legislation. Should the provisions of the Geneva Convention have been violated in German Upper Silesia, this can only be due to mistakes on the part of subordinate organs acting under a mistaken interpretation of the laws."[6]

This should, in theory, have ended the whole matter so far as the League Council was concerned. Everyone was let off the hook. Officials at the upper level in Germany could blame overzealous officials at the local level in Upper Silesia. Council members could take note of Germany's statement that treaty obligations could not be overridden by domestic legislation in the areas covered by the treaty. Franz Bernheim's insistence that the council look at National Socialist policy in general, and not only in Upper Silesia, could be quietly quashed by a simple and legal maneuver. Now that the German government had professed its willingness to abide by the terms of the Geneva Convention in the treaty area, Bernheim's petition could be sent back to Upper Silesia to be handled by the local procedures established under that same convention. The council could then, in good conscience, move on to other matters. But it did not.

At this stage of the proceedings, no one was willing to beard von Keller openly. He was, after all, their colleague. Nor was anyone willing to put him on the spot with the government he represented. Yet the statement he had presented from that same government did not really end the matter as he and his superiors had hoped and expected. Legally, the statement was perfectly correct. What it did not address, what it could not, within the usual diplomatic conventions, even begin to acknowledge, was the moral outrage provoked by German treatment of German Jews. The seasoned diplomats seated at the council table with von Keller were not immune to that outrage. Protocol or no protocol, they were going to keep the issue alive at least long enough to consider the Upper Silesian situation, if not German policy in general. The way they chose was one of the simplest of parliamentary maneuvers. Instead of referring Bernheim's petition back to local authorities, they referred the whole matter to a council committee for study. This meant that at some point a report would be brought to the full council and there would be an opportunity for discussion.

The chair of the council study committee was Sean Lester, an unflappable and experienced delegate from Ireland who, within a few years, would serve as acting secretary-general of the League and conduct a holding operation on its behalf throughout World War II. Lester had chaired the League committee that helped resolve the Letitia crisis, and he was currently engaged in League efforts to bring the Chaco War to a halt. He was accustomed to walking the narrow and treacherous path between national pride and international need, but the Bernheim petition presented problems of a different sort. The vocabulary of moral outrage was not part of conventional discourse, and the circumstances in which it could be used effectively were limited. The 1879 election campaign of William Gladstone in England, for example, with its searing condemnation of Turkish atrocities in Bulgaria, demonstrated the handling of moral issues at a high political level, but that was hardly a model to follow at the League of Nations in 1933. If Gladstone had been working side by side with Turkish representatives every day, as Lester was with German delegates at the League, he might well have couched his condemnation in the more oblique terms of formal diplomacy.

When the council met on May 27, Lester said that his committee was not yet ready to report "owing to the great difficulties raised by the question." Committee members wrestled with the difficulties for three more days, and on May 30 Lester presented the result of their labors. Anyone who had expected a highly colored account of National Socialist persecutions, did not know Lester or the ways of the League. Anyone who could read between the lines of the gray official prose in which the report was cast could see that

Germany stood condemned. The committee stayed on the solid ground of Upper Silesia, where the League had a right to comment. It noted that German laws regarding "the status of civil servants, the position of lawyers, notaries, and doctors, and the schools and universities" applied only to Jews. Any application of those laws in German Upper Silesia would run counter to the intent of the Geneva Convention, the governing international agreement for the area. The anti-Jewish laws were in conflict with the provisions of the convention that were expressly designed to protect minorities there.[7]

Thus did the restrained and somber prose of the Lester Committee report uphold Bernheim's position with regard to the illegality of actions against the Jews of German Upper Silesia. With his usual care, Bernheim had listed the provisions of the Geneva Convention that were being negated by such actions. These included the German government's treaty pledge to protect all inhabitants "without distinction of birth, nationality, language, race or religion," while assuring equal civil and political rights to all German nationals, again "without distinction as to race, language or religion." Discriminatory legislative and administrative acts were specifically prohibited in order that German nationals who were members of minorities could stand before the law "on the same footing as other nationals as regards the exercise of an agricultural, commercial or industrial calling or of any other calling." And finally, to emphasize the seriousness of the obligation, there was a repetition of the pledge of "full and complete protection" to all the inhabitants of the territory, no matter their nationality, race, language, or religion.[8]

Von Keller promptly said that he could not accept the report. Taking care to avoid any substantive issues, he set out his objections, which were chiefly technical. As he had pointed out earlier, council consideration of this petition was quite unnecessary. Once the German government had stated that Germany's internal laws could not affect its international obligations, that should have taken care of the matter. The council should have taken note of the declaration and then stated that "in so far as its general aspects were concerned, the petition was disposed of." As it was, he objected to the report on several grounds, an essential one being that the report seemed to accept what had yet to be proved, namely Bernheim's right to submit a petition at all. The German government, he said, had already begun an investigation of Bernheim. The man was not connected with Upper Silesia either by origin or by family. Further, even if Bernheim had suffered an alleged injustice himself, that did not authorize him to submit a petition on general questions of the application of German law since he was not an official or a representative of any sort.[9]

When asked by the president of the council if he wanted to respond, Lester replied that two of the points raised by von Keller could be resolved by experts in the law. He asked permission to refer to a committee of jurists the question of whether Bernheim belonged to a minority as defined under Article 147 of the Geneva Convention. The jurists would also be asked to rule on the separate question of Bernheim's right to petition the council. Having neatly turned von Keller's maneuver on the points of eligibility into a plausible procedural delay, Lester continued. His next remark was the first departure from strict League protocol since the Bernheim petition had come before the council. Quietly, without drama, Lester said that his addressing only two of the points in von Keller's remarks and not the others did not mean that he could "be held to agree with them in any way."[10]

Lester was too experienced a hand not to know the effect of his remark. Casual as the delegates might be in the corridors, cafes, and hotel rooms where much League business was conducted, they preserved all the formalities when seated around the council table. Day after day, the business before them proceeded on a wave of courtesies that masked essential disagreements and made it possible for these representatives of national pride to continue to work together. Any experienced delegate could pay graceful tribute to his "esteemed colleagues" while turning those same colleagues' statements to his own or his country's advantage. Lester's quiet remark was, therefore, like a rude shout in that refined atmosphere. But more was to come.

The next to speak was Anthony Eden, Great Britain's representative on the council. The debonair Eden looked as if he paid more attention to his immaculate appearance than to the business at hand, but anyone who took the appearance for the man made a great mistake. There was nothing soft or foppish about his mind and determination. He knew and supported the League, and he knew how to read the labyrinth of European politics that was reflected in its daily business. His colleague von Keller might preserve the courtesies of traditional diplomacy before the council, but behind von Keller was a new regime, one of open, brutish violence. Eden quickly seized the opening that Lester had provided. He supported Lester's proposal to refer to a committee of jurists the questions regarding Franz Bernheim's status and the admissibility of Bernheim's petition. He added that he would not attempt to answer all the points raised by von Keller. People should not, however, take this restraint to mean that he agreed with those points "for that was far from being the case."[11]

As if this second breach of League protocol were a signal, the general discussion that von Keller had sought to avoid suddenly took place. The delegate from France took the floor to bring into the open what had been obvious from the first and ignored from the first, namely that the Bernheim case "was only one aspect of a more general and more moving problem." Surely, he said, the League of Nations, "which had shown such legitimate anxiety for the rights of minorities belonging to nationalities within other frontiers, could not really ignore the rights of a race scattered throughout all the countries."[12]

The moral issue was raised by the Polish delegate in a particularly pointed fashion by distinguishing the moral aspects of the case from its legal aspects. He said that he knew very well that, legally speaking, the council could deal only with the position of the Jewish minority in Upper Silesia. This authority derived from the Geneva Convention, which had put the minorities there under the protection of the League. There was then no question of the council's right to deal with German treatment of the Jews in German Upper Silesia. The Jews in Germany stood in a different relationship to the council. Legally speaking, the council had no right to comment on their situation no matter how obvious it was that the same protection needed to be extended to them. But beyond legal rights were moral rights. All the members of the council had "at least a moral right to make a pressing appeal to the German Government to ensure equal treatment for all the Jews in Germany."[13]

It was obvious that feelings and thoughts that had been suppressed while the amenities were being observed were now being aired with a frankness totally at odds with the usual way of conducting council business. Not once did the council president rule the comments out of order, although they certainly went beyond the business at hand. As the Norwegian delegate remarked, this general debate, which was very wide in scope, "had somewhat unexpectedly arisen out of the discussion, which should have been confined to procedure." His comment was not intended to limit the debate. Rather, since the discussion had widened out in this unexpected fashion, he felt compelled to take part and to present an even stronger view of the League's responsibilities. "Norway," he said, "was interested in questions relating to the protection of minorities, because protection was one of the duties of the League, not a duty imposed upon it by certain treaties, but also a moral duty; for the protection of minorities followed from certain principles of justice which were dear to Norway."[14]

Clearly, this reference to justice did not equate justice with peace, the strongest identification made at the international level throughout the interwar period. Here the evocation was of a different meaning, one that encompassed both the League, on one hand, and minorities, on the other. The effects of the principle flowed in two different directions: downward to the minorities, who, if they received justice in this instance, were protected in their civil and political rights, and upward to the League, which, if justice were to be served, had the duty of protection. This might, of course, mean direct interference by the League in the internal affairs of a sovereign state, but, as the Norwegian delegate put it, times had changed: "There were no purely internal questions. Any problems that arose in a country might have, and in most cases, had such effects outside the country as to make of it an international problem. It was one of the elementary duties of the League never to forget that aspect of the question."[15]

The delegate from Czechoslovakia picked up on the theme of justice and carried it even farther away from its close identification with peace. By so doing he raised the concept to a level of abstraction that almost divorced it from anything concrete, but he then brought it back down to the individual level of the Franz Bernheims of the world. He noted that everything he had heard that morning had convinced him that "a civilized community of nations like the League could not disregard the claims of justice, not only international justice, but justice itself." Having made this grandiloquent flourish, he returned to the practical and the need for urgency in a situation in which German Jews were suffering even as the council debated its duty, if any, toward them. Action, he said, needed to be prompt since, although justice itself was indeed eternal, "the human beings who were entitled to enjoy and benefit by justice were not eternal."[16] It was this knowledge that had emboldened him to speak about the issues raised by the Bernheim petition.

And here the matter rested. Action against Germany for the treatment of German Jews was as much beyond the capacity of the League as it was beyond the political will of the states that would have to carry out any action. Moral indignation and the invocation of moral rights allowed the delegates around the council table to breach the customary forms of diplomatic discourse and express their dismay at happenings in Germany. But moral rights, and even legal rights, had almost no effect on the policies of countries that were sunk in economic depression and torn by political controversy. If Germany had refused to recognize its international obligations in Upper Silesia, what pressure could have been brought to bear? What country would have been willing to send one soldier or spend one penny to see that Franz Bernheim and his fellow Jews were reinstated in their positions and given protection from the mob?

The delegates around the League Council table in May 1933 were pushing hard against the limits of current conceptions of the sovereign state and the relation of that state's internal laws to some broader standard of judgment. But they could only push rhetorically. They had no weapons other than their anger, and when that was spent, they were done. The matter of Franz Bernheim continued through the processes that had been begun. The Committee of Jurists found that Bernheim was indeed a member of a minority as defined in Article 147 of the Geneva Convention and that he had a right to petition the council. That settled, there was nothing more for the council to do than accept Germany's word that it would see the matter through the local processes that had been established under the Convention. This it did.

Bernheim and the other Jews who had lost their jobs in Upper Silesia did not get their jobs back, but they did receive compensation. It was a very small victory for national compliance with international standards of behavior, but it was a victory. In the decade of the '30s, when flagrant disregard of international standards became almost the norm, the Franz Bernheim affair might have become the shining exception—except that it was almost unknown. Like many of the League's accomplishments, the handling of the Bernheim affair sank into obscurity or was overwhelmed by later, more dramatic developments. The basic problem with which the council had wrestled in 1933 did not disappear, however. The tension between the claims of sovereignty and the claims of humanity continued throughout the century. It was particularly acute in the 1930s, and, in the end, it forced a major rethinking of the concept of justice in international affairs.

CHAPTER TEN

Symbolic Interventions

Franz Bernheim, the German citizen who was dismissed from his job because he was a Jew, could appeal to the League of Nations for help because he was a resident of German Upper Silesia at the time of his dismissal. As a member of a protected minority there, he had the right of appeal to the council of the League. Although Bernheim tried to expand his personal right of appeal to cover the situation of Jews in general, both in Upper Silesia and in Germany proper, his attempt failed. Given the prevailing ideas about the freedom of a state in internal affairs there was no way that the League could justify official attention to Bernheim's broader claim.

Meanwhile, the truth of Bernheim's statement about the treatment of Jews by the National Socialist regime became more evident every day. "Already an enormous number of Jewish lives have been ruined," he said as he asked that his petition be treated as urgent: "If the tendencies at present prevailing in Germany continue to hold sway, in a very short time every Jew in Germany will have suffered permanent injury, so that any restoration and reparation will become impossible and thousands and ten thousands will have completely lost their livelihood."[1]

The "tendencies prevailing in Germany" did indeed hold sway throughout the spring and summer of 1933 until, as Bernheim had predicted, thousands of Jews had completely lost their livelihood. The National Socialists moved cautiously at first in their purge of Jews from the public arena, but their restraint was short-lived. As one scholar has noted, the law under which Jews were removed from office "was a relatively mild measure, but the destruction process was a development that was begun with caution and ended without restraint."[2]

The inability of traditional diplomacy to deal with the German situation is emphasized by the comments of two diplomats stationed in Berlin during the 1930s. William E. Dodd, who was U.S. ambassador to Germany in 1933, when Jews were being driven out of the professions, the civil service, and the work force, noted in his diary that he could do nothing about it. As an official representative of a government that maintained diplomatic relations with the German government, he could not possibly lodge a protest against German treatment of German citizens. When Professor R. G. Harrison of Yale University called at the U.S. embassy in August 1933 to ask Dodd's help on behalf of a distinguished woman professor at Berlin University who had been dismissed from her post and jailed because she was a Jew, Dodd made this bleak little comment in his diary: "As she was a German citizen I could make no move."[3]

The case was somewhat different with Sir Nevile Henderson, British ambassador to Germany in the late 1930s. Henderson was frequently at odds with his own Foreign Office because of what was perceived as his too great sympathy for German-inspired actions against the governments of Austria and Czechoslovakia. Uneasy as the British government might be about these moves, however, it was not until Germany breached a state boundary in September 1939 that uneasiness turned into official condemnation. By sending troops across the border into Poland, the German government violated a fundamental principle of the international system, one on which the political independence and territorial integrity of each state depended. Now indignation could find utterance. As Henderson observed in his final report to the Foreign Office, with the move into Poland, Hitler appeared "under his true colours as an unprincipled menace to European peace and liberty."[4]

And before that crossing of a state boundary? Before that there was an official desert, an expanse empty of effective action. The well-known brutalities of the National Socialist regime seemed so far beyond the reach of any other government that they might have been taking place on the moon instead of right in the heart of Europe. In order to be credible, any official protest from the world outside Germany would have had to rest on the threat of intervention, and that possibility *was* as remote as the moon. Even if economic depression and public opinion had not hobbled the governments of the states concerned, intervention was never a serious option. German treatment of German Jews, Communists, Socialists, and political dissidents of any persuasion was an internal matter and, as such, off-limits to official comment from outsiders. As Henderson noted in his final report, despite the "sickening technique of Nazism it was difficult not to concede to Germany the right to control her own destiny and to benefit from those principles which were accorded to others."[5]

The principles referred to by Henderson were the same ones that Japan had breached in Manchuria in 1931: peaceful settlement of disputes, no resort to war except in self-defense, and fulfillment in good faith of treaty obligations. These principles, as has often been noted, were state-centered. They were highly protective of the states that had devised them. Their purpose was to maintain an acceptable level of stability and order in the relations between independent, quarrelsome states. The principles had found expression in the covenant of the League of Nations and in the anti-war treaties of the 1920s, but they were not simply a static list of idealized norms. In the hands of many internationalists in the 1920s and early 1930s they had become the chief vehicle through which justice was being sought in international affairs.

So long as German leaders abided by these principles, they were protected from official criticism or action by the other states in the system—states that relied on those very same principles for their own protection. The unstated assumption of the whole state-centered normative system was that there would be no interference in a state's affairs so long as it carried out its treaty obligations, did not invade its neighbors, settled its external disputes peacefully, and so on. In certain respects, the German record on treaty obligations might have been open to question. Even under the Weimar Republic some German citizens had tried to focus international attention on secret German rearmament in violation of the provisions of the Treaty of Versailles. They had been jailed for their pains, and war-weary states had preferred not to take official notice of what was not officially acknowledged. Condemnation of the Treaty of Versailles by National Socialist leaders also might have given other states pause, but German pledges to seek change only by legal means reassured a world that desperately wanted to believe that the pledges were made in good faith.

A further barrier to official outside action against National Socialist brutalities within Germany's borders was the principle of self-determination. As Sir Nevile Henderson had put it, Germany had the right "to control her own destiny." It seems obvious today that this was a perversion of a principle that had been formulated to allow a free choice of government to national groups within eastern European empires. The perversion was not quite so obvious right after the National Socialists took power in early 1933. They made no secret of their repression of opposition parties. Instead they skillfully deployed the arguments of a different normative framework and appealed (as the Japanese had done) to the set of values associated with the need for social order. The Primacy of Order was a framework of ideas that had wide appeal in Germany after the disorders of the latter days of the Weimar Republic. There was no sign that Germans in general were ready to rise in revolt to protest National Socialist treatment of Jews or dissidents. And if the broad mass of Germans accepted National Socialism as their destiny, what were outsiders to do?

Officially, they could not do very much. Unofficially, there was no lack of condemnation of National Socialist domestic policies and of calls for governments or the League of Nations or some organization somehow to do something about the situation. In response to the treatment of Jews in Germany, Jews in other countries instituted a boycott of German goods and products. Mass meetings were called to hear German refugees and exiles tell of the atrocities being committed against German citizens by the regime. Unhampered by diplomatic protocol or reliance on principles protective of the state, journalists, editors, broadcasters, religious leaders, union officials, legislators, and members of many different professions publicly condemned Germany's internal policies and called on its leaders to change their ways.

Predictably, German leaders complained to the governments of the various countries where protests were taking place that these public outbursts constituted an unwarranted interference in Germany's internal affairs. Equally predictably, governments that had been constrained by protocol in their official reaction to the National Socialist regime blandly replied that because the protests were expressions of private opinions, there was nothing they could do about it. So the protests continued. Here, on a broad scale that transcended national boundaries, were passionate assertions of values that focused on the protection of human beings, rather than protection of the state. Direct intervention in Germany's internal affairs was out of the question for groups without governmental authority or power. They could, however, keep the issue before the public. They could point collective fingers of shame and, in various ways, dramatize the repressive nature of the National Socialist regime. If these symbolic interventions in Germany's affairs did nothing else, they at least served notice of a widespread belief that there were values beyond the state that were worth upholding and that these values were, or ought to be, of international concern.

IN THE LIKENESS OF LAW

The melodramatic elements in the explosion that set off the Manchurian Incident in 1931 were mimicked in Berlin in 1933. Again there was secrecy, again stealthy movements in the night. Then, as in Manchuria, actions taken in secret rose to a climax in public. On the night of February 27, the Session Chamber of the Reichstag building in central Berlin suddenly burst into flame. By the time the fire was put out, the grandiose hall with its great glass dome, its ranks of benches for the legislators, and its oak-paneled walls was a charred ruin. Architects might not lament the loss of a hall that one observer had described as a "ridiculous neo-Gothic crate,"[6] but a great many people could look back at the fire as the trigger for the losses in their own lives.

As dawn broke over the smoldering ruins in Berlin, arresting parties fanned out through that city and, in the next few days, through other cities as well. The three-man parties carried lists of people to put in "preventive detention." By the time the raids were over, hundreds of people had been arrested. Communists were the chief target, since the official line was that Communists were responsible for the fire. Government officials said loudly and repeatedly that Communists had set the fire as a signal for a general uprising. The "preventive detention" net was, however, broad enough to sweep into confinement many who were not Communists. These were people who were, or who might become, opponents of the National Socialists in the nationwide elections scheduled for March 5, just six days after the fire. Thus members of the Social Democratic party were arrested, as were journalists who had written critically about Hitler's appointment as chancellor and pacifists who had denounced German rearmament. Such prompt action by the National Socialists to eliminate opposition to their candidates has, naturally, led many to suspect them of setting the fire themselves. The question of official culpability was the focus of attention then, and the question has not gone away. It hung like a cloud over the trial of the five people who were eventually accused of setting the blaze, and it still stirs passionate controversy among those who do not accept either the trial findings or those of later investigators.[7]

Entangled with the question of responsibility for starting the fire was the question of how fair a trial the five defendants could expect to receive in the Germany of 1933. Opponents of the National Socialists had no doubt that the trial would be rigged in favor of the government's claims of a Communist conspiracy. Thus the question of the fairness of the Reichstag fire trial became for many, both inside and outside Germany, a critical test of the regime. But that was not its only effect. The trial also acted as a catalyst for a searching re-examination of the whole place of law in society conducted both by the National Socialists and by their opponents at home and abroad. The two sides came to wholly different conclusions about the spirit and the substance of law, a fact that profoundly influenced subsequent events. In the short run, however, public attention centered on the conduct of the trial. It was in that regard that those outside Germany made their unofficial and symbolic intervention. While preparations were going forward in Germany to hold the trial before the Fourth Penal Chamber of the Supreme Court in Leipzig, preparations also got under way to hold public hearings on the case in a courthouse in London.

The London hearings were conducted by a group of lawyers from seven countries: Belgium, Denmark, Great Britain, France, the Netherlands, Sweden, and the United States. The lawyers called themselves the Legal Commission to Inquire into the Burning of the Reichstag, but their profession and training were all that gave any color of reality to the word *legal* in their title. They had no authority from any public body. Their authority was that most dangerous spark in the dry tinder of statutory law: conscience. It was enough. Refugees from Germany, former German officials, and those exiled from their homeland for political reasons appeared willingly before the commission in London. These witnesses testified about the conditions in Germany that had driven them out. They described the Reichstag building, explained the security arrangements for the building, and told what they knew about the background and movements of the five men who were to stand trial in Leipzig. Most of the hearings were held in public, but at times the doors were locked and testimony was taken in private as a measure to protect the witness from possible retaliation by National Socialist sympathizers.

From a legal point of view, the proceedings were a farce. The London group could not subpoena witnesses or documentary evidence. There was no cross-examination, no challenge to testimony as being irrelevant or outside the personal knowledge of the witness. All this was admitted by Arthur Garfield Hays, the participating lawyer from the United States. It was, he said, a "pseudo-trial,"[8] but it was, nonetheless, an effective way to dramatize the threat to law—and therefore the threat to human life—in Germany. Looking back on this episode in his eventful life, Hays had no regrets about the pseudo-legal quality of the hearings by the commission of inquiry. The purpose was to keep the German proceedings as fair to the defendants as possible by keeping the Leipzig trial in the spotlight, and, further, to put pressure on the German prosecutors by gathering evidence that might otherwise be suppressed or overlooked.

The audience for these hearings was neither a jury nor a panel of judges. It was the public. And the defendant in that London courtroom was not any individual or group of individuals but rather the whole system of German government as it was developing under the Hitler regime. The arrests that had been made immediately following the Reichstag fire were only the beginning. Constitutional guarantees of civil rights were effectively set aside by an emergency decree issued in response to the fire. The emergency was then justified and extended by a drumroll of announcements of newly discovered "plots" that called for decisive action to protect the nation against its internal enemies: Jews, Communists, Socialists, Monarchists, and skeptics of every political stripe. It was "discovered" that these skeptics had found refuge in newspaper offices, labor unions, universities, professional associations, churches, even in courts of law. Since the regime was defining "criminal classes" in the broadest possible terms, the courts of the legal system were of particular interest to the German government—as they were also to the lawyers in London. To sharpen the focus of public attention, the hearings before the unofficial London Commission of Inquiry were held in September 1933, just a few days before the opening of the Reichstag fire trial in Leipzig. As Hays noted, the London hearings were, in effect, "a pretrial of a trial, involving German justice and the Nazi party."[9]

With this comment, Hays brought into the open the basic difference that was developing between the National Socialists in Germany and their opponents in countries such as France, Great Britain, and the United States, as well as in Germany itself. Hays's reference to "German justice" went straight to the heart of the matter. The term could be read in two different ways. Either it meant justice as administered in the Germany of 1933, or it meant justice in a specifically German form. It was clear that Hays and the lawyers on the London Commission of Inquiry acted on a concept of justice in which the accused in criminal proceedings was protected against the arbitrary exercise of power by the state. Thus the question for them and the whole impulse behind the hearings in London was whether the requirements of this ideal of justice would, or could, be fulfilled in the Germany of 1933.

Suppose, though, that "German justice" meant exactly that: a justice that was specific to Germany. The "German-ness" of various aspects of social and political life was one of the themes of National Socialism. The purge of non-Aryans from the civil service and the professions had been done in the name of the protection of the German character of those occupations and of

the public they served. Bonfires of books in Hamburg and Berlin were characterized by the regime as the spontaneous outrage of students against the
"Un-German spirit" of those books. Posters throughout Germany calling
for a boycott of Jewish shops and merchants urged customers to "Buy German," thus excluding from German-ness the German citizens who were
also Jews.[10] Thoughtful observers had reason to be concerned that this
same emphasis on German-ness would influence the proceedings in the
Reichstag fire trial and thus influence the concept of justice that would be
reflected there.

Clearly the National Socialists, even in those early days of their power,
were striving to make the legal system of Germany a policy arm of the state.
Doing so would harness justice to the party line and make it specific to the
German state under National Socialism just as, in the Soviet Union, Communist party leaders had created a concept of justice that was specific to
Russia under Communism. But in September 1933, at the time of the Reichstag fire trial, the National Socialists had not yet succeeded in blending
the state and their party into one as had been done in Russia. They were
moving as rapidly as they dared in that direction, but there was still a separation, small though it was, between party and state.

This became evident as the trial in Leipzig proceeded through weeks and
weeks of testimony, making it, in retrospect, not a clear-cut case of good or
bad, just or unjust, but, rather, an instance of conceptual confusion and conflict. On one hand there was still a lingering notion of justice as fair treatment for the accused, a notion that inspired a painstaking investigation of
the backgrounds of the five defendants and their movements on the night of
the fire. This search for the facts in the case, convenient or not to the powers that had arrested and charged the five men, was, however, offset by other
actions that seemed to put the court in the pocket of the government. Each
day the proceedings were opened with the Nazi salute, given even by the
judges. Then, too, there was such evident care for officialdom that prominent government officials such as Joseph Goebbels and Hermann Goering
were allowed uninterrupted blocks of time in court to repeat at length the
party line regarding responsibility for the fire and Germany's destiny in
general. These officials were particularly concerned that their charge of a
Communist conspiracy—on which many of their actions relied—not be
undermined by the London Commission of Inquiry. That group had concluded that "grave grounds exist for suspecting that the Reichstag was set on
fire by, or on behalf of, leading personalities of the National Socialist
Party."[11]

The trial was lengthy. Beginning near the end of September, it went on through October and November and well into December. Conflicting ideas of justice ran side by side throughout the proceedings, now one, now the other carrying the burden of events. This conflict of ideas can be summarized very roughly as a conflict between an emphasis on protection of the state and a concern for protection of the individual. In the end, despite significant gestures of submission to the state on the part of the court, the panel of judges acquitted four of the five defendants. The fifth, Marinus van der Lubbe, was found guilty of the charges of high treason, insurrectionary arson, and common arson. The verdict was a foregone conclusion since van der Lubbe had been found in the burning building and had, from the first, claimed sole responsibility for setting the fire.

The length of the trial, the prominence of some of the witnesses, and the attention that was focused on Leipzig both inside and outside Germany meant that the trial was as much a theatrical event as it was a legal proceeding. Excerpts were broadcast over the German radio each evening. There was extensive coverage in the foreign press by the numerous correspondents who crowded into the courtroom each day. Note was taken of the demeanor of the judges and of the splash of color provided by their scarlet robes against the backdrop of a large-scale floor plan of the Reichstag building. Exchanges between lawyers and witnesses were meticulously recorded and passed on to readers in conversational form as in the dialogue of a play. A dramatic climax was reached when Hermann Goering lost his temper during questioning by Georgi Dimitrov, the one defendant who conducted his own defense. So effective was Dimitrov that some headline writers began calling the whole affair the Dimitrov trial. As a piece of theater, the Reichstag fire trial had something for everyone, and it had this added fillip: in this play the stakes were real, and they were high. Treason was a capital crime, and every defendant faced the threat of execution[12]

No one was completely satisfied by the outcome of the trial. Even though the judges, in their discussion of their verdict, kept alive the suspicion of a Communist conspiracy, this effort was not nearly strong enough to satisfy the government. The official line was that Communist plots were an immediate threat that required strong countermeasures to protect the state. The trial strengthened the National Socialists' determination to gain complete control of the legal system they had inherited from the Weimar Republic, or, if necessary, to bypass that system completely and set up one that would reflect their own concept of justice. Defenders of Germany, on the other hand, saw the acquittal of four of those charged as proof that justice could still prevail in German courts. Their disillusionment was swift when the four were not released from "protective custody."[13]

What, if anything, had been accomplished by the symbolic intervention of the lawyers in London with their countertrial, or, as Arthur Garfield Hays had put it, their pretrial of the actual trial in Leipzig? It is impossible to establish with any certainty what might have happened if the London hearings had never been held and the lawyers from the seven different countries had simply stayed home. The drama of the fire had engaged public interest right from the start, and the National Socialist effort to make the trial a justification of their policies guaranteed increased attention to the proceedings. What then of London, and of the many other unofficial efforts to call attention to what was happening in Germany and mobilize public opinion against it?

One thing can be said for certain. Whether or not the London pretrial increased public awareness of National Socialist activities in Germany, it served as a platform for public witness against those activities. By their presence, the seven leading lawyers and the commission's supporting staff bore witness to a concept of justice that was being eroded in Germany. The spotlight of publicity was on the proceedings at Leipzig, but what was happening there was not the only concern in London. Ample evidence was coming out of Germany of arbitrary arrests, rigged court hearings, prolonged imprisonment, and inhumane conditions of confinement and labor, even when torture was not involved—as it frequently was. In this sense, the Reichstag fire trial was a smokescreen for the widespread assault on justice for individuals that was taking place in Germany. As Douglas Reed, covering the Leipzig trial for the *London Times*, pointed out: "Outside the courtroom men could be arrested and held for weeks, months or years without the preferment of charges or trial."[14]

Reed's comment highlights the central position of a trial in the minds of those who look to law as a bulwark against unrestrained force. Of all the forms the hearings in London could have taken to protest the actions of the National Socialists, that of a trial was the one chosen. This choice might be attributed to the legal training of the participants, but it might well signify more than that. The choice might also be a tribute to the ideal of a courtroom as a place where facts can be sifted from rumor and hearsay and where considered public judgment can take the place of private revenge or the arbitrary exercise of power. The notion underlying this ideal, that through trial procedures justice might be served, gives to the form itself an air of authority and authenticity, a fact that has had consequences outside the courtroom. Thus, public protests in the form of a trial have been favored by groups that have not the slightest color of authority. The Bertrand Russell tribunals of the 1960s and 1970s and the self-styled Permanent Peoples'

Tribunal have chosen the form for their protests against some aspect of international affairs.[15] Similarly, six months or so after the Reichstag counter-trial in London, another was held in New York city, this one billed as "The Case of Civilization against Adolf Hitler."

The reaction of Hans Luther, the German ambassador to the United States, can be imagined. As the date for the mock trial approached, he made repeated protests to the U.S. State Department. Official records note that Luther "earnestly complained against this sort of public proceeding against the Chancellor of Germany. . . .He indicated great concern and repeatedly expressed the opinion that he was helpless to make a satisfactory showing to his Government justifying his failure to prevent this mock trial." And on the day of the "trial", he made one final appeal "to stop this demonstration against the Chancellor of a friendly state." Officials of Germany made direct representations of concern as well. The German foreign minister, Constantin von Neurath, while acknowledging how "highly treasured" free speech was in the United States, nonetheless appealed to the U.S. government to curb the abuse of that freedom since it was being used to mount a "continuous American publicity campaign against the new German regime." Von Neurath's appeal was made through William Dodd, the U.S. ambassador in Berlin, who commented to his superiors in the State Department that the inspiration for the German appeal was "apparently the 'mock trial' to be held in New York tomorrow, which has made an extraordinary impression upon them."[16]

Secretary of State Cordell Hull responded to German protests against the "publicity campaign" in the United States with an unruffled demeanor and one of the sharpest barbs allowed in the courteous jousting of a diplomatic exchange. All that was needed, said Hull, for him to try to restrain public accusations of cruelty against the German government was to have conclusive evidence "to the effect that Jews had not been unfairly treated or seriously mistreated in Germany." With that evidence in hand, he could doubtless persuade prominent officials such as New York mayor Fiorello LaGuardia to stop accusing the National Socialist regime of doing just that. As for the so-called trial of Adolf Hitler, the people in charge of that were not "in any sense representing the Federal Government." However, noted Hull—with a flash of unexpected malicious humor—he was not letting the matter rest there. He had had "all the law books ransacked in an effort to find the complete international law relating to this sort of situation." So far he had been "disappointed" in the search for a definite law that would enable the federal government "to compel the abandonment of the mock trial." The State Department had not given up. Law books were still being examined, and "anything possible to be done in the light of international law would not be overlooked." [17]

Since the international law of the time could provide neither means nor justification for intervening in Germany to protect the victims of the National Socialist regime, it was not likely to provide the law of suppression that Hull said he was seeking—as he well knew. So the "trial" in New York went forward on March 7, 1934, a date chosen to mark the first anniversary of the National Socialists' assumption of power in the elections following the Reichstag fire. To open the proceedings, a bugler blew "Taps." The crowd of twenty thousand in Madison Square Garden observed a moment of silence to honor the memory of those who had been killed by the National Socialists. Then the "court" portion of the proceedings began, although it is difficult to tell exactly what century the organizers had in mind. A crier called the crowd to order: "Hear ye! Hear ye! Hear ye! All those who have business before this court of civilization give your attention and ye shall be heard. May I ask you to rise while the Court takes its place?"[18] The group of citizens who had been asked to speak filed onto the floodlit platform and took their seats. The "Case of Civilization against Adolf Hitler" was ready to begin.

If anyone found it odd that the speakers on the platform and the event itself were both called "the court," the fact is not mentioned in the accounts of that evening in Madison Square Garden. The affair was treated with the utmost seriousness by the participants. In a gesture of impartiality they had invited the German ambassador, Luther, to appear to defend Hitler and the policies of his regime. It was, of course, beneath the dignity of a representative of a sovereign nation-state even to reply to such an invitation. So the charges against Hitler went unanswered, and National Socialism was undefended except by a single voice that shouted "No!" when the question of guilt was put to a voice vote.

The charges against Hitler and his regime were specific and numerous. In twenty-one different counts the German leaders were accused not only of destroying civil liberties and subverting justice in Germany but of returning that nation to barbarism while threatening to plunge the whole world into war. Twenty different speakers brought "evidence" to support this comprehensive indictment and then spoke with deep feeling about the values and benefits of civilization. The theme running throughout the presentations was that civilization was under dire threat from what was described as "Hitlerism." Arthur Garfield Hays of the unofficial London inquiry was one of the speakers, as was LaGuardia, former New York governor Alfred E. Smith, former secretary of state Bainbridge Colby, and others prominent in labor, religious, reform, and public service organizations. The "verdict" of the proceedings was that the Hitler regime was guilty of crimes against civilization.

This came as no surprise. National Socialist actions, which German leaders defended as matters of internal policy, constituted prima facie evidence of guilt in the eyes of the organizers of the New York "trial." So the "verdict" was a foregone conclusion. What was surprising was the passion with which the crowd shouted its approval of the finding. The hour was late. The people were tired. But given the opportunity to make a united and vocal protest, there was, said a reporter for the *New York Times*, "a great swelling roar of approval from all over the hall."[19] Was Adolf Hitler guilty of the crimes with which he was charged? The reply was clear and overwhelming: "Aye!" Guilty as charged.

There was, of course, no binding force in this verdict, nor did the proceedings bear any relation to law except in form. The whole affair at Madison Square Garden on the evening of March 7 was an elaborate piece of make-believe that threatened no one with any serious harm, despite rumblings of diplomatic displeasure. This fact could hardly have escaped the speakers on the platform that evening. They were neither inexperienced nor unrealistic, and they could judge as well as anyone the very slight effect— if any—that their words and actions would have in the real world of international politics. Yet there they were in solemn conclave, as if the fate of an ambitious German politician depended on the outcome of proceedings in a cavernous arena in New York City thousands of miles from Berlin.

This was, indeed, an evening of make-believe, but it was a make-believe born of frustration. Despite undeniable evidence that the National Socialists were persecuting Jews and others defined by the party as "undesirables," an effective response seemed beyond the power or will of any other state or of the international community. Private individuals and organizations had no doubt that something ought to be done. If direct and official intervention was out of the question—as it seemed to be—then private, symbolic intervention would have to do. So, invoking the majesty of a law that could not, in 1934, bear the weight of their expectations, the people in Madison Square Garden tried the Hitler regime for its international crimes against civilization and found it guilty. The verdict served clear and passionate notice that, under extreme circumstances such as those in National Socialist Germany, the barriers of nationality had to give way to the claims of humanity.

Government officials in positions of responsibility might sympathize privately with this point of view, but in 1934 there was no way for them to do anything about it officially. The conceptual, institutional, and political barriers were much too strong to allow the direct intervention that the situation seemed to call for. The very idea of sovereignty forbade the states to interfere in each other's affairs. Under ordinary circumstances this was a prudent prohibition, a recognition that such interference might well be undertaken as much for political advantage as for any other reason. Even granted that the situation in Germany in 1934 was not ordinary and that ordinary rules would not serve, calls for official action would still draw a blank. Public opinion in France, Great Britain, and the United States was dead set against any move that might lead to war. Further, the weakness of the League of Nations, with its reliance on reason and persuasion, was most apparent when it came to situations that might require the collective use of force.

All of this meant that events in Germany took their course unhindered by those outside its borders. The verdict of the mock trial in New York City that there were times when justice required that the claims of sovereignty give way to the claims of humanity remained a private view until the end of the 1930s. Even then the change from the private to the public sphere was neither swift nor easy. For all the cruelties perpetrated prior to 1939, it took World War II, with its attendant and unspeakable cruelties, for this view to be taken up at official levels and for governments to begin to give serious consideration as to how they might translate this view into public policy.

CHAPTER ELEVEN

Morality in Thrall

There was little need for those involved in the unofficial "trials" in London and New York to make public statements about the concept of law under which they were acting. They could assume that the intended audience for these proceedings understood and shared their ideas of what law was supposed to be and the role it was supposed to play in society. Even militant labor leaders who might see law in general as a kind of cover for unequal power relationships could nevertheless participate in the mock trial in New York City on the grounds that some behavior did legitimately fall within the domain of criminal law. They, and the thousands in Madison Square Garden the evening of March 7, 1934, had no doubt that the behavior of the National Socialists was indeed criminal and that those responsible should be punished. To them it made no difference that the actions were taking place within Germany's borders, just as, to the lawyers on the London commission of inquiry, it had made no difference that the Reichstag fire trial was being held within Germany. The feeling was strong that certain standards ought to apply, no matter the site of action.

The people involved in these two symbolic interventions were asserting the universality of standards regarding the treatment of human beings by the governments under which they lived. These universal standards had long been expressed in national documents such as the Act Declaring the Rights and Liberties of the Subject (England, 1688), the Declaration of the Rights of Man and of the Citizen (France, 1789), and the Bill of Rights (United States, 1791). Internationally, in the early 1930s, there was nothing

147

comparable, but this did not by any means soften the widespread unofficial criticism of German actions. The feeling was strong that a declaration of human rights did not create those rights. It simply recognized an existing state of affairs. Therefore, whether there was a statement or not, the standards regarding the treatment of human beings were the same, inside or outside Germany.

Under these standards, there could be no arbitrary arrest and imprisonment for those accused of crimes. If a legitimate arrest were made, the conditions of detention were to be decent, and certain rights were to be observed: a full disclosure of charges, the right to counsel, and the right to be brought quickly to public trial. Punishment, if any, was not to be cruel. The National Socialists were subverting or ignoring every one of these standards every day. Their record was no better when it came to protecting citizens' rights of expression and association. Publishers and broadcasters were under the thumb of the state—which was, increasingly, a tool of the National Socialist Party—and labor unions, opposition parties, and professional associations were being systematically destroyed or transformed into organized offshoots of the party. As the organizers of the mock trial in Madison Square Garden put it, Hitler and his followers had "exterminated every vestige of the hard-won liberties of the forgotten men and women whose defense and protection has made up the progress of civilization."[1]

Authors of this indictment might well have argued about fine points in the definition of *civilization* that they held up as a contrast to the National Socialist regime. They might even have argued whether *civilization* was the proper term. They would, however, have agreed that, whatever name was used, major themes in human history were the efforts to restrain the strong members of society and protect the weak, to control the powerful and shield the powerless, and to make the law a system in which all stood on equal ground. The moral universe that they inhabited, and from which they drew their strength, was an inclusive one. *All* were to be citizens of that universe. *All* were to have the same rights, be subject to the same duties, and stand before the law on the basis of their actions, not on the basis of their opinions, possessions, social standing, or racial or ethnic origin.

Few in 1933 and 1934 would have argued that these goals were fully realized in the societies where criticism of the National Socialists was strong. Criticism could be, and often was, just as strong against their own societies. Arthur Garfield Hays, who took part in both the London Commission of Inquiry and in the New York City trial, was counsel for the American Civil Liberties Union. In his private practice he spent much time defending those who were victims of a system that did not live up to its own ideals. When the civil liberties of ordinary human beings were threatened in the United States in the interwar period, there Hays was to be found. He helped to defend Sacco and Vanzetti, John T. Scopes, Frederick Sweet, the Scottsboro Seven, and a number of obscure others whose cases never attracted public attention.[2] In each case the defense rested on the same standards, since each case, in a different way, tested the U.S. commitment to the values of inclusion and equality. The law could not mandate either equality or inclusion. These were essentially moral values. But the substance of the law, and the way that the law was applied or ignored, interpreted, or enforced, could help create— or destroy—a context in which equality and inclusion might be attained.

Over against the claims of this inclusive moral universe, with its standards of equality and universality, were set the claims of a different moral universe. Critics of the National Socialist regime did not recognize this different universe as having anything to do with morality, but it, like theirs, created a system of values and judgments that was internally consistent and that could appeal to people's need for a sense of direction. Force and intimidation could go only so far in the establishment of a new regime, particularly a regime such as that of the National Socialists. To survive, it needed the cooperation and support of many people who were repelled by brute force: the respectable middle class, the laboring poor, church leaders, teachers, members of the professions, small-scale industrialists, the officer corps of the old-line army. The party had to offer a great deal more than anti-Communist street brawls and gigantic floodlit rallies to attract and hold this vast middle level of society—people who were home-centered, oriented to private life, and weary of domestic violence.

The party offered a complete moral universe with clear standards of right and wrong, good and evil. Unlike that of its critics, the moral universe of the National Socialists was uncompromisingly exclusive. There were insiders and outsiders, the chosen and the rejected. Much of the history of the party from 1933 onward can be seen as a drawing of ever stricter boundaries of separation between those who were to build a new and greater Germany and those who, through malice, weakness, ignorance, or perversity, were a threat to that great project. The very existence of these people was not to be tolerated. In the National Socialist philosophy, these outsiders were more than just an antisocial element. They were criminals whose crime was even worse than simply breaking a law. Their actions transgressed the moral boundaries that had to be maintained if the German people were to be great and strong again, free of the guilt, confusion, and paralyzing weakness of the Weimar Republic.

One of the boasts of National Socialist thinkers was that they had closed the gap between law and morality. Instead of the tension between the law as it was and the law as it ought to be, there was harmony between the two. The stated basis of the National Socialist program was that law and morality were equal partners in the grand undertaking in which the German people were engaged. Where the law was lacking or incomplete, morality was there to provide guidelines for acceptable and unacceptable behavior. The standard of measurement was the well-being and strengthening of the Volk, the people, which is to say, all those who were within the circle of the elect. This was not a random selection. These were people uniquely fitted to repair the tattered social fabric of the German nation and return the country to greatness.

The possible outcome of making a moral universe congruent with the boundaries of a specific nation-state was not apparent in the early 1930s even to the most outspoken critics of the National Socialist regime. They could not imagine the lengths to which this philosophy of German-ness would be taken. Nor were they the only ones who found this outcome difficult to foresee. Some of the Germans who were counted among the elect in the '30s had a similar failure of imagination. They were shocked when various actions of the regime that they had found personally distasteful but, perhaps, necessary in a time of revolutionary change grew into trends that could not be controlled, with consequences that they deplored. For many others, ambition, fear, patriotism, and a measure of willful blindness combined to make keeping quiet a more attractive course of action than speaking up. Patriotism was an especially strong defense against doubt and, for some, a sufficient answer to scruples. What, after all, was wrong with pride? With wanting the German nation to be strong again and take its place among the other nations of the world? What was wrong with an emphasis on the community and its needs? Hadn't the emphasis on the rights of the individual led, in many instances, to social fragmentation, hedonism, and a careless disregard for anyone but oneself? Wasn't it time and past time for a change?

Thinking such as this in Germany in the early and mid-1930s helped develop what the German scholar Ernst Fraenkel has called "the dual state."[3] It was a state in which, at one level, the legal system continued to function with every appearance of normality, while, at another level, various centers of party power used tactics of terror to gain their ends. Thus there existed, side by side, the administration of law and the arbitrary exercise of power. This duality made it possible for those who wanted to dissociate themselves from violence to give their support to the National Socialist program of reform and strengthening, while privately regretting the excesses of such groups as the Gestapo and the SS. The result was that life in Germany came to resemble an elaborate masque in which the deadly work of terror and persecution was hidden by the trappings of normality and the demands of the daily routine.

Concentration camps and Christmas trees, beatings and baptisms, torture sessions and excursions by tram—by concentrating on the second element in these disquieting pairs, the first could be ignored or denied. Life had to go on, didn't it? People had to be married, babies to be baptized, children to be educated, wills to be probated. There were meals to get and beds to make, the sick to tend, anniversaries to celebrate, the family to be gathered together to affirm old bonds and welcome new relationships. So life went on in Germany, and the appearance was not so different from what it had been in the past except that there were more public ceremonies and more uniforms evident in the streets. For those who could look beyond the daily activities it all seemed a little unreal, but many did not want to look and many feared to do so. By the mid-1930s the pattern of duality was set, as was the widespread denial that it existed.

The surreal quality of this determined emphasis on normal life and activities was nowhere more strikingly demonstrated than in Berlin in 1935. In August of that year there was a gathering of prison officials from around the world for the eleventh meeting of the International Penal and Penitentiary Congress. Of all people, they would be most likely to look with critical and informed eyes at the workings of the legal system in Germany under the National Socialists. With this in mind, the regime deployed some of its big guns to present the formal, legal aspects of their program. Reform was the chosen framework of explanation. The immediate audience was the assemblage of prison officials and those interested in problems of criminal justice, but the larger audience was the world. In 1935 the National Socialists still needed and wanted recognition of their regime as the legitimate and lawful government of a resurgent Germany.

The Reich minister of justice addressed the congress, as did the president of the German Supreme Court, the head of the German Academy of Law, the leading criminal law expert in the Ministry of Justice, and the Reich minister for public enlightenment and propaganda. The speakers were introduced with the customary laudatory remarks about their accomplishments and the importance of the work in which they were engaged. There was applause for their speeches, and thanks were tendered to them, again in the laudatory mode. The masquelike quality of daily life in Germany was thus faithfully preserved in the hall of the Kroll Opera House, where the plenary sessions of the congress were held. Parliamentary procedure provided the masks that helped create the illusion of normality. It might have been any international gathering, an occasion for professionals to discuss the papers that had been circulated beforehand, a place to exchange ideas with their German colleagues and with each other.

For the most part this illusion of normality was maintained, both at the meetings of the congress and throughout the study tour of German prisons that followed. There were one or two instances in which a recognition of the reality that lay behind the speeches of the German officials threatened to break through and disrupt the proceedings. But the courtesies of professional discourse managed to contain the outbursts and channel them into parliamentary maneuvers regarding the wording of various resolutions. In subtle ways the delegates were in a bind. They were not constrained by their positions, as the members of the League Council had been in the Franz Bernheim affair, but the constraints on speech were almost as strong. They were guests of the German government. They had been welcomed at a grand reception in the former imperial palace. The hall where the Reichstag met when in session had been turned over to them for their plenary sessions. They were taken on an excursion to Potsdam and Sans Souci and given "a delightful supper" after seeing the sights of the park and the castle and visiting the tomb of Frederic the Great.[4] At what point, in the midst of all this, was it appropriate to insult their hosts by suggesting that the Germany that was being presented to them was not all the Germany there was? It was a question that the delegates to the Eleventh Penal and Penitentiary Congress did not know how to answer. Nor were they alone in their inability to handle a situation of confusing duality. The problem for anyone dealing with Germany in the early days of National Socialism was deciding when it was time to put aside the assumption of normality and the persistent hope that, in the end, all would be well. And, supposing these *were* put aside, what then? No one seemed to have a plausible alternative. The policymakers of the various states did not. The tired men at the League of Nations did not. The impasse was frightening to observers such as the poet A. M. Klein: "Most miserable world!" he exclaimed, "which had to lean, Upon the dotards of this dying scene!"[5] There seemed to be little the dotards or anyone else could do about the situation. For a few more years, the masque of normality continued to be acted out, and many, inside Germany and out, continued to pretend that all was—or would be—well.

A FAIR PUBLIC FACE

The Berlin meeting of the Penal and Penitentiary Congress had many advantages for the National Socialists' presentation of their program of legal reform. They were assured of an audience interested in criminal law in all its aspects. They were assured also of wide dissemination of their message. Delegates from almost fifty countries were in attendance at the congress. They came from countries as distant and varied as China, Japan, Egypt, Turkey, Iraq, Peru, Mexico, and Canada, the United States, and most European countries. In the audience were prison officials, legislators, members of justice departments or ministries, judges on the highest courts of appeal, practicing lawyers, parole officers, university teachers, consular officers, and journalists. The fact that the meeting was held in Berlin gave the National Socialists another advantage, which they used to the full. The local venue meant that many more Germans could attend than would otherwise be the case. On votes that were taken by individual count, the large numbers of Germans had a decisive effect.

The occasion and the setting were perfect for the National Socialists' purpose. Not since the Reichstag fire trial had so much attention been concentrated on the question of the place of law in Germany. At the time of that trial, two years before the Berlin congress, traditional views of justice and traditional legal forms had still had an influence on the proceedings. When the presiding judge at the trial, Wilhelm Buenger, was asked by reporters how the trial would be conducted, he replied sharply that it would be conducted "according to the German penal code and the rules of German criminal court procedure." He had added, "I am astonished that such a question should be put to me. Law and justice still rule in Germany."[6]

For the National Socialists to retain the support of middle-level Germans and at the same time present an acceptable front to the world, it was important to show that law and justice still ruled in Germany. For this, it was imperative that appearances should not alarm, that familiar forms should be kept as a reassurance that all was much as it had been, only better, more vigorous, more attuned to the times. So, although the Weimar Republic was no more, the National Socialists did not abolish the constitution under which the republic had operated. Rather, they preserved the constitutional form while altering the spirit of government beyond all recognition. It was the same with the Reichstag, the popularly elected legislative body. It still met, debated, and passed legislation. None of these laws went against the party line, which only showed, said the National Socialists, what a community of like-minded feeling was being engendered in the new, vigorous Germany. As for the laws themselves, the spiritual renewal that was taking place throughout Germany would transform dry, outdated legal forms into living instruments of justice—as Reich minister of justice Franz Guertner explained to the delegates at the International Penal and Penitentiary Congress when he addressed them on the opening day of their meetings, August 19, 1935.

Guertner's position in the German government, and the fact that these meetings usually opened with a talk by an official of the host country, reinforced the air of normality that surrounded the proceedings of the congress. What could be more innocuous than a discussion of penal theory, especially one conducted with such care for the niceties of professional discourse? Following Guertner's "most interesting address," he was elected honorary president of the congress—and this by acclamation.[7] The election was presumably an honor routinely offered on such occasions, a tribute to his office, if not to his message. Such gestures, however, helped keep the mask of normality in place and made it more difficult to see and acknowledge the unflinching use of arbitrary power at the core of the message brought by Guertner and other party officials.

Even as Guertner spoke to the delegates, now-infamous laws were being prepared for presentation at the National Socialist party rally to be held in Nuremberg the following month. These laws were to strip German Jews of the rights of citizenship and forbid marriage between Jews and non-Jews on pain of criminal prosecution. Guertner did not discuss the Nuremberg laws, however, nor any of the anti-Semitic laws already in place.[8] His focus was not on specific legislation but on the philosophy that underlay that legislation, giving it validity within a specified frame of reference. He gave a clear and detailed outline of the legal frame of reference being developed in Germany under the rubric of "penal reform."

As minister of justice, Guertner was in a good position to make this kind of exposition. His office had the primary responsibility for seeing that the German penal code was recast along new lines. Guertner undertook this task with great seriousness and an awareness of its importance in the new German state being shaped by the National Socialists. He indulged in neither false modesty nor excessive pride. He was simply a professional doing the job he had been given: "Since the Führer and Reich Chancellor entrusted me about two years ago with the task of elaborating the draft of a new German Penal Code for the Cabinet, the work of reform has been undertaken energetically and pursued without intermission."[9]

This energetic attention to reform had resulted in sweeping changes that affected far more than the details of criminal procedure. Guertner's talk was titled "The Idea of Justice in the German Penal Reform." It quickly became clear that justice in the German context departed drastically from the concept of criminal justice in most of the countries represented at the congress. Theirs was the principle *nulla poena sine lege*, which is to say, no punishment without a law. Justice on this basis meant that no one could be punished for an act unless that act had first been defined by law as a criminal offense. In Germany this was to change, said Guertner. Instead of nulla poena sine lege, the underlying principle would be *nullum crimen sine poena*. In Germany there was to be no crime without punishment. Guertner was clear about this: "Everyone who commits an act deserving of punishment shall receive due punishment regardless of the incompleteness of the law. . . . National Socialism imposes a new and high task on Criminal Law, namely the realization of true justice."[10]

The most striking aspect of Franz Guertner's presentation of this theory of justice was its calm, low-key delivery. Here was no rabble-rouser screaming abuse into a microphone, no booted storm trooper demanding that everyone, foreigners included, return the Nazi salute. Here was an ordinary-looking, fifty-two-year-old bureaucrat, conscientiously carrying out the duties of his office, which, in this case, involved overturning much that had been won in years of struggle against tyranny. Gravely, pedantically, Guertner pointed out the advantages to be gained: Of "fundamental importance" was the fact that judges would no longer be hampered by gaps in the law. Whereas, under the present system, a judge's actions were restricted to acts that the legislators had, through specific laws, made a criminal offense, in the future this would no longer be true: "The future German Criminal Law will release the German judges from being closely bound by the text of the law."[11]

If not the text of the law, then what would judges be bound by? What would guide their deliberations as they pondered the fate of those who appeared before them, charged with crimes that were not on the books? Guertner had an answer for that, as he had an answer for most of the questions that might arise in response to this reformulation of the ideal of justice. He was nothing if not thorough, and in this professional setting, where ideas could be discussed in a detached and dispassionate manner, he was quite willing to spell out the details of the German penal reform. Further, his text made it clear that he was, in a quiet and seemly way, proud of German aspirations to achieve "true justice." By so doing, the separation of morality and legality could be overcome. The two could be brought into harmony with each other, and "the valuable forces of ethics" would then become a firm support of the criminal law.[12]

As for guidance for the judges under the new concept of justice, that was only a problem for those who still believed that a legal system should be centered on individuals. Such emphasis on individuals' rights and protection, said Guertner, had in Germany encouraged so much leniency in sentencing and laxity in pardoning that there had been an enormous increase in criminal behavior: "Criminal justice was absolutely threatened with bankruptcy." But no more. The proposed penal reforms were already in their second reading before the special commission that Guertner had appointed, and it was certain that the "great work of reform will be completed at no distant date. Germany will then have created a system of modern criminal legislation in accordance with the political and cultural views now prevailing in this country."[13]

In other words, there was to be a specifically German justice. And, since the political and cultural views prevailing in Germany as Guertner spoke in August 1935 were views that were defined, promulgated, and enforced by the National Socialist Party, justice in Germany was, in practical effect, to be what the party said it was. Guertner did not flinch from that assertion, but he did not put the case that baldly, either. Rather, he elaborated a theory of society and the state, and of the leadership of the state, that made the will of the party an expression of the will of the people and that found the highest and truest expression of national life in a leader who could speak for all. This leader, this Führer, "lays down the fundamental ideas, and the officials of the administration and the judges work within the framework of these provisions. . . . As the leadership in Germany is constantly endeavouring to be the incorporated expression of the people's will, the judge finds, both in the Führer's will and also in the national consciousness, bearings from which he can obtain the guiding line for his decisions." The judge thus becomes not only the servant of the legislator "but also his independent assistant who thinks out the ideas of the law in their application to individual cases."[14]

One did not have to be an extremist or a social misfit in the Germany of 1935 to believe in the primacy of the state and in the duty of the law to reflect the will of the state—a will that was, by extension, the will of the people. Guertner's advocacy of this position helps explain the appeal of National Socialism on a level distinct from that of the uniformed bullies in the street. Guertner had nothing to do with those swaggering exponents of a philosophy of hatred. An accomplished lawyer, trained at the University of Munich, he was poles removed from the street-level rank and file of the National Socialist Party. He was not even a member of that party but, like many other well-educated and conservative members of the legal profession, belonged to the German National Party. It is certain that he did not see himself as simply a mouthpiece for the National Socialists when he spoke to the Penal Congress in Berlin.[15]

Guertner's loyalty was to the German nation, and his concern was for that nation. In his view, the German nation—the Volk—constituted a natural, organic community, the unity of which was threatened by enemies from within. Like other members of the German National Party, he supported the National Socialists because they shared this view of the nation and were prepared to use the powers of the state to act in defense of the nation's unity and integrity. The views of both parties concerning methods to be used in that defense did not coincide, but in 1935 it was still possible for a conscientious government official to believe that the more extreme methods of the National Socialists could be modified or even that these methods would eventually disappear as the consolidation of power made them unnecessary. And Franz Guertner was a conscientious official.

He believed totally in the theory of justice that he was at such pains to explain. And it was precisely this that helped keep the mask of normality in place at the Penal Congress. Exchanges of views concerning principles of justice and their practical application in the field of criminal law were what these meetings were all about. In such a setting it was easy to view the appearance of Joseph Goebbels as an aberration, an unfortunate political move on the part of the National Socialists. Seen this way, Goebbels's speech to the delegates could be dismissed as so much propaganda on the part of a man whose position as Reich minister for public enlightenment and propaganda gave him license to expound such views. Few from outside Germany were going to cheer his statement that "We have got rid of the other parties because we considered them superfluous."[16]

No such extreme and provocative statements came from Minister of Justice Franz Guertner, nor from Erwin Bumke, president of the Supreme Court of the Reich and also outgoing president of the congress. It was all but impossible to associate these solid, serious citizens with a man like Goebbels, whose reputation as a vituperative purveyor of hatred preceded him into the meeting hall. Erwin Bumke was known to many there. Quite aside from his position as president of the congress, he was honored as a friend and colleague. He had attended the congress in London five years earlier and established personal contact with others in the field. The decision to go to London was, he said, not an easy one because any form of international collaboration had fallen into disrepute in Germany. "For this very reason the surprise I experienced in London was all the more joyful." He discovered like-minded professionals whose concern for the workings of justice was as great as his own. And now he had "the inestimable privilege" of welcoming the congress to his own country. This was all the more satisfying because he deeply felt that "the position held by the German Science of Penal Law and the standing of the German Prison System" entitled

Germany to host this august gathering where there could be a fruitful exchange of views.[17]

Here, too, as with Franz Guertner, there was no doubt that the speaker meant what he said, and sincerity went far in such a situation. It was difficult to go public with basic objections when colleagues and friends were speaking, to disrupt proceedings and sever friendships by making protests from the floor. In the smaller, more private sectional meetings in which designated subjects were discussed and resolutions formulated, some attempts were made to make the resolutions reflect a different view of justice, one that had at least as much care for the individual as for the community, however defined. The attempts were only partially successful. In some instances, as in a resolution dealing with the treatment of convicted criminals, no compromise was possible between the views of those who favored a strict regime of punishment for these dangerous, antisocial elements and the views of those who favored a program of re-education and rehabilitation.[18] They avoided a potential rift by agreeing that they could not agree on a resolution to bring before the whole group for a vote.

The close of the congress found harmony restored. A congenial party of delegates embarked on a week-long study tour of German prisons as guests of the German government. Every care had been taken for a trouble-free, enjoyable journey. The way was smoothed by the fact that Justice Minister Guertner and his wife, plus one of Guertner's deputies, Roland Freisler, and his wife accompanied them. Businesslike visits to prisons were punctuated by more social occasions: formal dinners and luncheons, receptions, concerts, excursions to castles and sites of historic interest. By "a pleasing coincidence," they were in Regensburg, the birthplace of Guertner, on the day of his birthday, and the company extended to him their "warmest good wishes and congratulations."[19] All in all, it was a delightful trip, long remembered by those who took part, but remembered, perhaps, with altered perceptions as the extent of National Socialist terror became well enough known in later years to undercut the assumption of normality on which the tour had rested.

Even in 1935, however, a measure of willful blindness must have been involved. Unless those on the study tour had been in isolation in their own prisons, they had heard enough about conditions in Germany to know that the penal establishments they visited were not the whole of the German prison system. As in Berlin, professional courtesy and their role as guests combined to engender silence, if not acquiescence, and the masque went on throughout the tour. Never was normality more insisted on than here, where it was most needed. Never was the mask of everyday routine gripped with such determination or pressed down with such force as it was against the death's head that grinned at the edges of the route on which they traveled. In Munich, where they had a "delicious supper" and heard "a highly artistic performance by the world famous pianist Elly Ney,"[20] they were about twelve miles southeast of the concentration camp at Dachau. If anyone on the tour thought about or mentioned Dachau during their entertainment in the Palace of the Residency in Munich the evening of August 26, 1935, that is not recorded in the official account. Entertainments had a role in this elaborate masque, but concentration camps did not. They were quite outside public notice, as the people in them were quite outside the German state—the state that had been their birthplace but was now no longer their home.

BEHIND THE MASK

Dachau was one of the first concentration camps established after the National Socialists came to power in 1933. It was known for the brutality of the regime established there by its commandant, Theodor Eicke, a high-ranking officer in the Schutzstaffel (SS). In later years, Heinrich Himmler was to make the SS into a powerful instrument of cruelty and oppression, and the beginnings of this program could be seen at Dachau in 1935. Prisoners there did not know why they had been arrested and interned. They had no idea when, if ever, they would be charged and brought to trial. They were fed inadequately, forced to perform hard labor with primitive tools, and were beaten if they faltered or complained. The creation of what one scholar has called an "order of terror"[21] was part of a deliberate plan. It was Commandant Eicke's boast that he had trained the SS Death's Head units guarding the camp to feel no pity for the prisoners. Indeed, the guards had been trained to see the prisoners as creatures less than human, a drag on the new Germany that was rising under the leadership of the Führer. This being so, there was no place for the prisoners in the new Germany. They were outsiders in the most literal sense of the word, reduced from human status to that of labor units, pure and simple—and poor ones at that since most of them were professionals, not used to manual labor. If they could not perform the tasks assigned to them, they were expendable.[22]

Justice Minister Guertner did not try to explain how Dachau fit into the legal reform movement of which he was so proud, nor in what way calculated brutality could further the new German union of morality and the law. Officially, the subject did not come up, either in the meeting in Berlin or on the study tour. If it had, Guertner might have pled lack of jurisdiction.

Dachau was outside the authority of the Ministry of Justice. In 1935 there
was a great deal of confusion about the several concentration camps scattered about Germany, a legacy from the first sweeping roundups of pre-
sumed enemies of the state in 1933. It was not clear who was in overall
charge of the camps, nor who would win the struggle for control of them
that was taking place between different organizations of the National Socialist Party and various units of government, both state and national.

In this struggle, the Ministry of Justice was not much of a contestant.
Little by little it was being pushed into the role of a respectable legal cover
for other, less respectable activities. The sober, conscientious Franz Guertner could not begin to match the skill and ferocity of party officials such as
Himmler or Hermann Goering in their bureaucratic battles for extension
of their power. He could not even weigh in against a lower official such as
Eicke, who, in 1934, had been made an official inspector of concentration
camps. By 1935, when the party of prison officials took its blinkered tour of
Germany, the "Dachau system" of brutality and terror was rapidly becoming the model for the other camps under SS control: Esterwegen, Lichten-
burg, Sachsenburg, and Moringen.[23] As those within the camps passed
into the hands of the SS, their hard life became even harder, and their
hopes for the future became limited to the hope that they would make it
through the day.

Whether or not the prison officials on the tour knew the details of the
camps, they surely knew in general what was common knowledge outside
Germany: namely, that political dissidents and social undesirables were being confined in Germany without trial and with little prospect of release. If
the officials had not been aware of the situation in the early days of the National Socialist regime, they would have had it brought to their attention in
1934. An international campaign was begun that year on behalf of one of the
concentration camp prisoners, Carl von Ossietzky. It was a high-profile campaign, launched and supported by such people as Albert Einstein, Bertrand
Russell, Jane Addams, Nicholas Murray Butler, Harold Laski, Thomas
Mann, and Romain Rolland. Their immediate purpose was to persuade the
Nobel Committee to award Ossietzky the Peace Prize. Their larger goal
was to focus public attention on the concentration camp system in Germany
and, by extension, on the whole National Socialist program of intimidation
and terror. Governments around the world might be in a state of paralysis,
mesmerized by their own economic woes and straitjacketed by their rigid
conceptions of sovereignty, but private individuals and organizations were
not. As with the mock trials in London and New York, the campaign on behalf of Ossietzky was conducted by private individuals who found that the

only thing worse than the situation in Germany was the fact that nothing was being done about it.

So far as Carl von Ossietzky was concerned, the campaign met with a certain success. A journalist, a pacifist, and a relentless foe of German militarism, Ossietzky had been picked up in the sweep of arrests following the Reichstag fire in February 1933. No evidence could be found connecting him to the fire, but he was not released. He was simply kept in "preventive detention," a term that covered and officially justified the incarceration of anyone the regime wanted to keep in custody. Even before the fire, Ossietzky had been a marked man. During the Weimar Republic he had insisted on publicly condemning the republic's rearmament effort as a clear violation of the Treaty of Versailles. Officialdom under the National Socialist regime took due warning and, with the Reichstag fire as an excuse, took steps to silence this potentially dangerous critic. When the international campaign began on his behalf, Ossietzky was imprisoned—without benefit of trial—in one of the Emsland camps near the Dutch border. There he was laboring in the peat bogs that the Emsland prisoners were supposed to reclaim for agricultural purposes. Since his health was poor he was, in effect, working out a sentence of death.

German officials responded to the Peace Prize campaign with protests about interference in Germany's internal affairs. They were, however, not completely immune to outside criticism, and they feared public reaction if Ossietzky were to die in a concentration camp on the eve of the 1936 Berlin Olympics. Overwork and abuse had made the journalist's health precarious. They transferred him to a prison hospital in Berlin and then to a private sanatorium where in May 1938 he died. Ossietzky lived long enough to learn that he had been awarded the Nobel Peace Prize for 1935, but neither his health nor his government would allow him to go to Oslo to receive it.

In the speech of presentation the chair of the Nobel Committee paid tribute to the journalist's devotion to peace. He pointed out that Ossietzky's life and work were "dominated by the theme of peace," hence this award. Even so, there was a note of caution. In an attempt to head off the obvious conclusion that the award was a slap at the German government, the tribute concluded, "In awarding this year's Nobel Peace Prize to Carl von Ossietzky we are therefore recognizing his valuable contribution to the cause of peace—nothing more, and certainly nothing less."[24] Despite the ambivalence and the care not to offend, the award to Ossietzky was a brave move in an age when gestures of support at this level were rare indeed.

In the 1930s, a campaign by those outside of Germany and an award made in a city far from Berlin were the best that could be done on behalf of

Carl von Ossietzky. And what of the others in German concentration camps, those without prominent friends abroad? By 1938, when Ossietzky died, twenty-four thousand were being held in camps that the SS had built and controlled. These included political prisoners, both Jewish and non-Jewish, and a large and growing category that the SS defined as "asocial"—beggars, Gypsies, alcoholics, prostitutes, homosexuals, traffic offenders, "fault finders," and those who were "work-shy." There were, moreover, several thousand Jews who had been sent to the camps as part of a policy of the "Aryanization" of business, meaning that they would be held until they agreed to turn their property over to the government. They would then be released and allowed, as paupers, to emigrate. A combination of abuse and squalid camp conditions killed hundreds of Jews before they could agree to anything. The Aryanization" of 1938 was the first step in what became a deliberate policy of extermination of Jews.[25]

For the thousands in concentration camps in the 1930s there was no prize and no rescue even of the limited kind that had allowed Carl von Ossietzky to spend his last days in a hospital. Mostly unknown outside Germany, these Germans were arrested, they worked in the mines and factories near the camps, they suffered and died. Many others had already left the country when they saw what was happening to Jews and to opponents of the National Socialist regime. This latter-day exodus had results perhaps not foreseen by German officials. The exodus created a situation that, by the standards of the day, was a matter of legitimate international concern. Governments might hesitate to criticize German internal policies, but when German refugees began arriving in numbers on their doorsteps, that was a different story.

As early as the fall of 1933, the governments of neighboring countries began to take official notice of the refugee situation, and the League of Nations appointed a high commissioner with special responsibility for German refugees. Even then, care was taken to make the office an independent entity, separate from the League, lest the German government take offense at being singled out for special attention. As the months went by and the number of refugees mounted, James G. McDonald, the American who had accepted the post of high commissioner, found himself operating an office with a high purpose and a low budget and with no international authority. By December 1935 he had had enough of the begging and persuasion that were his only tools for the job of resettling the refugees. He had had enough also of tiptoeing around the situation in Germany lest international relations be strained and sovereignty be put at risk. In his letter of resignation McDonald sounded a note that would not be heard again at an official level until the agony of a second world war had shown the prophetic insight of the statement he made in 1935.

In Germany, he said, a "terrible human calamity" was taking place and would grow even worse unless something was done to stop it. The League of Nations, its member states, and other states of the world must take immediate action, if only in their own defense, for this human suffering would spill over into neighboring countries. Indeed, it was already doing so. But more than self-interest was involved. Much was known about German policies and their disastrous effects. McDonald was convinced that the time for official silence was past: "When domestic policies threaten the demoralization and exile of hundreds of thousands of human beings, considerations of diplomatic correctness must yield to those of common humanity."[26] When next the claims of humanity were heard in such a clear, unambiguous way, it was in the war crimes trials that followed World War II. Some of the defendants in those trials were men who had sat in the hall of the Kroll Opera House in Berlin in 1935 and listened to Justice Minister Franz Guertner praise the new union between law and morality in Germany. By the time of the trials Guertner was dead, as was his deputy, Roland Freisler, who had accompanied the prison officials on their guided study tour. Supreme Court President Erwin Bumke had committed suicide as Allied forces closed in on Leipzig, a method of escape followed by many of the more prominent in Germany, including Adolf Hitler himself.[27]

But many remained alive to be tried for crimes against that common humanity of which James McDonald had spoken with such passion in 1935. Franz Schlegelberger, an attendee in Berlin and acting minister of justice following Guertner's death in 1941, was found guilty of war crimes and crimes against humanity for his complicity in the persecution of Poles and Jews. He was sentenced to twenty years in prison. Ernst Lautz, also an attendee and chief public prosecutor at the People's Court in Berlin, was found guilty of the same crimes. Among other acts, he had filled one of the gaps in the law of which Guertner had spoken by extending Germany's law of high treason to cover the acts of a Polish citizen *in* Poland *before* the beginning of the war in 1939. Lautz was sentenced to ten years in prison.[28]

The list could be extended to others who attended the Penal and Penitentiary Congress in Berlin in 1935—people who would later become notorious for their part in National Socialist programs of Aryanization, aggression, and extermination. Theodor Eicke, the brutal commandant of Dachau, was there, as was Werner Best, later to become Reich commissioner for occupied Denmark. English and American prison reformers such as Alexander Paterson and Sanford Bates shared meeting space with the likes of Otto

Thierack, vice-president of the Reich Supreme Court of Justice at the time of the congress. Later, as minister of justice, Thierack was an active collaborator in the SS program of working whole populations to death in the camps. Then there was Hans Frank, Reich minister without portfolio, who, within four years of the meeting in Berlin, became the scourge of conquered Poland, and Kurt Daleuge, head of the police in the Prussian Interior Ministry, who would wage ruthless war against dissent in the former Czechoslovakia.[29]

Lawyers, prosecutors, prison administrators, government officials—on one level the congress was an ordinary meeting of people concerned with the problems of their profession. On another it was like a miniature replica of the international system of the day, in which the authoritarian few who were to become architects of terror were opposed, not very openly or successfully, by those who supported political freedom and the rights of the individual. Until the end of World War II approached it was not clear whether justice in the postwar world would be defined by those who were concerned to protect and increase the authority of the state or by those whose concern was for the well-being and protection of the individual.

CHAPTER TWELVE

The Puzzle of Evil

The word *evil* was rarely heard in the Assembly Hall of the League of Nations in the 1920s and early 1930s. If anyone at the League Council table had characterized the actions of some state or individual as evil, an embarrassed silence would have ensued. This would have been more than an unfortunate choice of words or a lapse in manners. It would have been a breach of diplomatic protocol, the formalized set of standards for discourse between states that helps keep channels of communication open even when the states are in basic disagreement. The contempt shown for protocol and the harsh language used by Soviet officials in the early years of the Soviet Union contributed much to the difficulties of fitting that new, revolutionary state into the existing framework of international relations. Even in the midst of the Manchurian crisis, Chinese officials did not call the Japanese evil. Neither they nor anyone else involved in the crisis wanted to go to such a rhetorical extreme, as if to banish the Japanese from the realm of civil discourse and suggest the fruitlessness of further attempts to resolve the crisis peacefully.

The concept of evil did not fit the assumptions of the times. Those assumptions have been spelled out in detail in earlier chapters. Here it is only necessary to point again at the prevailing reliance on reason and persuasion. No situation, no conflict was considered unresolvable. Great effort went into the establishment of mechanisms through which time might be gained and tempers cooled so that negotiations could begin. Some early successes with commissions of inquiry, panels of arbitration, and similar methods of settlement strengthened belief in orderly—if uneven—progress toward a new and different world. It would be a world of cooperative endeavors, of arbitration and adjudication, of nations under the law—in short, a world that was the very expression and vehicle of international justice.

Nicholas Politis, one of the good, gray men who helped the League achieve its modest successes, shared fully the assumptions of his times. He was not blind to the rivalries that divided nations, nor to the fact that they remained armed and suspicious of each other. But he believed in what was commonly called "the progressive development of international law," which, for this Greek statesman, meant the gradual erosion of the emphasis on sovereignty and the rights of states. Replacing these would be an emphasis on the rights of peoples and a recognition of the interdependence of states. As for international justice, that, too, was in the process of development. What was required, said Politis, was the development of different attitudes and habits of thought: "The work is very long and exacting. One is well advised to be armed with patience." But "when one knows history, one can have confidence in the future."[1]

That was the outlook of an informed and realistic observer of international affairs in 1924. Seventeen years later another observer, standing in that very future that Politis had attempted to foretell, looked at an international scene for which no one had been prepared and felt the need to bolster confidence with prayer. Speaking at a meeting of the American Bar Association, Supreme Court Justice Robert H. Jackson invoked an ancient liturgy: "Grant us grace fearlessly to contend against evil, and to make no peace with oppression; and, that we may reverently use our freedom, help us to employ it in the maintenance of justice among men and nations."[2] Evil had arrived on the scene, and with it a changed conception of justice in international affairs.

Jackson was to have a chance to contend against evil since, in the spring of 1945, President Harry Truman appointed him the chief U.S. prosecutor for the trial of the major German war criminals. Thus, Jackson not only contended against what he and most of the world saw as evil actions on the part of Germany, he came face to face with the men who had initiated and directed those actions. And he, like many others who observed the twenty-one men in the dock at Nuremberg, where the trial was held, was troubled by what he saw.[3] *These* were the men who had dragged the world into war? It was at *their* instigation that millions had suffered, lost homes and families, been tortured, worked to death, or killed outright for no reason other than being what they were or being in the way? Surely the power they had wielded, the bargain they had struck with ruthlessness should have left some mark on these men, some small sign of the evil they had done. Instead, they looked completely, terrifyingly commonplace—people one might pass on the street without a second glance.

A young British major, Airey Middleton Neave, served the indictments on the defendants in their prison cells in Nuremberg. He has left vivid portraits of the men as, in their individual ways, they received a copy of the charges against them. "So it has come," said Hermann Goering, once the commander-in-chief of the Luftwaffe, president of the Reichstag, and prime minister of Prussia. Until a quarrel with Hitler in 1945, Goering had been the second most powerful man in the Third Reich, the one hand-picked by Hitler to succeed him. "So it has come," Goering repeated. "The words," said Neave in his account, "seemed very ordinary, not like the end of twelve years of absolute power."[4]

To each defendant Neave handed three documents: a copy of the charges, a copy of the charter establishing the international military tribunal that would conduct the trial, and a list of German lawyers from which they could choose for their defense. Some of the defendants were nervous, some blustering, some uncomprehending, some resigned, some indignant, some sly, but none gave a sense of great inner power, of the uncommon strength of character that might help explain the years of unparalleled cruelty and suffering they had inflicted on the world. In a religious context, evil has frequently had some quality that is larger than life, a remaining spark of nobility that has been flawed by pride. If any nobility remained or had ever been present in these men, it was not apparent to those who observed them at the trial.

What happened under the National Socialists before and during World War II has been well documented, but understanding what happened is difficult. Understanding is made more difficult by the thousands of words that have been written about the twenty-one men who stood in the dock in Nuremberg. Analyses galore screen from view the human beings who made decisions, signed orders for policies of extermination (which, at the trial, they claimed not to have read), and devised plans of assault against their neighbors. It is all too familiar, too set in a mold to allow for a fresh look. For that, it is more useful to turn away from the top men in the National Socialist regime and from their trial. There were hundreds of other trials and thousands of other defendants. What, if anything, can be learned from them about the appearance in Germany of what the people who had to face it could only call evil? And what can be learned of the widespread efforts to contain that evil and bring it under the rule of law?

CENTERS OF REFERENCE

The war crimes trials conducted by the Allied nations were, at the most obvious level, trials about behavior. What was acceptable behavior during a war? What was acceptable in preparing for war? Considering the sustained efforts made in the 1920s and 1930s to provide alternative means for settling disputes, was war itself even permitted anymore? If so, what kind of war? When would recourse to arms not bring, at the least, condemnation and, at the most, a military response? Finally—most difficult of all in a world of assertively sovereign states—what was acceptable behavior on the part of governments in relation to their own citizens? Did humanitarian interventions by individual states in the past offer any guidance for present attempts at a collective response? For that matter, did past efforts to control the use of force, both domestically and internationally, offer any guidance at all for a world exhausted by war and appalled at the devastation and brutalization left in its wake?

These were some of the questions thrashed out in war crimes trials held by the Allies in scattered locations around the world following World War II. The trials of the major war criminals, held in Germany and Japan at Nuremberg and Tokyo, were the focus of news reports at the time, and they have become the chief subjects of the controversies regarding the trials that began then and that continue today. The Tokyo and Nuremberg trials were, however, a very small part of the effort to determine what was acceptable behavior, internationally speaking, and to assess responsibility for breaches of those standards. In trials in Singapore, Manila, Kuala Lumpur, Yokohama, Shanghai, Oslo, Rome, Prague, Lyon, Paris, Wiesbaden, Hamburg, Lüneburg, Strasbourg, and a dozen other cities, large and small, the work of clarification and assessment went on.[5]

The undertaking was vast. Resources were inadequate and qualifications uneven. Nevertheless, efforts were made, on an international scale, to bring the manifold specific circumstances of a worldwide war within reach of general legal principles that had never before been subjected to a test of such intensity and scope. The fury and weariness of people who had had to fight even though their fathers had fought to end war altogether—these passions were to be brought under control and subjected to the discipline of the law in hundreds of courtrooms throughout Europe and Asia. The records of the United Nations War Crimes Commission contain the proceedings of more than two thousand war crimes trials conducted by ten different countries, and the commission's records are admittedly incomplete.[6]

From the fall of 1943, when the commission was established, to the spring of 1949, when the last of the trials held by the United States in Nuremberg came to a close, there were ongoing battles about the legal principles that were to legitimate the trials, govern their conduct, and determine the grounds for guilt or innocence. In this sense, the Allied war crimes trials were about much more than behavior. Courtrooms around the world became the scenes of debates with profound philosophical and practical implications. The scope and legitimacy of international concern was a question that had the power to stir strong feelings both at the policy level and in the courtroom. Denial of the legitimacy or the application of international concern was by no means confined to the defendants and their lawyers. Debates among various Allied officials and legal experts were as sharp during the planning stages of the trials as were the debates between the prosecution and defense in the trials themselves.[7]

What was at stake was nothing less than the definition of the international system itself. With due allowance for complexities of thought, the debate can be seen as proceeding from two totally different centers of reference. On one side was the state as the center of thought, activity, and authority. Here the international system was not much more than a collection of individual states, each pursuing its own interests under the light restraint of rules that were subject to voluntary compliance. The other side of the debate was more complicated. It was also often confused, since activity on its behalf and what authority it might have was just then in the process of definition. The arguments on this side by no means ignored the state but placed equal emphasis on individual human beings and on the international system as a whole. The assumptions and ideas that flowed from this locus of thought, while respectful of the state, diverged in significant ways from those that began and ended with the primacy of the state.

These two competing centers of reference were the hidden protagonists in the war crimes trials, the common element that bound them all together despite their particularities. They helped explain the arguments about the legitimacy of the trials and, if the trials were accepted as legitimate, the arguments over what legal principles were to be applied in them. Yet they do not explain everything. Added to the incompatibility of these controlling centers of reference was another element, the lack of precedent and example. Even in well-established polities with institutions for the promulgation, enforcement, and interpretation of laws, there are still arguments about what the law is and how it should be applied. It is, then, hardly surprising that there were (and are) disagreements over such matters where there were no such institutions and where the very existence of an international polity with rights and authority of its own was a hotly contested part of the argument.

Much of the discussion that follows relies chiefly on records of war crimes trials that took place in Europe. This is not to say that the trials in Asia, including the Tokyo trial, are less important or less worthy of examination than the European trials. It is simply to say that the Asian trials have not been studied to the same extent as those in Europe, nor are their records as widely available. Besides this, the very nature of the National Socialist regime stimulated debate on the philosophical and legal issues underlying the trials and still stimulates debate today. The regime's state-sponsored programs of terror and extermination bring into sharp focus the differences between those for whom the state was the center of thought and action and those whose center encompassed the protection of individual human beings and international peace as well.

There was no intrinsic reason for an emphasis on the state to have the outcome it did in Germany, since the state was central in the thought of the times and was the basic form of political organization. Large parts of the remaining empires as well as most of the mandates under the League of Nations were, it was generally assumed, on their way to becoming states— someday. So Germany was not unique in its focus on the state and the well-being of the state. When, however, the concept of the Volk and its purity was blended with that of the state, the stage was set for exclusionary policies. Two possibilities in this dual emphasis were already clear in 1935. They can be perceived in the speeches made by two of the German officials mentioned above, who addressed the congress of prison officials in Berlin in August of that year.

Each speaker emphasized the nation as a whole and expressed concern for its well-being. Their approaches, however, could not have been more different. For Justice Minister Franz Guertner, "any attack on the interests of the national community" was what he called a "material wrong," to be suppressed through the courts by careful evaluation of what was necessary for the "demands of national life." Reich Minister for Public Enlightenment and Propaganda Joseph Goebbels had no patience with such procedures. The need was too great and the threat of "anarchy" too immediate for such time-consuming measures. "Antisocial" elements were to be simply excised from "the community of the people" and isolated in camps where, if possible, they could be made "once more useful members of human society." There was the well-being of sixty-six million people to consider. In view of that, "what does it matter, after all, if a few thousand individuals hostile to society are taken into custody?"[8]

In 1935 it was not yet clear which of the two possibilities in a state-centered policy would come to the fore. By the end of the war it was clear that the Guertner approach of caution and legal procedures had lost, and lost badly, to the Goebbels approach. That approach, crude as it was, had coarsened still further in the course of the war. Confinement and "re-education" had become deliberate programs of forced labor and extermination. Extreme measures to combat social "emergencies" had become a routine way of governance. The circle of those who counted was drawn more narrowly every year. The result was an atmosphere in which people accepted acts that, under ordinary circumstances, they would have condemned. Their selves turned inward while outwardly they conformed, fearing to depart in the smallest way from what was required of them. These tensions and attitudes, and a concomitant separation from the suffering of others, spread throughout society and penetrated to its lowest levels. The effect of this penetration can be seen in the accounts of some of the war crimes trials that took place away from the blaze of publicity that surrounded the major trial at Nuremberg.

INSIDE THE NARROW CIRCLE

Georg Hessling and Heinrich Gerike, both German citizens, stood trial before a British military court in Braunschweig, Germany, in the spring of 1946 on the charge of committing a war crime. With six other defendants, Hessling and Gerike were accused of killing more than eighty Polish babies through willful neglect "in violation of the laws and usages of war." Those laws and usages were the same ones that had been set out at the 1899 conference at The Hague. The 1899 rules had been modified slightly at a second Hague conference in 1907 but were essentially the same. Thus it was that the terms of a treaty signed in The Netherlands almost half a century earlier were brought to bear on conduct in the obscure German village of Velpke, where it put Hessling, Gerike, and six others into the dock.

In 1944, the German authorities had brought Polish prisoners to Velpke to labor in the fields and raise food for the German war effort. While in Velpke, some of the Polish women had babies. The babies were taken from their mothers shortly after birth so as not to interfere with the women's ability to work. Separated from their mothers, the babies died. Eighty-four of them died in a corrugated iron shed that had been built for a barracks. In his summation, the British prosecuting officer made the connection between events in the German village of Velpke and the proceedings at The Hague: "There is a definite rule laid down in the Hague Rules of 1907, Article 46, that family honour and life must be respected by the occupant in time of war in the territory which he has occupied. It was wrong to bring those people;

it was wrong to exploit their labour; and it was wrong, above all, to so wrongly disregard their children, when children were born, that they died from the direct result of that neglect."[9]

Both Hessling and Gerike were found guilty of the deaths of the babies through willful neglect, and thus, under the rules of the Hague Convention as applied by the British military court, were each guilty of committing a war crime. Each was sentenced to death by hanging. Gerike showed no emotion, but Hessling was obviously distressed. He had not fared well in the cross-examination by counsel for the prosecution. The cross-examination had been searching and severe since, as administrator of the home where the babies were placed, Hessling was directly responsible for its operation. When asked by counsel what steps he had taken to save the life of even one child, he had replied that, if a child was sick, a doctor was to be called.

Counsel: Did you give that order?

Hessling: No, not myself.

Counsel: I am asking what steps you took to save one child's life.

Hessling: That did not come in my duties.[10]

Both Gerike and Hessling were members of the National Socialist Party. Gerike was the local party leader with overall responsibilities for the district. Under orders from the regional party leader to separate the Polish babies from their mothers and establish a home where they could be placed, he had picked the corrugated iron barracks as the best accommodation available under crowded wartime conditions, and he had appointed Hessling as administrator. Beyond that, he seems to have troubled himself as little as possible, never once visiting the place, despite the fact that the conditions there and the mounting death toll were common knowledge in the district. Counsel for the prosecution bored in on this apparent indifference. He pointed out that when party members took the babies from their mothers, they then became "*in loco parentis* to these children." Party members had assumed the care and responsibility for all the Polish children that they directed to be put in the Velpke home. And what happened? "They are the parents of some hundred-odd children, of which they allow 84 or more to die."[11] As for the home's administrator, "All that Hessling can say is, 'It was not my job; I was only concerned with the finances.'"[12]

So the sentences for the two party members were handed down: death by hanging. And a visibly distressed Georg Hessling was led from the courtroom crying out, "Warum, warum? (Why, why?)."[13]

Hessling's question resonates with more than personal meaning. Since 1933 people have been asking "Why?" Why were the National Socialists so successful? Why were they able to turn a culturally rich, industrially developed country into a pit of persecution, a sink of suffering that was denied and disregarded even by those who knew what was happening? There are multiple answers to what, after all, are questions about an extremely complicated set of events and circumstances. There are numerous variations on the theme of German national character. Beyond that, blame is spread with a generous hand on the victors in World War I, on economic nationalism, on the intransigence of both the Right and the Left, on the feebleness of the Weimar Republic, and on the French, the British, and the Americans for policies that scarcely looked outside their own borders or beyond the next election.[14]

The records of the war crimes trials suggest another element in this complicated mix. Georg Hessling was not alone in his lack of comprehension. He is simply a dramatic instance of it. Even after thirteen days of testimony about the neglect and bureaucratic buck-passing that had contributed to the deaths of the eighty-four Polish babies, he still did not understand why he should be blamed in any way, much less found guilty. Wasn't there a matron in charge of the daily operation of the home? True, she was often not there and, true, she was completely untrained. Still, as administrator, his primary job was to keep the books in order, to see that the proper forms were filled out, to be sure that money was collected from the Polish workers to pay for the costs of upkeep—and burial.

The counsel for the prosecution would not let either Hessling or Gerike off the hook. He elicited damning evidence of the lack of supervision and of the failure to follow through and then, with one question, went to the heart of the matter: "When German women worked on farms their children did not go to the Velpke barracks, did they?"[15] The responses to this question made it clear that the matter had never once been considered. German children were in a different category altogether. The hardships and shortages of wartime that had made it difficult to do anything much for the Polish children apparently did not apply to German children. When German children were sick, they were sent to a clinic or a hospital or attended by a doctor at home. They were allowed to stay with their mothers, who could nurse them and care for them, even if that meant reducing the women's effectiveness as labor in the fields—where they were badly needed, most of the men being away in the army. German children were inside the circle of primary concern. Polish children were outside. That was a fact of life in 1944, the fifth year of the war, so much a part of the milieu that it was hardly noticed, much less questioned. Hence, Hessling's lack of understanding and his cry, "Warum, warum?"

Little by little, since 1933, the circle of concern of many ordinary Germans had been steadily narrowed by National Socialist policies of exclusion and intimidation and by the hardships of war until by war's end, for some, that circle was exceedingly small. For some, indeed, it encompassed only the self and the immediate family. One of the German lawyers at the Velpke trial admitted that he knew that terrible things were happening in Germany. And what did he do? "'Nothing.' Why not? I could not have helped anybody; I could not have changed anything, and would have had only one success, that my family would never see me again."[16]

Jews and Communists were the first to be excluded officially from the circle of those who counted in society, and from that time it became dangerous for any German to show concern for them. As the months and years of National Socialist rule went on, the list of exclusions grew: Social Democrats, pacifists, homosexuals, beggars, the crippled, the senile, the retarded, the mentally ill, Gypsies, Poles, Russians, Slavs of any nationality and, of course, anyone who opposed the regime, who spoke out against its cruelties and abuses of power—as some brave Germans did. The range of responses was varied. Some people lay low, attracting as little attention as possible, and waited for the storm to pass. Some, like Franz Schlegelberger at the Ministry of Justice, held on to their official positions in the belief that by so doing some of the worst excesses of the Hitler regime could be stemmed from within.[17] Others, like Georg Hessling and Heinrich Gerike, simply inhabited the world that had been created for them by the National Socialists and did not question its narrow limits. The trial of the personnel of the Hadamar Institution is another case in point.

The charges against the defendants in the Hadamar trial would be unbelievable in any context other than that of Germany under the rule of the National Socialists. Seven people were brought before an American military tribunal in Wiesbaden, Germany, in the fall of 1945, charged with "violation of international law" during the period from July 1, 1944, to April 1, 1945. Specifically, they were charged with aiding or participating "in the killing of human beings of Polish and Russian nationality, their exact names and number being unknown but aggregating in excess of 400, and who were then and there confined by the then German Reich as an exercise of belligerent control."[18] In other words, the victims were prisoners of the Germans, civilians from Poland and Russia who had been brought into Germany as part of the vast forced removal of slave labor from lands the German armies had conquered. Some had become tubercular and could no longer work. Some were simply unlucky. At any rate, the prisoners were sent in batches of fifty or sixty to the Hadamar Institution in the village of Hadamar near Limburg, expecting care and treatment because that was what they had been told, both before being sent and after their arrival. There, as was clearly brought out in the trial, they were given doses of drugs, either by injection or by mouth, that killed them. Four hundred lost their lives this way within a few hours after their arrival—men, women, and children, without distinction.

All seven defendants were found guilty of the charge of violation of international law through participation in the killing of the Russians and Poles. Three were sentenced to death and four to terms of imprisonment. All had testified that they believed that what they were doing was lawful. Earlier in the war, at Hadamar as at other German institutions, a policy of killing Germans who were deformed or incurably insane or simply unwanted had been carried out. So far as the defendants in the Hadamar trial were concerned, the Polish and Russian prisoners were in the same category: sick and socially undesirable people. According to one of the defendants, orders had been given "that these patients, just like the German patients, were to be put aside according to the law."[19]

Not one of the defendants had ever seen the law, nor had they received any orders in writing. They were simply told that the prisoners were to be killed, and, with varying degrees of participation, the defendants carried out this policy. They were also told that the policy was not to be discussed outside of the institution, an order that none of them found inconsistent with the assertion that they believed that the killings were "according to the law."

Neither the Hadamar nor the Velpke defendants were concentration camp guards, thriving in a climate of cruelty and sadism. These were people who bent with the wind. They may have had doubts, but they went along. If the law thrust entire groups of people outside the circle of the living, well, that was the law. If Polish babies were to be taken from their mothers, well, so be it. If Poles and Russians were to be killed, it had to be done. One kept one's head down. One hoped to stay hidden, if not in a briar patch at least in a thicket of rules and regulations strictly observed. Much that happened was, of course, too bad.

The matron of the Velpke Baby Home was sorry that the Polish babies died. The administrator of the home was sorry. The district party leader regretted the deaths. But the public health officer had been told not to visit the home because "It did not come under his duties." The local Evangelical pastor did not visit the home because it was not in his parish. People in the village made no complaint to party leaders or to the health authorities although "we were very sorry about what was happening there." Prosecuting Counsel: "If it had been a Home for German babies what would you have done?" Witness: "We would have complained and had the matter examined." Since they were Polish, the babies remained outside the narrow circle of the villagers' concern, and the babies died. Poorly housed, inadequately fed, emaciated, diseased, and unwashed, they died. They were buried in a mass grave outside the regular churchyard—from which the British disinterred them to give each an individual grave plot and burial.[20]

As at Velpke, so at Hadamar. No one was outwardly cruel to the Poles and Russians who were brought there to be "put aside." The travel-weary, apprehensive prisoners were taken into one of the wards in the building, soothed with promises of treatment, given drugs that killed them, taken out, and buried in a mass grave. The process was "completely painless," said Adolph Wahlmann, the only medical doctor at the institution. He did not administer the drugs himself—that was done by two male nurses—but his was the knowledge that made sure that the dosages were lethal. He also made out the death certificates, giving tuberculosis as the cause of death, although he had not, in fact, examined any of them for that disease. Prosecuting Counsel: "Then how could you certify that they had died from tuberculosis?" Dr. Wahlmann: "I was in a very bad position. I had to go through the same thing all these two years before that. Throughout these two years I had to make these same false statements about German mentally diseased. The Russians were brought in under the same kind of law as the German mentally diseased."[21]

The National Socialists' success in narrowing the circle of those who counted can be measured by statements such as this in towns and villages such as Velpke and Hadamar. At the lowest level of society, far from the centers of power, these obscure functionaries carried out the policies of high officials whose very names they might not even know. The distance between Dr. Adolph Wahlmann at the Hadamar Institution in the village of Hadamar and Leonardo Conti and Philip Bouhler in the Ministry of the Interior in the capital city of Berlin was far greater than could be traced on a map. Conti, and then Bouhler, were architects of the means to carry out Hitler's program to rid society of "useless" people. The wheels were set in motion in Berlin, and, in time, busloads of mental patients were rolling through the streets of Hadamar, where even the children knew what was happening. "There comes the murder-box again!" they would cry, as yet another distinctive gray bus headed up the hill toward the institution.[22]

The exclusion of "undesirables" was a two-stage process. First, those to be eliminated from society were removed from peoples' mental worlds, even at the village level. "Do not get excited," the matron of the Velpke Baby Home is reported to have said in regard to the deaths of the Polish babies, "after all, they are only enemies."[23] Having first suffered psychological removal as "enemies," "undesirables" or "useless mouths," the victims were then removed from the world altogether, and functionaries such as Adolph Wahlmann were there to falsify the death certificates. At Hadamar the "mentally diseased" came first, and then the Russian and Polish laborers and their children, and all were swiftly removed. Many Germans must have lived in fear that one day they would wake to find that they, too, had been excluded from this ever-narrowing circle of people who counted in society, people who were true members of the Volk and who would, therefore, be allowed to live.

One effect of the war crimes trials, whether intended or not, was to repudiate this narrow circle of concern, to push back its constricting limits. The message was this: Polish babies count, even if their care is inconvenient; Polish laborers count; Russian laborers count; their children count. By no rule or regulation, official or otherwise, can these people be thrust outside the boundaries of the human race. You cannot deprive them of the protections of law and society, for these are part of their heritage as human beings.

The message was a resounding affirmation of the value of human life. Its effectiveness was somewhat muted by the conceptual restrictions of the time: these people count, yes, and we, the Allies, will seek retribution for their deaths and inhumane treatment—since that treatment and those deaths occurred in wartime. That was the key. That was the justification for bringing the defendants to trial and sitting in judgment on them. The atrocities had happened in wartime. There were international agreements regarding wartime conduct and behavior in occupied territories. Prosecutors and judges could fall back on the Hague Conventions on the Laws and Customs of War on Land and the 1929 Geneva Conventions regarding care of the sick and wounded and the treatment of prisoners of war. Beyond that, the judges in the trials under Allied authority would not go. Despite strenuous efforts by the prosecution in several of the trials to bring German victims of German policies within the circle of international protection, the judges refused. If the actions took place prior to the beginning of World War II in September 1939, they were outside the courts' jurisdiction.[24]

Germans had been the first to be thrust by the National Socialists outside the bounds of human society. Concentration camps were filled with Germans before other groups were brought in. But if retribution were to be found for these mostly unknown compatriots of Carl Ossietzky and Franz Bernheim, that retribution would have to come through German actions in

German courts. What had been true in 1933 in the case of German victims who did not, like Bernheim, happen to live in Upper Silesia was still true in the mid-1940s for Germans who had been victimized before the war began. Those German victims of German policies were, in the immediate postwar period, still outside the circle of effective international concern.

A Conservative Compass

When the Hadamar trial opened in Wiesbaden on October 8, 1945, the defense team moved quickly to the attack. All seven defendants were charged with a violation of international law in the killing of the more than four hundred Polish and Russian laborers at the Hadamar Institution near Limburg, Germany. In his opening statement, the chief defense counsel asked the U.S. military commission hearing the case to dismiss the charge against all seven defendants. He gave four reasons for this sweeping request. First and foremost was his contention that the defendants could not have violated international law since "there is no rule or law existing under International Law" that would cover the actions at the Hadamar Institution. Second, the United States did not have jurisdiction over the matters in the charge, namely the killing of Russian and Polish workers by Germans. Third, the Polish victims were no longer under the protection of the Geneva Convention since Poland, as a conquered nation, was under German law. The Russian victims were not protected, either, since Russia had never signed the convention. Fourth, the charges against the defendants were too vague to allow for a "legal, fair, and impartial trial."[1]

On the surface, these were arguments about jurisdiction. At a deeper level, the arguments raised questions about the law itself and, specifically, about the law on which the war crimes trials were based. Thus, even before the opening of the trial of the major German war criminals at Nuremberg, defense lawyers in the obscure Hadamar trial in Wiesbaden raised questions that were asked again and again, not only in these places but in war crimes trials around the world. What exactly was international law? Who or what was subject to it, and under what conditions? If it was to be enforced, who had the right to enforce it?

International law was no stranger to a courtroom, as evidenced by the Permanent Court of International Justice in the Peace Palace at The Hague. But the differences between proceedings at the Permanent Court and proceedings in the war crimes trials were profound. Only states were represented at the Permanent Court, and they sent representatives only if they chose to do so. Further, those states stood on grounds of legal equality, and they appeared before the court as equal claimants for justice—justice as they understood it. At Hadamar, as at Nuremberg and elsewhere, the defendants were individual human beings who were standing trial in order that a different kind of justice might be done. It was against this conception of justice that the defense counsel moved in the Hadamar trial, arguing that international law did not and could not deliver retributive justice in this case, since that law did not apply. Therefore, they asked that the charges against the seven defendants be dismissed.

The defense team consisted of three members of the U.S. armed forces and four German civilians. All were grounded in law, but not necessarily in international law. Their attempt to place the Hadamar defendants beyond the protective reach of the Geneva Convention suggests that international law was not their primary field. As a statement of the law that the defendants were charged with violating, this 1929 convention on the treatment of prisoners of war would have been a weak support for the prosecution. The convention's focus was on the treatment of military prisoners of war, and it would have been a stretch to make it cover the women and children who were put to death at Hadamar. As it turned out, the prosecution was relying on a wholly different statement of international law, but this argument on the part of defense counsel is important as an indicator of one aspect of these trials. Very few of the policymakers who had planned the trials and very few of the prosecutors, defense lawyers, or judges in the trials were experts in international law. There was much hasty boning up on that law by people whose basic training and experience were in other legal fields. By the end of the trials, these participants' habits of thought and argument and the legal procedures to which they were accustomed in domestic criminal law had helped shape international law and broaden the concept of what justice might mean in an international setting.[2]

In this sense, the planners and participants in the trials were pioneers, although they were, for the most part, very cautious pioneers. Nothing in a lawyer's training, whether on the European continent, in Great Britain, or the United States, encourages bold leaps into the unknown, nor does the profession attract many whose temperament is impatient of detail and precedent. The flashy performer is the exception, not the rule, and, although one such might have swept into the major Nuremberg trial on a wave of self-confidence, he would have left the courtroom a much quieter, chastened person. Sir Geoffrey Lawrence, the British judge who was president of the international military tribunal hearing that trial, kept firm control of the proceedings. He had a hawk's eye for any action or word that might detract from the dignity of the law as he understood it or the fairness of the trial over which he was presiding.

Lawrence was determined that the critics of the trial should not, through any lapse of his, be able to criticize the smallest detail of its conduct. His exchange with Robert Kempner, a member of the U.S. prosecuting team, brings this out clearly. It was Kempner's task at Nuremberg to present the case against Wilhelm Frick, German minister of the interior from 1933 to 1943. Kempner presented evidence to show that Frick was responsible for the policy according to which thousands of "unfit" Germans were killed at Hadamar and other nursing homes and sanitariums, and that Frick's policy was then extended to the "unfit" Russians and Poles killed at Hadamar as well. To support his argument about Frick's responsibility for this policy, Kempner introduced a copy of the charges that had been laid against the defendants in the Hadamar trial—which had taken place in Wiesbaden three months earlier. Kempner pointed out that sanitariums and nursing homes such as that at Hadamar came under the jurisdiction of Frick's Ministry of the Interior.

"I follow that," said Lawrence, "but this document does not refer to nursing homes." And, indeed, the charge made at the Hadamar trial did not use those words, although the evidence had made it abundantly clear that it was at the Hadamar nursing home that the killings had taken place. The wording of the charge, however, was for killings "at Hadamar, Germany." In vain did Kempner explain that "Hadamar is a common name for the so-called Hadamar killing mill, which is a nursing home." Lawrence would not have it. The document was not specific enough, and the connection with the Frick policy was too tenuous: "Until Dr. Kempner produces something to show that this was a nursing home and in a time during which the Defendant Frick was Minister of the Interior, the Tribunal will not treat it as being evidence which implicates Frick."[3]

It would be overreaching the mark to claim that all the war crimes trials were conducted with a similar regard for the niceties of law. The times made it difficult to conduct quiet, orderly proceedings. The war was over but its effects were not, and violence was not far below the surface of what passed for everyday life. Amid the ruin of cities and the disruption of farming and transport, normal life was almost impossible, and this was as true for the conquerors as for the conquered. Key witnesses for the trials could not be found. Key defendants were dead, many by their own hands: Hitler, Goebbels, Himmler, and a host of others down to the local party officials who had given the orders carried out by people such as Georg Hessling at Velpke or Adolph Wahlmann at Hadamar. On every side in postwar Germany were the sick to be tended, the hungry to be fed, repairs to be made, ordinary police functions to be carried out, and a whole civil society to be created out of the wreckage. This was the turbulent context for Allied efforts to establish courts and cases that could withstand the scrutiny of future generations as well as the verbal assaults of contemporary critics.

For effective cases to be brought to court, it was not enough to state in general terms what was common knowledge: that the National Socialists had committed acts of destruction and brutality that went far beyond any justification by military necessity. At the upper levels of German officialdom, it was necessary to show the direct responsibility of specific officials for specific policies. At the lower levels, it was necessary to link specific individuals to specific acts, and, if possible, to tie those down to particular dates and places. Was there brutality at Bergen-Belsen, at Auschwitz and Dachau, and other concentration camps? The films taken by the Allies when they freed those camps showed the horrifying results of the treatment of the inmates, but the films, in themselves, were not evidence enough to indict a single person, much less to support a guilty verdict. For that, different kinds of evidence would be needed.

To seek that evidence, teams of investigators fanned out across the devastated countryside, picked through the rubble of buildings, gathered up files that had not been destroyed, and searched for the places—basements, caves, mine shafts, false walls, wine cellars—where incriminating documents had been hidden. The investigators were themselves or were accompanied by German speakers and experts in German history. They collected, catalogued, and translated thousands upon thousands of pages of documentary evidence. They interviewed hundreds of witnesses and took affidavits under conditions designed to meet any objections that defense lawyers might make once the trials got under way. It was an extraordinary effort to meet what was felt to be an extraordinary need, and it was unique in the history of international law.

Suddenly international law found itself the focus of widespread attention. Suddenly this field, which for many years had been the province of the obscure and the earnest, was overrun by outsiders who were determined to haul it into the very midst of the battles about policy toward the defeated nations. More, these outsiders were sure that somewhere in international law there was guidance for the unparalleled problems with which they were faced. Many of the actions of the National Socialists were of such magnitude and cruelty as to be almost beyond belief. Were those actions also beyond the reach of the law? If so, then where was justice for the millions who had died, justice for those who had, directly or indirectly, caused those millions of deaths?

The answers to those questions would be given in the closing days of the war, when the trials were planned, and in the three or four years immediately following, when the bulk of the trials were held. And the answers would, for the most part, be given by lawyers trained in national, not international, law. They moved carefully in this field, concerned to follow paths already there so as to avoid the charge of making new law and applying it retroactively. And where there were no paths, no guidance for those who sought to define international wrongdoing and bring wrongdoers to book, they trusted to their training to bring them through. Short of deciding to sit back and do nothing whatever about those who had plunged the world into suffering and war, a more conservative compass than standard legal training could hardly be found. How this compass functioned in practice can be seen by looking at some of the war crimes trials in more detail.

THE LIE OF THE LAND

The objections of defense counsel at the Hadamar trial were answered with due form and courtesy by the chief prosecutor, whose title, according to military form, was trial judge advocate. Filling this role at Hadamar was Leon Jaworski, a Texas lawyer with the wartime rank of colonel. Thirty years later, Jaworski would stand before the U.S. Supreme Court as special prosecutor in the Watergate scandal involving President Richard Nixon. His arguments before that court would be made in the hot light of intense public interest. In 1945, before the U.S. military commission sitting to hear the Hadamar case, Jaworski's arguments were of interest chiefly to the defendants and their counsel and to the Allied representatives who had come to Wiesbaden to observe this, one of the first war crimes trials.[4] The arguments made in that bare, unpretentious courtroom offer a revealing look at the legal means that were available to those who asserted an international interest in National Socialist policies and actions, even when those actions were confined to Germany, as was the case at Hadamar. Jaworski first addressed the defense argument that international law did not apply to the defendants.

It would, he said, be an anomalous situation—indeed, a tragic situation—"if our network of International Law were so inherently defective as to be powerless to bring to justice the murderers of over 400 victims." That, however, was not the case. The long and painful effort to establish law among nations had provided the tools necessary to see that justice was done at Hadamar. As the defense no doubt knew, much of international law was based on the "custom and usage" of civilized nations, and these, in themselves, would be enough to support the charges against the Hadamar defendants. But the prosecution did not need to depend on the "unwritten law" of custom and usage. There were specific international agreements on which they could rely, agreements that had been signed by all the countries involved in the trial. The Geneva Convention mentioned by the defense did not apply in this case since it dealt with prisoners of war and the care of the sick and wounded. What did apply, and applied directly, were the Hague rules of warfare.[5]

Here, in 1945, the work of the delegates at the Hague conference of 1899 bore unforeseen fruit. The rules of warfare they had articulated—rules that had been picked up and incorporated in the 1907 convention on land warfare—formed the basis of the prosecution's case. One rule in particular told against the seven Germans who were charged with participating in the killing of more than four hundred human beings. The rule was expressly designed to protect the inhabitants of occupied territories such as Poland and eastern Russia under German occupation. Jaworski read the rule aloud in court: "Family honour and rights, the lives of persons and private property, as well as religious convictions and practice, must be respected."[6]

When he read this provision aloud, Jaworski paused after the words "the lives of persons" and interjected "—get this—" before repeating, "the lives of persons." He then finished the passage. The implication was clear. If the lives of the Polish and Russian workers had been respected, they would not have been torn from their homes to be put to forced labor in Germany, and they would not have been killed. But there is more in this statement than Jaworski's obvious abhorrence of the killing and his determination to make as strong a case as he could. He referred to the Hague rules of warfare as the source for the international law governing the trial, but he did not quote directly from those agreements. Rather, he read from the U.S. Army's basic field manual Number 27-10, *Rules of Land Warfare*, in which the Hague stipulation regarding protection of the inhabitants of occupied territory had been incorporated, word for word.[7]

This two-tiered approach, in which national law gave specific, enforceable form to principles and regulations that had been expressed in international undertakings, was congenial to conservative lawyers such as Jaworski. It also fit well into prevailing concepts of the sovereignty of the state as an entity that made and enforced its own rules, answerable to no outside authority unless it chose to be. Nothing in the Hague Conventions defined failure to abide by the rules of warfare as a crime, nor were there any provisions for the trial of those who broke the rules. Who would have tried them? No international criminal court existed in 1899 or 1907 when the conventions were signed, nor did one exist in 1945 when the Hadamar defendants stood trial. The two conventions, like most international agreements of that time (and later), upheld the sovereignty of the state, but they also placed on the signatory states the responsibility for incorporating the conventions' rules of warfare into the instructions to their own armed forces.[8]

Here international declaration feeds into national practice, and regulation and enforcement become a joint venture. The specification and punishment of war crimes was a long-established practice of states, in regard to their own military forces and also those of their opponents. The Hague Conventions did not break new ground. Through long hours of negotiation, the delegates at the 1899 Hague conference had produced a treaty that both reflected the existing rules of warfare of the participating states and set standards by which the future conduct of war could be judged. The rules and standards were, in turn, incorporated with only slight changes into the 1907 convention. The basic contention of the prosecution at Hadamar, as at other war crimes trials, was that the actions of the defendants had fallen so far short of meeting those standards—had, in fact, so directly defied and denied them—that their actions could only be characterized as criminal. And justice required that criminal behavior be punished. But who was to seek out those responsible and try and punish them?

The task could not be entrusted to German courts. After World War I, German courts had made a mockery of the trial of suspected war criminals.[9] The situation after World War II was even less conducive to trust in German courts because they had allowed themselves to be bent to the purposes and policies of the National Socialists. German courts being out of the question, and there being no international criminal court, the Allies assumed the tasks of investigation, indictment, and trial. But punishment was not the only goal. There was a pressing need to head off any action by those who had been so deeply injured by the National Socialist regime that, if nothing else were done, they would take revenge on any German within reach. It was essential, therefore, to identify beyond all question those who were responsible. Beyond that was concern about the future. For the sake of generations yet to come, it was imperative that a full record of the actions of the National Socialists be compiled for the trials and then preserved, both as a warning of what could happen and to give the lie to those who might claim that such actions had never taken place.

Morally speaking, the Allies were on solid ground. At Hadamar, as at other trials, even the defense lawyers said as much. "I am certain that there is not one of you who has listened to these proceedings who does not feel shocked by the crimes that have been unfolded here," said Hans Laternser, German defense counsel for two of the defendants at the Hadamar trial. It might well have been made at any of the other trials where the nature of the National Socialist regime became fully known and documented. Hermann Jahrreiss, a professor of law who was a defense lawyer at the trial of the major German war criminals, said frankly that the revelations at that trial put him through the most difficult times of his entire life. The unfolding tale of cruelty, with atrocity piled upon atrocity on a scale almost beyond the capacity to comprehend, was simply too much: "I have no way to express my horror and to describe this sufficiently in any language."[10]

What then? That was the very question that the Allies were trying to answer, and they were determined to answer it by legal means. That intention had been publicly expressed in such documents as the St James's Declaration, by representatives of the Allied governments in exile (1942), the Moscow Declaration, issued by the leaders of Great Britain, the Soviet Union, and the United States (1943), and numerous other public statements leading up to the Allied agreement of 8 August 1945. That painfully worked-out agreement provided the basis for the establishment of an international military tribunal to try the major German war criminals. It was signed by representatives of France, Great Britain, the Soviet Union, and the United States. Within four months, nineteen other states had signified their acceptance of its provisions "for the trial of war criminals whose offenses have no particular geographical location whether they be accused individually or in their capacity as members of the organizations or groups or in both capacities."[11]

The legal means chosen by the Allies ran the danger of being rejected as inadequate by those who equated law with the commands of a sovereign, whether that sovereign was a ruler or a legislative body. The chief defense counsel at Hadamar seemed to be operating on that concept of law in his objections to the trial and, later, when he commented on the prosecution's answer to his objections: "From the moral standpoint the argument is very good; from a legal standpoint it is not any good. The Prosecution has failed to show us any law that permits the Commission here to hear this case or to disprove a single one of our motions. There is no specific law in point."[12]

But the concept of law that underlay the arguments of the defense at the Hadamar trial was not the only possible one. A completely different view was the very basis of the trials. There being no ruler with power or authority over the states of the international system, and no international body to enact global legislation, a concept of law that was tied to specific, citable statutes was, in these circumstances, beside the point. International law could not be treated that way. That did not mean that nothing could be done about the actions of those in Europe and Asia who had wrought such havoc in the world. It only meant a different approach to the problem of defining what, exactly, constituted an international crime.

It meant looking at what the states themselves had been concerned about and had agreed to since at least the beginning of the century and then applying the results of that examination to the problems of definition. It was not by accident that the states had given the term *law* to their deliberations and agreements. That it was a law among equals rather than a law emanating from a superior authority did not rob it of force or significance. It did set it off from the internal law of individual states, but, under ordinary circumstances, the two kinds of law rubbed along in an uneasy, constantly shifting partnership. The problem for policymakers at the end of World War II was that the circumstances were not ordinary. The National Socialists in Germany and, to a lesser extent, the military leaders in Japan had thrown this partnership so out of balance, had asserted so strongly the preeminence of their own national goals, that the whole relationship was thrown into question.

So what *was* this law under which the defendants in the war crimes trials were charged and tried? It was a law whose boundaries were always in dispute, outside and inside the courtroom. It was a law of custom as well as treaty, of authoritative writings as well as judicial findings and arbitral decisions. Since the end of World War I, it had been a law in quickened process of development, yet that development was frequently stymied by entrenched concepts, particularly with regard to the prerogatives of sovereignty. Like prevailing ideas in economics and politics, the concepts embedded in international law could not keep up with the rapid changes of the twentieth century that were bringing the states of the world into ever closer contact where they shared danger and distress, as well as opportunity. By mid-century international law was a law in movement, a law in process of change as the states of the world tried to adjust their rules as well as their behavior to the changing circumstances of the times. The case against those charged at Nuremberg, Hadamar, and elsewhere rested on the assertion that that movement clearly encompassed the crimes with which they were charged.

At the Hadamar trial, Leon Jaworski put it this way: "If the contentions of the Defense were sound, International Law would be an empty shell; it would be a meaningless thing. It is not that, because it is a living, growing body of law and it is not limited to the boundaries of any treaties or conventions, and there can be no doubt but what under the unwritten rules of International Law, under the written rules as set forth in the Hague Convention, and under the recognition of the rules of International Law as set out by Germany in the *German War Book*, there can be no doubt but that an offense as here charged is punishable under International Law."[13]

The defendants in the Hadamar trial, unlike the defendants at Nuremberg, were scarcely known outside their small, local circles. The positions they occupied could not compare to those of the defendants at Nuremberg, where, for example, the former president of the Reichsbank and the former Reich minister for armaments and war production stood in the dock. At Hadamar it was a doctor, a bookkeeper, three nurses, a handyman, and the administrator of an institution for the mentally ill who stood in the dock. Yet their defense was much the same as the defense at Nuremberg. For one reason or another, they were not responsible. Responsibility lay elsewhere. The administrator was only carrying out orders. The doctor only signed the death certificates. The bookkeeper only made out the certificates for the doctor to sign. The handyman only removed the bodies and buried them. The female nurse only prepared the drugs, she did not administer them. The two male nurses did administer the drugs but as a kindness to put the Russians and Poles out of their suffering. Besides—and this was the basic contention of the defendants—that was what was to be done with these people.

But this defense of higher authority, of legality under German law, was contemptuously rejected by Jaworski in his closing argument: "If German law could be invoked as the guiding influence upon which the prosecution of war criminals was to be based, we would soon find that there could be and would be no war crimes trials." A nation could simply pass laws that approved any expedient act, no matter how cruel, and anyone charged with committing that act would get off, scot-free. But neither German nor American law was controlling in this case: "The thing we look to is International Law, as it has grown up through the ages and as it has been promulgated through treaties and conventions." And in international law it was clear that the defense of "superior orders," even in a military situation, was no defense for acts such as those at Hadamar, where prisoners under the control of the German Reich were wantonly killed.[14]

All of the defendants in the Hadamar trial were found guilty in that they did "wilfully, deliberately and wrongfully aid, abet and participate in the killing of human beings of Polish and Russian nationality"—in number more than four hundred. The administrator of the home and the two nurses who had given the drugs were sentenced to death, the other defendants to various prison terms. One of the nurses, Karl Willig, even as he was being led to execution, clung to the shield of the German state: "I did my duty as a German official. God is my witness." As with Karl Willig at Hadamar, so with Alfred Jodl at Nuremberg. On learning of his death sentence, the former chief of the operations staff of the Armed Forces High Command affirmed his utter loyalty to the German state: "For I believe and avow that a man's duty toward his people and fatherland stands above every other. To carry out this duty was for me an honor, and the highest law."[15] The question at Nuremberg, at Hadamar, and elsewhere was what that state could reasonably command that the citizen could, with honor, obey.

LINES OF DEVELOPMENT

Criticism of the war crimes trials has been extensive, with the sharpest being directed against the charges in the trials of the major war criminals in Nuremberg and Tokyo: crimes against peace, war crimes, and crimes against humanity.[16] Most critics, no matter how conservative, have no trouble accepting the charge of war crimes. Many are willing to accept as well the charge of crimes against humanity since the brutalities committed against civilians were so extensive and well-documented that to ignore them seems almost to make one an accessory. The crime against peace is the sticking point today as it was at the time of the trials. To charge that the defendants committed a justiciable crime by waging an aggressive war is, in the critics' eyes, to bring a charge under *ex post facto* law.

When, at the close of the Hadamar trial, Leon Jaworski was invited to Nuremberg to help prosecute the major war criminals, he refused. He was, he said, bothered by a clause in the tribunal's charter in which aggressive war was defined as an international crime: "That clause bothered me no end. The Allied powers had all of these crimes against humanity, and here was an effort to put a new wrinkle into international law. I thought it was a serious mistake."[17]

Jaworski's comment is illustrative of much that was in dispute at the trials and in discussions of those trials today. The lines of demarcation between national and international law were not (and are not) clear. If a person disputed some of the lines that had been laid down for the trials of the major war criminals—as Jaworski and many others did—then personal judgment, based on training and experience, became the standard for evaluation. At Hadamar, Jaworski had no difficulty accepting and vigorously prosecuting the imprecise charge of "violation of international law." This he took to mean a violation of the standards for the conduct of land warfare as set down in the Hague Conventions. He was comfortable with this since he could immediately shift ground to national laws as set down in the U.S. and German codes for the conduct of their armies. But even these, by themselves, would not completely serve. They only stated general principles such as the protection of lives and property in occupied territory. Like lawyers at the much higher level of the major war criminals trials, Jaworski was forced to bridge the gap between a statement of general principles and the particulars of certain actions. And the bridge that he used was an explanation of the distinctive nature of international law, which was, he said, "a living, growing body of law and it is not limited to the boundaries of any treaties or conventions."[18]

The paths through this murky area of contested authority and disputed law were poorly marked, if marked at all, and there was much disagreement as to which way would lead to justice. Jaworski would not set foot on the path of treating aggressive war as a crime. He was, however, willing to follow the war crimes path because it was the best marked, although not without its uncertainties when it came to the murders at Hadamar. Actions that were "shocking to all humanity"[19] pushed Jaworski onto the separate path of crimes against humanity although he would have been hard put to point to the clear markers of specific statutory law that, as a lawyer, he craved. Travel on that path had to rely on the general purpose behind the military codes of conduct and on the international precedent of some humanitarian interventions. And this reliance was, of course, the very method of argument that gave confidence to the prosecution at Nuremberg as they attempted to show the validity of the third path, that of crimes against peace.

The case was best put by Sir Hartley Shawcross, chief British prosecutor at the trial. Shawcross relied mainly on the Pact of Paris (the Kellogg-Briand Pact) of 1928 and on the fact that the Axis powers had, in this pact, officially renounced war as a means of achieving national goals or settling disputes: "What statesman or politician in charge of the affairs of nations could doubt, from 1928 onwards, that aggressive war . . . was unlawful and outlawed? What statesman or politician embarking upon such a war could reasonably and justifiably count upon an immunity other than that of a successful outcome of the criminal venture? What more decisive evidence of a prohibition laid down by positive international law could any lawyer desire than that which has been adduced before this Tribunal?"[20]

Both Shawcross and the judges on the bench in the proceedings at Nuremberg could simply have relied on the charter that had established the international military tribunal hearing the case. The charter stated that a war of aggression in all its stages, from planning to waging, was a crime against peace, as was a war in violation of treaty agreements. But reliance on the charter would not have satisfied the desire that was marked throughout this trial: the desire by all concerned to make clear the reasoning that lay behind the arguments made and the positions taken. The defense, the prosecution, and the judges all had their eyes on future evaluations of this key trial. It was as central for those such as defense lawyer Hermann Jahrreiss, who argued that international law did not yet cover war as a crime, as it was for those who argued that it did. Thus, when the judges accepted the criminality of aggressive war they did not simply point to the jurisdiction article in the tribunal's charter. They spelled out in detail the international statements and agreements on which they based their conclusion that aggressive war was indeed an international crime. As for the defendants:

"At least some of them must have known of the treaties signed by Germany, outlawing recourse to war for the settlement of international disputes; they must have known that they were acting in defiance of all international law when in complete deliberation they carried out their designs of invasion and aggression." And aggressive war was, in the opinion of the judges, "the supreme international crime differing only from other war crimes in that it contains within itself the accumulated evil of the whole."[21]

There were eight judges on the bench in the trial of the major German war criminals, one judge and one alternate from each of the four countries that had established the tribunal: France, Great Britain, the Soviet Union, and the United States.[22] These judges were by no means a rubber stamp for the prosecution. They were concerned to establish their own independence. They were concerned also to put this trial on the soundest possible legal footing. There were to be no forays into uncharted territory, no application of *ex post facto* law as they understood it. In their meetings and in their judgment, professional caution was their guide and they took the narrowest possible view of the provisions of the charter.

This meant that one of the prosecution's main contentions, that of a general conspiracy to commit all the other enumerated crimes, was reduced to conspiracy with respect to the single crime of aggressive war. This narrow reading of the charter also meant that they refused to take jurisdiction of crimes against humanity, no matter how blatant or well-documented, unless those crimes were committed in connection with or during the course of aggressive war, which is to say, committed after September 1, 1939. The judges also acquitted three defendants against whom the prosecution had proceeded with vigor. And no defendant whom they sentenced to death was sent to the gallows solely on the strength of guilt on the controversial counts arising from the charge of crimes against peace: the common plan or conspiracy, and planning, preparing, initiating, and waging aggressive war. In each case, there was also guilt on the counts under the charge of war crimes, crimes against humanity, or both.[23]

Conservative themselves, the judges on the international military tribunal gave a conservative reading to the charter and to their task under its provisions. And this cautious approach to the task of assessing guilt and punishment for the horrors of World War II was reinforced when the task passed out of the hands of these eight judges into the hands of the judges in the subsequent war crimes trials at Nuremberg. These trials, too, relied on international law, and in these trials, too, it was hoped that it could be shown beyond all question that there were limits to the freedom of action conferred on states by their sovereign standing. And here, too, caution prevailed.

There were twelve subsequent trials, conducted by Americans before American judges under the authority of the four-power Control Council, which was the putative government of Germany during the period of occupation. Control Council Law No. 10, which authorized the trials and established their powers and jurisdiction, was an international undertaking, and the law that was applied in the trials was international law. The chief prosecutor, Telford Taylor, felt a deep sense of responsibility in regard to these trials since the proceedings would be the first test of the Nuremberg principles in different courts with different lawyers and judges. In light of this, Taylor and his staff worked especially hard on preparing for those trials, in which they planned to bring indictments under the charge of crimes against peace—the crime that, in the words of the international military tribunal, was the supreme international crime. Specifically, some of the defendants in those trials would be indicted for planning, initiating, and waging aggressive war and taking part in a conspiracy to commit crimes against peace.

The defendants in the subsequent trials were from neither the top nor the bottom of German society but belonged to the great middle level of those who had helped make the National Socialist programs possible. Indictments regarding aggressive war and conspiracy to commit crimes against

peace were brought against defendants in four of the twelve subsequent trials. The sixty-nine defendants in those four trials were industrialists, military leaders, and high government officials. No defendant was found guilty
under the conspiracy charge, and in three of the four trials no defendant was
found guilty under the aggressive war charge. The judges refused to find
guilt under this charge against any of the military men or any of the industrialists. And only five of the seventeen diplomats and government ministers
so charged were deemed to have positions powerful enough that they could
have initiated or effectively influenced policy and, hence, might be said to
be guilty of crimes against peace.[24]

In this initial test, the Nuremberg principle regarding crimes against
peace was taken in hand by men whose training and outlook inclined them
to caution, and they treated it with great reserve. Panels of three judges
heard each of the four cases in which indictments were brought under the
charge of crimes against peace. The twelve Americans entrusted with judgment in these important proceedings had reached high positions in the
court systems of their respective home states, but—like most others in these
trials—had little or no experience in international law.[25] They knew the
rules of evidence, however. They felt that they knew a war crime when they
saw it, and they were willing to entertain charges of slave labor, spoliation,
and crimes against humanity so long as these occurred in connection with
or during the war, and not before. The charge of conspiracy to commit any
of these crimes they treated with such caution as to render it effectively null.
And crimes against peace?

Well, that was a different matter. The judges obviously felt that guilt
under that charge required overwhelming evidence of personal involvement and responsibility. It would have been difficult for them to dismiss the
charge entirely, since the international military tribunal had strongly supported it and had backed that support with extensive discussion. They
could, however, tiptoe around it by staying, for the most part, on the safer
ground of war crimes and crimes against humanity. It was obvious that these
crimes had been committed on a large scale, so the question at issue in the
trials was the relation, if any, of each defendant to the crimes committed. As
for the charge of crimes against peace—that could, in most cases, be quietly
put aside. It might be, as the international military tribunal had said, that
that crime contained within itself "the accumulated evil of the whole," but
the judges in the subsequent trials were reluctant to assess responsibility for
that particular evil. So the Nuremberg principle that waging aggressive war
was an international crime for which instigators could be punished was

weakened, not strengthened, by the caution of these judges. The principle
was, at any rate, an awkward legacy for sovereign states and one that, for
much of the rest of the century, they found it convenient to ignore.[26]

The lawyerly caution that was evident in many of these war crimes trials
did not disappear in the years following. If anything, it became stronger as
peacetime activities claimed the attention and energy of most of those who
had taken part in the trials and as international law passed again into the
care of the old hands in the field. Still, the seeds of that law's development
along certain lines had been sown in the trials, especially with regard to individuals within sovereign states. Whether as subjects with international responsibilities or as objects of international protection, individual human
beings stood in a different relation to international law after the war crimes
trials than they had before. Some aspects of the changes in this relation will
be examined in the following chapters. Here it is enough to say that, whatever the arguments about the trials, they had at least made abundantly clear
the depths to which people could descend in their treatment of others, given
the appropriate conditions, the approval of authority, and the lack of international oversight and action.

In his opening address at the trial of the major German war criminals in
Nuremberg, chief prosecutor Jackson found the words to describe what was
at stake in the trial and in the postwar world in general. "The real com-
plaining party at your bar is Civilization," he said,[27] summing up in that one
word the centuries-long effort to contain and control violence and to create
a world where people—all people—could flourish in peace and justice. And
this was exactly what the organizers of the unofficial trial in New York City
had said eleven years earlier when they had tried Hitler for crimes against
civilization. It had taken a world war and untold horrors and suffering before some of the states of the international system came to that same conclusion. But they finally got there.

CHAPTER FOURTEEN

Sovereignty's Hard Shell

On the battlefields of World War II new ideas about the international system began to take shape. In particular, there came to be a new understanding of what it might mean to place justice in an international context. If only during the war and for a short time after, *justice* came to have an unambiguous, well-understood meaning. It meant retribution. It meant that those responsible for starting the war and for committing criminal acts in the course of that war should pay the price for their actions. This determination found expression in the Moscow Declaration, issued by the leaders of Great Britain, the Soviet Union, and the United States in the fall of 1943. Those who had plunged the world into war were there put on official notice that they could not escape judgment, "for most assuredly the three allied powers will pursue them to the uttermost ends of the earth and will deliver them to their accusers in order that justice may be done."[1]

This wartime definition of *justice* considerably narrowed the scope and reach of the term from the definition that had prevailed in the interwar period. The interwar merger of justice and peace had given the abstract concept of justice a particular home in the affairs of human beings and had allowed it to be attached to a myriad of activities tending toward international peace. Peaceful settlement procedures such as adjudication and arbitration could gain luster from their strong association with justice as well as with peace. Defining justice as retribution cut it off from these wide fields of action and focused it tightly on the capture, trial, and punishment of those responsible for atrocities in the war and for the war itself. Justice as retribution also tied the concept tightly to law and to the legal system. And therein lay a problem for those who hoped that the war crimes trials would spark a move toward an international system of justice under the law.

The problem was both practical and philosophical. Internationally, there existed no legal system comparable to those within states. This was difficult enough. Philosophically, the matter was even more difficult. Throughout the postwar period the tension caused by this difficulty bedeviled all attempts to give operative meaning to the concept of justice. The tension went beyond disagreements over definitions. Such disagreements were, after all, as old as the concept itself. The tension derived from a deep uncertainty about the base from which to operate in the continuing search for justice. Was the base to be national? International? Both? Some mixture of the two? Or was there to be a competition for the primary base of thought and action—a competition with few established rules and with no referee? When the Allies were no longer allies and were no longer willing to force the issue as they had in the war crimes trials, what then? Much of the history of the postwar period can be seen as a struggle to answer these questions, and by century's end no clear answer had emerged.

At the time of the war crimes trials, the necessity for a strong international base seemed much more obvious than it did even five years later. The wartime hopes of the Allies were well expressed by Sir David Maxwell Fyfe, the British deputy chief prosecutor at the trial of the major German war criminals in Nuremberg. Fyfe carried the burden of the presentation of the British case so he was thoroughly familiar with the issues of legality and justice that had been raised at Nuremberg and in other war crimes trials as well. Fyfe spoke of the longing for "a better world" that was intense and widespread at the end of the war. He noted that people who shared this desire came from different national, religious, and political backgrounds, yet they were at one in their desire for change. Many also believed that justice between individuals and between those individuals and the state had to be based on an ordered system of law within the state. It followed that justice outside the state required such an arrangement as well. Hopes for a better world thus depended on the establishment of an ordered system of law in the international sphere. The majority of mankind, said Fyfe, hope "to see an effective system of international justice set up to regulate the relations between States, and be a crown and unifying principle of municipal systems of law."[2]

Fyfe's invocation of international justice was obviously heartfelt. It was also vague. This combination of characteristics was not uncommon in the postwar period as people's desire for a better world came up against the barriers to achieving it. Conceptually, there was the persistent difficulty of sorting out the various strands of authority that were entangled in the concept of justice when that concept was attached to the idea of law. Even as *international justice* came to mean more than simply retribution—as it obviously did in Fyfe's statement—it still retained the association with law that had been made during World War II and immediately after. And the *law* part of this association carried overtones of coercive power that were missing entirely, both from the international system itself and from similar invocations of international justice and law that had been made before World War II. It was the hope of the Allies that the future would be different.

As Robert H. Jackson had put it, even before he became chief prosecutor for the United States at Nuremberg, in the future there must be an international order based on law, "equipped with instrumentalities able and willing to maintain its supremacy." Lawyers, especially, were called to dedicate themselves to that order and to the task "of pushing back the frontiers of anarchy and of maintaining justice under the law among men and nations."[3]

The assumption that some sort of coercion was a necessary corollary of law is not surprising in the thought of lawyers who were trained in various systems of municipal law, whether Continental or Anglo-American. But that assumption and the hopes that it embodied, however heartfelt, left unanswered some basic questions, and, in fact, added complications to an already complicated mix of ideas and levels of authority. The question of how, exactly, an international order was to be equipped with instrumentalities capable of maintaining the supremacy of law was not even addressed, nor was there any indication of what those instrumentalities might be. Similarly, it was not at all clear how a system of international justice could ever become the "crown and unifying principle" of municipal law, as David Maxwell Fyfe had put it. Nor was it clear what the relation between the two systems of law might be, should that day ever come to pass. Granted, the purpose of many pronouncements made during the war and immediately after was not to lay out courses of action but to provide spurs to action. Still, the majority of the participants in the war crimes trials shed their wartime preoccupations as quickly as they could when the trials were over. It was left to others to try to take grand, general concepts such as international justice and international order under the law and give them a definite structure and particularity so that they might be felt as an actual presence in the rush of human affairs.[4]

THE RESISTANT PAST

Henri Donnedieu de Vabres was the French judge on the bench in the trial of the major German war criminals at Nuremberg. He was also the quietest

judge and one about whom very little was known, at least by those who have
written accounts of the trial. Telford Taylor, a member of the U.S. prosecuting team, expressed surprise that the French government had appointed
this obscure law professor to sit on the bench at such an important trial.
Francis Biddle, the U.S. judge, found the Frenchman's sweeping mustache
and his command of English to be subjects for witty comment. The literary-
minded Rebecca West, who was covering the trial as a journalist, was reminded of characters in the plays of Molière and Marivaux, the speeches of
Lamartine, and the lawyers in the drawings of Daumier. People at the trial
remembered the ancient black Citroen in which de Vabres and members of
the French prosecution team took weekend tours because the car frequently
broke down, leaving the Frenchmen stranded by the roadside. They remembered that de Vabres was referred to as *"Nom de Dieu,"* although not to
his face. Beyond that, their ignorance filled in the blanks with comments on
his appearance and his demeanor. Not one seemed aware that Henri
Donnedieu de Vabres had been thinking about questions of international
criminal law and wrestling with such practical difficulties as the definition of
aggression while most of them were still in school or just beginning their careers.[5]

   This ignorance about the pre-war career and accomplishments of de
Vabres is a measure of the gap that separated the field of international law in
the mid-1940s from the lives and awareness of those who were involved in
making and carrying out high-level policy—especially in Great Britain and
the United States. In France the name of de Vabres might call up vague associations with criminal law and with the University of Paris, where de
Vabres had taught for twenty years. But that was scarcely enough to assure
him recognition at Nuremberg. There he was a quiet, reflective scholar
among active, busy men whose intelligence had, throughout their careers,
been directed to other pursuits than those that had occupied de Vabres.
They might have been mildly interested to learn that as early as 1922 he had
published a book on international criminal law or that he had long urged the
establishment of a criminal chamber in the Permanent Court of International Justice, but the information would have been marginal to the immediate demands of the trial they were conducting. From this vantage point, the
lifelong efforts of de Vabres and his colleagues to achieve effective enforcement of international criminal law were ancient history. If anything, the international military tribunal hearing the trial of the major German war
criminals could be seen as the crown of these efforts.[6]

   De Vabres's colleagues on the bench, although not trained in international law, were experienced lawyers. They were also intelligent, conscien-

tious, and concerned to conduct the trial fairly within the basic framework of international law. The charter that had established the tribunal gave them solid guidance in this task, and they could assume that its authors had grounded it firmly in international law. Indeed, they had to make that assumption. That the charter's view was not the only view was quickly made clear by the defendants' German lawyers. The trial, they said, raised many contested and difficult points of law. Therefore, all the defense counsel joined in the request that "the Tribunal direct that an opinion be submitted by internationally recognized authorities on international law on the legal elements of the Trial under the Charter of the Tribunal."[7]

The tribunal rejected the request because it, in effect, questioned the legal foundation of the trial itself, a challenge the charter specifically prohibited. But the issue did not go away. It surfaced again and again in this and other trials. It was brought up in the comments of defense lawyers and in the testimony of practioners and teachers of international law who were called by the defense as expert witnesses. The issue was basically philosophical. As the international lawyer Quincy Wright noted, people's opinions of the validity of the trials were a direct reflection of their theory of international law.[8]

Such theoretical issues were the professional concern of scholars and academics such as Wright and de Vabres and the bane of practical men of affairs such as most of the others involved in the trial. At one point in the private deliberations of the judges on the Nuremberg tribunal, the Soviet judge dismissed a question raised by de Vabres with the cutting remark, "We are practical, not a discussion club."[9] But the trial itself, as well as the practicalities of its conduct, rested on certain assumptions about international law, particularly in regard to individual responsibility under that law. Quincy Wright could have spelled out these assumptions and showed how they fit into a complex theory of law. But by the time he joined the legal team as an adviser to U.S. judge Francis Biddle, decisions had already been made in the ongoing contest over the nature of international law. The view that emphasized the centrality of the sovereign state and held that the state's freedom of action could not be restricted except through its own explicit consent had been rejected. It was not rejected easily or without argument in the bureaucratic battles through which a war crimes policy was finally put together. But it was rejected in favor of a more dynamic model that emphasized the development of law on the basis of stated international principles, norms, and agreements. This was the theoretical underpinning for the charges in the trials, the foundation on which practical men took their stand. But even those who prided themselves most on their practicality had to abide the consequences of theoretical thought. Answers to a key question in the trials depended on the theoretical starting point. The question was simple, and its centrality obvious: In international law, where did responsibility lie? Did it lie with the state? Or was it the burden of the individuals who carried out the state's policies? Before World War II, state responsibility was simply assumed. Now that assumption was being called into question. For many, the assumption had been shown to be positively harmful, a shield for the human beings who had planned Germany's barbarous policies and for those who had carried them out. Not so, said others, pointing to the fact that international law—as it had existed for many years—was a law *of* states, *for* states.

The German international law expert Arthur Wegner had no doubt where responsibility lay. Indeed, he was passionate on the subject. Called in as an expert witness in the *Peleus* trial, one of the war crimes trials conducted by the British, Wegner argued that international law relieved the defendants of any responsibility for their acts as agents of the state. On trial were the commander and crew of a German submarine. They were charged with violating the laws and customs of war by killing the unarmed survivors of the ship they had torpedoed and sunk. Wegner threw the whole blame back upon the German state: "It has been a well-established rule of International Law that an individual forming part of a public force and acting under authority of his own government is not to be held answerable as a private trespasser or malefactor." The responsibility, if any, rested not with the individual but with the state.[10]

Similarly, in the trial of people who had been guards at the concentration camps at Belsen and Auschwitz, an English expert on international law, Herbert Arthur Smith, argued, "In International Law the general principle is that the State and not the individual is responsible." That being so, the German government was responsible for "paying the fullest compensation to every non-German subject who has suffered in these concentration camps, or to the dependents of those who have perished." As for the defendants who were charged with the actions that had caused suffering and death in the camps, their trials should not be held under international law but under the national law of the countries where the actions had taken place.[11]

The most learned presentation of this state-centered view of international law was made by the German lawyer Hermann Jahrreiss, defense counsel for General Alfred Jodl in the trial of the major war criminals. Whereas Wegner had been overwrought and Smith had been defensive, Jahrreiss was markedly calm and reasonable. He spoke on behalf of all the defense counsel, and he spoke well. His tone and his manner invited all in the courtroom to look together at the issues raised by the trial and to consider them in their historical and legal context. One by one he raised the points that had been made by the prosecution, and one by one he subjected them to analysis. He was like a surgeon whose purpose was to save the patient by removing cancerous growths, the patient in this case being international law itself. Given his assumptions about its state-centered nature, his arguments were convincing. The problem was that not the judges, nor the prosecutors, nor the charter on which the trial rested shared his view that the sovereignty of the state trumped every other consideration.

Still his presentation was impressive: Did the prosecution rely on the 1928 Pact of Paris? True, it had outlawed war as an instrument of national policy. True, Germany had signed the pact. But—let us consider the many reservations that were made by the signatory states. Would they have signed if the pact had specified punishment for a breach of its terms? Let us also look at the late 1930s, when even its strongest supporters admitted that the pact was dead. If we suppose that the prosecution arguments are valid—that the pact remained in force despite its being ineffective—what then? Are individuals to be held responsible for actions they have committed when those actions were authorized by the state? This brought Jahrreiss to the heart of the disagreement between the defense lawyers and the underlying charter:

> Should things reach the point where, according to general world law, the men who participated in the planning, preparation, launching and conduct of a war forbidden by international law could be brought before an international criminal court, the decisions regarding the state's final problems of existence would be subject to super-state control. One might, of course, still term such states sovereign; but they would no longer be sovereign. . . . What the Prosecution is doing when, in the name of the world community as a legal entity, it desires to have individuals legally sentenced for their decisions regarding war and peace, is . . . incompatible with sovereignty.

Such an action, said Jahrreiss, destroys the very "spirit of the state."[12]

What Jahrreiss was defending was classical international law with its emphasis on a sovereignty that reserved to the state the right to be a judge of its actions in matters touching its own vital interests. He was not in any sense defending the actions that were charged against the defendants in the major war crimes trial. It was clear that he abhorred much of what had been done in the name of the state. What he was attacking with considerable intelligence and skill was the idea that there was an international community with the authority to bring a state to book through a trial of that state's agents and organizations. But this idea and the assertion that it was true were precisely what drove the trial and kept the prosecution in heart through many weary days of argument and gut-wrenching evidence.

Robert H. Jackson, the chief U.S. prosecutor, put it well in a reflective backward look at the trials: "In these war crimes trials we no longer regard International Law as exhausting its force upon states alone. It is considered to penetrate through the shell of sovereignty into the state and to be able to call individuals to account for its violation." This is exactly what was feared by Jahrreiss and rejected by the international law that he espoused. Jackson knew this quite well: "Of course, this principle of individual responsibility is a negation of the old and tenacious doctrine of absolute and uncontrolled sovereignty of the state and of immunity for all who act under its orders. The implications of individual accountability for violation of International Law are far-reaching and many old concepts may be shaken thereby."[13]

Long after Jackson's death in 1954, the implications of individual responsibility under international law were still a subject for passionate argument. Jackson could not have foreseen the length and bitterness of the struggle between state authority and international authority, but he saw clearly the conceptual weapons in the hands of those who opposed the idea that international law could "penetrate through the shell of sovereignty." During the planning stages of the trial of the major German war criminals he remarked that he would have to depend on young men, men who could look to the future, since all the older international lawyers were against him.[14] The observation—which was not made in public—was more sweeping than the situation warranted, but it did reflect Jackson's frustration at the entrenched conservatism of the closed and cautious discipline on which he had to rely in the trial. An encounter in the spring of 1945 with the views of Jules Basdevant reinforced Jackson's frustration and his impatience with what he called the old school of international law.

At that time Jules Basdevant was legal adviser to the French Foreign Office and to the French delegation at the San Francisco conference where the United Nations Charter was written and signed. Basdevant's interest in international law had been stimulated by the French expert Louis Renault, whose efforts at the Hague Conferences of 1899 and 1907 had helped make possible their achievements in arbitration procedures and in setting out the laws of land warfare. Basdevant's intellectual roots were deep in the Continental tradition of exhaustive examination of the agreements and actions of states in the international system in order to determine what international law actually was. He came from a line of lawyers who had established the prestigious Institute of International Law in the late nineteenth century, had helped establish the Permanent Court of International Justice following World War I, and had pled cases before that court in the interwar period. Basdevant himself, during the conference at San Francisco, helped write the statute of the new International Court of Justice, to which he was appointed as a judge the following year. He was, therefore, very much an established and secure member of an international set of lawyers who were experienced in and devoted to international law. Compared to Basdevant and his colleagues, Jackson and other Allied war crimes policy planners were rank newcomers. And, Jules Basdevant, although polite, was in definite opposition to some of the ideas of those newcomers. Having examined the U.S. arguments for the criminality of aggressive war and the international law sources on which that charge was to be based, Basdevant gave his considered opinion. The arguments were, he said *"très fragile."*[15]

Basdevant was sixty-eight years old when he gave this opinion, an opinion that strengthened Jackson in his belief that all the older international lawyers were against what the Allies were planning to do at Nuremberg. And, since Basdevant and many of those in international law were also university teachers, Jackson was also strengthened in his dislike of those who mainly talked about law while he and his colleagues mainly practiced it. When he faced the bench in the trial of the major German war criminals, however, he faced a glaring contradiction to his belief and his dislike. There on the bench was Henri Donnedieu de Vabres, also a university professor, also in his sixties, also secure in his standing in international law. And de Vabres had no doubt that international law had moved far beyond nineteenth-century suppositions and formulations regarding the sovereignty of states. For de Vabres, there was a new law, a law for the twentieth century. This new law was the product of sustained and widespread international efforts—in which the Axis powers had taken part—and it was the legal basis for the major war crimes trial. Thus, for de Vabres, the question to be decided at Nuremberg was not whether international law applied in the case but, rather, the involvement and culpability, if any, of each of the defendants in the crimes with which they were charged.[16]

De Vabres was proud to take part in the trial. In many respects it was indeed the culmination of years of obscure struggle undertaken by him and others to clarify international criminal law and give it an institutional presence in international affairs. At last at Nuremberg an international criminal court had come into existence, and at last the whole array of court proceedings was actually taking place before the bench where de Vabres sat with his American, British, and Soviet counterparts. Said a friend who visited him in Nuremberg, "It was an unforgettable sight!"[17]

But de Vabres did not forget that the court was temporary and that much remained to be done if law was to be an effective component of justice in the international system. He knew, as apparently Jackson and other prosecutors did not, the toughness of the conceptual shell of sovereignty that protected the state from outside interference. In his reflections on the trial, he said that the judgment of the tribunal had proved that municipal law had to defer to international law and that states were bound by that law even when it was not spelled out in formal treaty agreements.[18] But he did not leave the subject at that. He knew that the judgment of even so prestigious a judicial body as the International Military Tribunal would not secure the dominance of international law. Further action would be needed, and to the best of his ability he would try to see that that action was taken.

From the fall of 1946, when the International Military Tribunal delivered its judgment, to his death in February 1952, de Vabres worked to bring to completion the task that had been begun at Nuremberg. The work there was promising, but it was a beginning only. Two more things were necessary: the codification of international criminal law and the establishment of a permanent international criminal court. In pursuit of this goal, de Vabres tried to influence the opinions of professionals by working through private law organizations such as the International Association for International Penal Law. He also tried to influence state officials by working through the newly formed United Nations. As a member of that organization's Committee on the Progressive Development of International Law and Its Codification, he was indefatigable in urging member states to establish an international court of criminal jurisdiction.[19]

In this task of persuasion de Vabres was joined by others including Sir Hartley Shawcross, chief British prosecutor at Nuremberg, and Vespasian V. Pella, a colleague from the days before the war. It is another mark of the distance between those who had long been active in international law and those who were making policy based on that law that the name of Pella did not figure in the discussions when Allied war crimes policy was being worked out. If anyone in the 1940s could be said to be a better-known authority on international criminal law than the Frenchman Donnedieu de Vabres it would be the Romanian Vespasian V. Pella.[20] They had worked closely together before the war as members of a group of lawyers, mainly European, whose membership and interests transcended national boundaries. The fortunes of war had separated them—Pella as minister to Switzerland, de Vabres as a citizen of occupied France—but the war's end allowed them to resume their joint campaign for the codification of international criminal law and the establishment of an international criminal court. They had first-hand knowledge of the resistance of states to any curtailment of sovereignty, but they thought that surely the experiences of World War II would make obvious, even to sovereign states, the need for such a code and for a court to enforce it.

It was not to be—not, at least until long after the deaths of most of those who had been involved in the war crimes trials. The immediate postwar years saw a number of efforts to get sovereignty to share its space with more broadly based standards of international behavior, but this period of activity was brief and was hotly contested at the time. For many years the longed-for goal of "justice under the law" seemed an ever-receding vision. Even the attempt to spell out the principles of law that had informed the trials at Nuremberg gave pause to the traditionalists who were rapidly establishing themselves on the various commissions and committees of postwar international organizations. After the Nuremberg principles were affirmed (but not defined) by the General Assembly of the new United Nations, they wandered for long periods in the wilderness of official committeedom as part of an effort to draft a comprehensive code of international criminal law. It took the return of mass slaughter near the end of the twentieth century to bring the Nuremberg principles again to the fore and return international attention to courts for the trial of those accused of international crimes.

This belated effect was not, however, the only legacy of the war crimes trials. The experience of those trials also affected the ways in which people thought about the concept of justice in an international setting. In particular, the trials helped change the framework of ideas within which international affairs were viewed. These changes fell far short of what had been hoped for by many who were involved, but they were still significant. First, the trials made retribution an active component of the mix of assumptions and ideas that swirled around the central concept of justice like so many planets orbiting a star. This was not retribution in the sense of tit for tat: "gore my ox, and your ox is at risk; expel my diplomat, and yours will be sent packing." This was retribution with an international face. It rested on the assumption that damage to one was damage to all and that in the name of that "all"—however defined—punishment must follow. The Allied prosecutors had attempted to make a very large jump. They had tried to move from a self-help system wherein retribution often resembled nothing so much as a petty feud raised to a national level to a system of cooperative endeavor within well-defined guidelines on behalf of the entire community. This was far too large a jump to last once the trials were over, but the experience was there, and it served as an example and a precedent in the last half of the twentieth century.

The second change given impetus by the trials also was linked to the idea of retribution. If retribution was to have any international meaning and if retributive justice was to be served internationally, then certain acts had to be defined in an appropriate manner. They had to be defined not simply as crimes but as international crimes. From this it followed that everyone had an interest in the suppression and punishment of these crimes just as everyone had an interest in the suppression and punishment of crimes in a neighborhood or nation. Given the lack of comparable governmental and legal institutions, this comparison would not stand close analysis, but it was deeply felt, nonetheless. And this meant that the idea of international criminal law gained a standing it had never had before.

In the interwar period such men as Donnedieu de Vabres and Vespasian V. Pella had rowed hard against the prevailing winds of sovereignty to gain some recognition for courts and codes of international criminal law. They had ended about where they had started: far from the centers of power. In vain they had urged that international condemnation of piracy and slavery was sufficient precedent for recognition that some acts were internationally criminal and of international concern. Until World War II, this remained an unargued but also unimportant sidelight in international thought, of interest chiefly to law societies and publications. The experiences of the war brought the matter of international criminal law to the forefront of postwar attempts to define and achieve international justice.

One part of the legacy of the war crimes trials was especially sensitive and controversial. That was the question of an international criminal court. Here, quite clearly, support in the postwar period was eroded by uncertainty over that court's relation to national legal systems. Even a supporter of international criminal law might balk at such a court on the grounds that the means of enforcement should stay strictly in the hands and institutions of individual states. The idea of an international criminal court—so obvious a necessity to men such as de Vabres and Sir Hartley Shawcross—was a matter for alarm on the part of other people no less concerned for justice. When, for a time, the establishment of such a court seemed an immediate postwar possibility, the vehement opposition of such groups as the American Bar Association made it clear that the time for it had not come.[21]

Putting aside the chauvinistic elements in such opposition—and at times these elements were prominent—there were still too many unresolved questions of authority and accountability for widespread acceptance of an international court, even though that might seem to be the logical crown of a system of international criminal law. In this respect, the war crimes trials set an example that was not, until the near the end of the century, even seen as a precedent. In the intervening years the issue did not, of course, disappear. What *was* to be done about international criminal behavior when a state that was theoretically responsible refused either to take action against the perpetrators or offer compensation in any form? The question reflected the continuance in the postwar years of the tug-of-war between national and international authority that had figured prominently in the war crimes trials.

Justice as retribution, certain actions defined as international crimes, the question of an international criminal court, individual responsibility under international law, international enforcement of that law—the legacy of the war crimes trials was complex and far-reaching, and that legacy was added to an already complicated mix of international justice issues. Much remained to be worked out in the postwar period, but one thing was clear. Although the hard shell of state sovereignty had not been cracked open by the trials, they *had* succeeded in leaving a nick in that shell—a nick that would gradually widen as subsequent events showed the relevance and importance of the issues that had been raised and argued in courtrooms around the world.

PART FOUR

THE LONG ROAD HOME

CHAPTER FIFTEEN

A Grotian Moment

Nineteen forty-five. The end of World War II. It was a time of exultation and frustration, of myriad personal adjustments, of hope and weariness. It was also a time of determination that the mistakes of the past would not be repeated. Any claims the past might make on the present were to be put aside as quickly as possible. Chief among these was the League of Nations. Logic would suggest that the League simply pick up where it had left off before the war, with an expanded membership and, perhaps, expanded powers. It had maintained a skeleton wartime existence under Sean Lester, acting secretary-general, and a small, dedicated Supervisory Commission. Its new and scarcely used building in Geneva's Ariana Park could, with a modest expenditure, be made suitable for a resumption of League activities. Time, effort, and money could be saved by reviving the League of Nations and making it the center of international cooperation that its founders had hoped it would be.

This kind of reasoning was valid only in the abstract. At San Francisco, where the charter for the United Nations was being drafted in the spring of 1945, this reasoning carried no weight at all. The very name "League of Nations" was so fraught with controversy in the United States that any mention of U.S. membership in that organization was little more than a proclamation of political ineptitude. The Soviet Union, too, did not feel kindly toward the organization from which it had been expelled in 1939. Recognizing these political difficulties, the states that had been members of the League were willing to leave it behind along with the failures for which it had become both symbol and scapegoat. In April 1946 there was a final meeting of the League Assembly. Then arrangements were made for the United Nations to take over the League building and its contents. Besides the equipment necessary for operations on a worldwide scale—typewriters, telephones, and the like—there were tapestries, paintings, sculptures, and precious materials that had been the gifts of member states.[1] It was a huge material legacy from the days when the League had seemed the best hope for peace and justice in the world.

But this was not the League's only legacy. Unrecognized as such, because so widely accepted as the norm, was the ideological legacy from those days of hope. The very basis of the League's existence was the sovereign state. The same was true of the United Nations. Members came together in the League to cooperate for certain stated purposes, but the association was free, unforced, revocable at any time. The same was true of the United Nations. There were key differences between the two organizations, and it was on those differences that people pinned their hopes. But the ideological underpinning was the same. Neither in the planning stages at Dumbarton Oaks and Yalta nor in the drafting stage at San Francisco was there serious consideration of forming the new United Nations on any other basis than that of a free association of independent sovereign states. It was a powerful, subtle legacy that the League of Nations bequeathed to those who were determined to avoid its mistakes and failures.

A MOMENT IN CONTEXT

The three years that followed the establishment of the United Nations in 1945 were critical in the search for justice in international affairs. For this brief period, the crust of custom was broken. Vigorous ideas that had lain beneath the surface of international affairs came to the fore and found expression in forms that remained even after custom resumed its sway. In short order, the United Nations General Assembly affirmed the principles of law of the Nuremberg and Tokyo war crimes trials, declared that genocide was an international crime, and set in train the work that would give these ideas explicit and formal expression. Equally early in the life of the United Nations was the establishment of a Commission on Human Rights with the clear and urgent mandate to draft an international bill of rights.[2]

These were striking departures from anything the League of Nations might have done, or, indeed, anything that would have been possible in the interwar period. But that was precisely the point since it was, of course, the experiences of those years and of World War II that made such departures possible. The period right after World War II was what one scholar, in another context, has termed a Grotian moment. That is to say, it was a time when old ways of thought and old institutional arrangements were so obviously inadequate—as they had been in Grotius's time—that something different was required. In 1625 the Dutch scholar could only call for change. In 1945 and the years immediately following, people set change at the heart of some of their international arrangements. As it turned out, they got considerably more change than they had bargained for, but that was far in the future and could hardly have been foreseen. At the time, many observers thought that the early United Nations had not gone far enough in the direction needed if peace were to be preserved and justice somehow obtained.[3]

The immediate postwar period saw other achievements as well. The enormous labor of putting together a new international organization and getting it up and running was accomplished in those years. Even though elements of Cold War hostility were becoming evident on the Security Council, the organization's executive body, and in the much larger General Assembly, there was still an air of seriousness and purpose that was missing in later years. The delegates were engaged, and felt they were engaged, in a monumental effort whose outcome they could not see but were determined to influence. Theirs was not the hopeful world of 1919 but the damaged world of 1945. The veteran French diplomat Joseph Paul-Boncour, who had experienced the aftermath of both world wars, was struck by the difference. In 1945 he did not find "the enthusiasm and faith which animated our work in the great days of the League of Nations." Hanging like a cloud over the whole enterprise was the specter of failure: "The setback suffered by this organisation [the League] helps to undermine faith in the destinies of the other."[4] The tasks of the new organization were to repair the damage done to the idea of international cooperation, restore public confidence in international undertakings, and—above all—avoid failure. The framers of the United Nations Charter thought they had found a way to accomplish all this. They put their faith not in the new initiatives in the field of human rights and international criminal law but, rather, in the structural innovations they had built into the organization.

Their approach was twofold. First, permanent seats on the Security Council were assigned to five wartime allies: China, France, the Soviet Union, the United Kingdom, and the United States. Nowhere does the charter call these states the great powers, and nowhere does it say that these states have a veto over decisions taken by the council. What the charter says is that council decisions, except on matters of procedure, require seven affirmative

votes "including the concurring votes of the permanent members."[5] The
studied neutrality of this language fooled nobody. At the San Francisco conference where the final version of the charter was drafted, there were stormy
debates over the "great power veto," debates led by the smaller powers and
fueled by resentment at this arrogation of privilege.

With privilege, however, and with power, went responsibilities. Even the
grudging had to admit that in case of future aggression it was the states with
the most power that would have to furnish the most means to repel it. The
arrangement was, then, simply a recognition of what Andrei Gromyko, one
of the Soviet delegates at San Francisco, called an "obvious fact." The Security Council had to have the means necessary to maintain peace, and that required that the council have as permanent members "those countries which
have sufficient resources in men and material necessary for the successful
and effective fulfillment of its duties." Further, the effort to halt aggression
in the future, just as in the recent war, would require the cooperation of all
the countries with permanent seats: "Without such co-operation, it would
be impossible in the future to carry out the task of preserving peace."[6]

The privilege granted to the five permanent members of the Security
Council was thus an implicit recognition that, in the future, force might be
required to repel aggression and maintain peace. Elsewhere in the charter
the recognition of the role of force was made explicit. The framers' second
structural innovation was the one of which they were proudest and the one
that inspired the most confidence at the time. In case of a threat to peace,
members of the United Nations were to provide armed forces to the Security Council so that action could be taken to meet the threat. Further, in order to facilitate quick action, members were to "hold immediately available
national air-force contingents for combined international enforcement action." A Military Staff Committee was to be a permanent fixture of the organization to give expert advice and assistance to the Security Council in its
primary job of maintaining international peace and security.[7]

These arrangements spoke more of World War II, still being fought as
the charter was planned and written, than it did of any future need for collective action. That war was so much on people's minds that they projected
its conditions and characteristics into the future: a clearly defined enemy, a
specific goal (unconditional surrender), and allies thoroughly committed to
the attainment of that goal. If the planners had looked more deeply into the
inner conflicts of the war in which they were engaged, they might have anticipated the difficulties that immediately emerged in the United Nations.
All was not serene in the Allied camp, even when engaged in a desperate
struggle with the enemy at their doorstep. And if this was the case when an

ongoing war was compelling a choice between cooperation or disaster, what would be the situation when that compulsion was gone—when people had to agree on what constituted a threat to peace before they could agree on what to do about it? Small wonder that the arrangements in the United Nations Charter regarding the collective use of force quickly became little more than an expression of wishful thinking. Agreements for the furnishing of military forces were not forthcoming. No state reported air-force contingents being held in readiness. The Military Staff Committee finally stopped meeting altogether, since it was obvious that there was no use for their particular expertise.

The framers of the charter were not naive. Indeed, they thought of themselves as supremely realistic in the arrangements they had made to stop any future aggression. Looking at the League of Nations, they saw its reliance on reason and persuasion and forgot or glossed over why its provisions for the use of force had so seldom been called on. Now things would be different. Reason and persuasion, yes. But force when force was needed. It was this determination that the framers of the United Nations Charter tried to build into the structure of the new organization. The means they chose did not reflect naiveté so much as a misperception about the long-term effects of the total struggle in which they were then engaged. The rapid return to peacetime institutions and attitudes cut the ground out from under their expectations, and thus undercut the arrangements they had made for the collective use of force. But that is not all the story. Any study of the search for international justice in the postwar period must take into account the thinking that gave rise to these arrangements, since it was that thinking that helped set the context in which the search for justice would take place.

Planning for an international organization to replace the League of Nations had begun early in the war. In the U.S. State Department, the British Foreign Office, and in many private organizations as well, thought was given to the new organization's powers and structure. Planning was thus well along in the late summer of 1944 when representatives of four Allied powers met at Dumbarton Oaks in Washington, D. C., to work out a draft that could be submitted to other Allied governments for study and comment. The Dumbarton Oaks Proposals formed the basis for discussion and revision at the San Francisco Conference in the spring of 1945, in which the United Nations Charter was put into final form. The proposals make perfectly clear the thinking of those who labored over every word during long sessions at Dumbarton Oaks. They were thinking about war and the prevention of war.

The word *justice* does not even appear in the Dumbarton Oaks text except in the section dealing with the proposed International Court of Justice, and in that section it is a label, not a goal. What *does* appear again and again, like a mantra that will gain effectiveness through repetition, is the phrase "the maintenance of international peace and security." The first purpose of the organization is "to maintain international peace and security." Members of the organization are to see that nonmembers comply with its principles "so far as may be necessary for the maintenance of international peace and security." The General Assembly may consider, discuss, and recommend action on any matter "relating to the maintenance of international peace and security." The Security Council, the very name of which reflects the thinking of the time, is given primary responsibility "for the maintenance of international peace and security." The Council is to decide on measures to be taken "to maintain or restore international peace and security." Members of the organization undertake to contribute "to the maintenance of international peace and security" by cooperating with those measures.[8] The depth of longing, fear, and determination that gripped people planning for the postwar future can be gauged by the number of times this prayerful invocation is scattered throughout both the Dumbarton Oaks Proposals and the United Nations Charter. It is a poignant appeal. "O peace," it seems to say, "O security, come dwell among us and we will set our guard about you, and lay down our very lives and honor in your defense." The experience of war lay heavily on this generation.

But the experience of war could have other effects as well. This became evident at San Francisco. Delegations from many countries, and observers from many private organizations as well, made it clear that they viewed the Dumbarton Oaks Proposals as only a starting place. The proposals as they stood were an inadequate guide to the future. Where did they say anything about law? About justice? About the kind of world for which the war had been fought? Peace and security were all very well, but peace and security for what? "We have fought for justice and decency and for the fundamental freedoms and rights of man," said Jan Christian Smuts, the respected South African leader who had been one of the spiritual founders of the League of Nations. Smuts called for a charter for the new organization that would make it clear that "this was not a mere brute struggle of force between the nations but that for us, behind the mortal struggle, was the moral struggle, was the vision of the ideal, the faith in justice and the resolve to vindicate the fundamental rights of man, and on that basis to found a better, freer world for the future."[9]

The keynote for this broader approach to the drafting of the charter had been struck at the very beginning of the San Francisco Conference by Harry S. Truman. Struggling to fill the role of president of the United States, a role into which he had been thrust by the death of Franklin Roosevelt only thirteen days earlier, Truman seemed, in this speech, to reflect a little of his predecessor's oratorical skill. His customary plain speaking stretched itself to match this far-from-plain occasion. "The world," he said, "has experienced a revival of an old faith in the everlasting moral force of justice." Noting that the delegates at San Francisco represented "the overwhelming majority of all mankind," he spoke of the "powerful mandate" that had sent them there to prevent, "if human mind, heart and hope can prevent," a repetition of war. "If we should pay merely lip service to the inspiring ideals and then later do violence to simple justice, we would draw down upon us the bitter wrath of generations yet unborn. . . . The sacrifices of our youth today must lead, through your efforts, to the building for tomorrow of a mighty combination of nations founded upon justice for peace. Justice remains the greatest power on earth. To that tremendous power alone, will we submit."[10]

Many of the changes made in the Dumbarton Oaks Proposals at the San Francisco Conference reflected the beliefs and hopes of people such as Smuts and Truman. The preamble that was added to the charter spoke of fundamental human rights, of justice and law and freedom. The stated purposes of the organization were expanded to include the promotion and encouragement of respect for human rights and fundamental freedoms. Not only was peace to be preserved, it was to be preserved in accordance with the principles of justice and the law. Further, the whole operation was to be based on respect for the principle of equal rights and self-determination of peoples. Not included in the charter was the Bill of Rights that many wanted, but there was a clear understanding that the drafting of such a bill would be one of the first tasks of the new organization.[11]

The charter that emerged from the San Francisco Conference was thus significantly different from the Dumbarton Oaks Proposals. The changes that had been made created a document at odds with itself in the same way that the postwar international system was at odds with itself. The basic structure of both was determined by the primacy of the sovereign state, a fact that was reflected in the wariness of relationships, and in the organization's emphases. Liberty of action was the watchword. That liberty was limited only by agreement not to disrupt the peace of the world or infringe on the liberty of other states. Beyond that, a state was free to make agreements and to withdraw from those agreements. It was free to arrange its internal affairs as seemed best to it, and no other state had the right to interfere. For

years this had been at the very foundation of sovereignty, a principle invoked to reject criticism of internal affairs, much less intervention. In 1933
the principle had found expression in a formal treaty signed by most of the
countries in the Western hemisphere. "No state has the right to intervene
in the internal or external affairs of another," read Article 8 of the 1933
Convention on Rights and Duties of States, a treaty still in force when the
United Nations Charter was written. And Article 2.7 of the charter repeated the same basic idea: "Nothing contained in the present Charter
shall authorize the United Nations to intervene in matters which are essentially within the domestic jurisdiction of any state or shall require the
Members to submit such matters to settlement under the present Charter."
In other words: Hands off. Within its borders, the state is accountable only
to its own.[12]

Yet in the charter, as in the international system, there were signs of a different framework of values, one that did not begin and end with the sovereign state. The state was incorporated within this different framework, but
as agent, not as principal. The key word is *within*. As a principal, engaged in
brief, uneasy alliance with other principals, each state was the independent
arbiter of its own actions. The situation changed when each state was seen
as an agent, set with other states within a framework of values that provided
both goals for action and standards by which to judge the actions taken. Human rights. Fundamental freedoms. Justice. The obligations of law. These
signs of a world beyond the horizons of sovereignty, to which sovereignty
might contribute but which it could neither encompass nor deny, were far
too strong to be ignored at San Francisco.

So the charter went forth, astride two horses, as it were. People were familiar with state-centered values and were comfortable with them. Yet, essential as they were to the functioning of both the international system and
this new international organization, they had somehow managed to inspire
two horrendous world wars. So, obviously, there had to be something else.
For the drafters of the Dumbarton Oaks Proposals and for many at San
Francisco, that "something else" was a prompt and, if necessary, a forceful
response to any act of aggression or threat to peace. This seemed more vital
than ever with the revelation of the destructive power of atomic weapons
in the summer of 1945. The consequences of a third world war were now
too terrible for most people to contemplate. They clung to the forceful-
response provisions of the charter as to a life preserver that would keep them
from being swept into that dreadful abyss. None of this, however, challenged the centrality of the state or the primacy of state-centered values. It
simply attempted to preserve a hard-won status quo.

What, then, about those other values, the ones dismissed by many as soft, or irrelevant, or so much empty rhetoric? People were not sure about them, although they, too, were familiar coin. They were, of course, of very ancient lineage, far more so than state sovereignty. Their lineage could be traced all the way back to ancient Greece, if not beyond. Wasn't it Aristotle who had said that justice was the perfect virtue? And then there were those equally ancient religious assertions of the essential worth of individual human beings. Even if religion were put aside, there were still a number of highly regarded secular declarations of the rights of human beings on which to rely. And yet . . . And yet . . . With those references to a different system of values tucked into the United Nations Charter, now what? Internationally speaking, what did those values mean? There was argument enough about their meaning in a domestic context. How then could they be transferred into a system with different institutions and modes of organization? Did those values, admirable as they were, have any meaning at all in a system of sovereign states, and, if so, how was that meaning to be applied?

In the three years immediately following the end of World War II there were strong movements, both inside and outside the United Nations, to answer those questions. It was this determination that created a moment, a brief Grotian moment, when possibilities for fundamental changes were seized and acted on. Memories of the war were still fresh. There was general, if short-lived, agreement about the lessons to be drawn from that war beyond that of avoiding at all costs another Munich-like surrender to the demands of an aggressor. The lacks that the war had made clear had to be addressed, and provisions to fill what had turned out to be gaping holes in the conventional system of self-help and reciprocity had to be made.

It was obvious now that some acts were criminal acts in an international sense. The implications of this for the future were not at all clear, but there was, in this brief period, a drive to consolidate and expand on the work that had been done for the Nuremberg and Tokyo trials. Related to this was a sense of urgency about human rights. They needed to be spelled out. It needed to be made clear that they were universal, that they were the birthright of every human being. How this was to be done, whether they should be enforceable in a court yet to be established, whether they should include rights to be demanded *from* governments, as well as rights of protection *against* governments—all of this was yet to be worked out. The point is that in this Grotian moment there was a ferment of ideas and a sense of possibilities that was not to be repeated for many years. Before memories faded, before Cold War tensions diverted thought and paralyzed action, the long effort to place and define justice in an international context was picked up, given new life, and set in new forms.[13]

SEIZING THE MOMENT

The link between international justice and international peace had been exceptionally strong for many years. Sometimes, as in the period before World War I, justice was seen as the prerequisite for peace. It was felt that only if justice were the arbiter of the disputes that were bound to occur among nations could there be any chance for peace. The Permanent Court of Arbitration was the chosen instrument for this approach. Through a just resolution of conflict, peace would be secured. The voluntary nature of the process, and the exceptions made for questions of national honor and vital interests, insured the irrelevancy of the court in matters that could—and did—lead to war. Failure did not sever the link between justice and peace, however. The link remained so strong that in the interwar period the two, for all practical purposes, blended into one.

Peace was not simply a goal in the years between the two world wars. Peace was the very form that justice had to take in an international system wherein war had become so destructive that it had to be avoided at all costs. This was the lesson drawn from World War I, in which the memory of the thousands who fell for a few feet of muddy ground haunted those in power. This helps explain their extraordinary efforts to keep the peace and their reluctance to use force against Japan in Manchuria, Germany in the Rhineland, Italy in Ethiopia. It also helps explain their extraordinary efforts to provide means through which conflicts might be resolved: mediation, good offices, commissions of inquiry, arbitration, temporary international administration of disputed areas, and—the achievement that, in their view, crowned them all—adjudication through the Permanent Court of International Justice. The success of some of these methods has been detailed in this study. Their failure is well known.

Where did all this leave international justice at the close of World War II? It still seemed to be, as Aristotle had said, the perfect virtue in that it incorporated abundant possibilities that could be seized and acted on. And people moved quickly to seize them. Three separate lines of development can be distinguished in the rush of postwar plans and ideas. The first retained the strong tie with peace that had been prominent since the end of the nineteenth century. This line of development found its basic expression in the United Nations Charter, the whole thrust of which was to keep the peace, preferably by the methods that had been developed between the wars, but if not by them, then by force. Here, too, as in the interwar period, a court was seen as the crown of efforts for the peaceful resolution of conflicts between states. Here, too, as in the past, states proved reluctant to take serious disputes to a court, in this case the new International Court of Justice, which was to replace the old Permanent Court. Nonetheless, the court was there, an institutional expression of the close and apparently unbreakable link between justice and peace.

The second line of development derived from long-standing concerns about social justice. Many possible objects of concern were bundled within this overarching concept, including the one that came to be emphasized in the immediate postwar period: rights. The strong link that was formed between justice and rights found its basic expression in the Universal Declaration of Human Rights, approved by the United Nations General Assembly in December 1948. This pairing of justice and rights, like the pairing of justice and peace, created a relationship in which first one, then the other was given emphasis. Sometimes justice was seen as the progenitor of rights: if justice were done, then people would be granted the rights due to them. At other times, as in the Universal Declaration, justice was made to depend on the recognition that human beings had certain "equal and inalienable rights" to which, without exception, they were entitled. This recognition was presented as the necessary basis for justice, and for freedom and peace as well.

The relationship of justice and rights was thus one of mutual interaction, so close in operation that the boundaries of the two were in constant movement, now overlapping, now drawing apart from the pressure of the needs and preoccupations of the times. In the interwar period, the rights and protection of minorities was an ongoing concern for the League of Nations. In the same period, the International Labour Organization focused on the rights and protection of workers. Both efforts helped establish the legitimacy of international concern in the field of social justice. This concern had the potential to shake sovereignty to its foundations, but the drafters of the Universal Declaration were very careful not to rouse this particular sleeping bear. Their comprehensive listing of rights to which everyone was entitled was not accompanied by any enforcement provisions. Indeed, the declaration was not even a treaty that states might sign. It was just what it said, a declaration, and it was offered as "a common standard of achievement" to which all might aspire, states and peoples alike.[14]

The third line of development in the immediate postwar period was the linking of justice with law in a way that was intended to be not ad hoc, not specific to a particular need or situation as in the Nuremberg and Tokyo trials, but permanent. This line of development found its basic expression in

the Convention on the Prevention and Punishment of the Crime of Genocide, adopted by the General Assembly in December 1948. Unlike the Universal Declaration, the convention *was* a treaty, opened for signature and
ratification by sovereign states, with all that that implied about their formal
commitment to its provisions. The convention's definition of genocide
is clearly indebted to the definitions of crimes against humanity in the
Nuremberg and Tokyo charters, as is the concept of genocide as an international crime. Under this convention, actions intended to destroy whole
groups of people could no longer shelter under the protective cover of "internal affairs," beyond international reach. The key provision that made
specific the tie between justice and law was the one that stated that persons
charged with genocide "shall be tried." Not "may be tried" but "shall be
tried by a competent Tribunal of the State in the territory of which the act
was committed." The link here is to law as it is generally understood in a domestic context, which is to say, law that can be enforced against a law-
breaker, with or without the consent of the party so charged.

   This provision went even further, and in so doing, made an extraordinary
jump from a national to an international base for enforceable law. Given the
prevailing framework of state-based thought, and given the fact that the
convention was an agreement between states, this jump was both difficult
and unlikely. Only in this brief Grotian moment, when war memories were
fresh and national egos slightly subdued, was such a provision possible.
Even then, the wording that emerged from the drafting battles in various
committees was cautious in the extreme. Beyond the trial in a national tribunal for persons charged with genocide was another possibility: that of
trial in an international tribunal. And here caution hastened to add a limiting qualification: "such international penal tribunal as may have jurisdiction
with respect to those Contracting Parties which shall have accepted its jurisdiction."[15]

   Even in a moment of possibility, this hedged and tentative mention of an
international penal court was the best that could be wrung from states concerned to maintain their prerogatives and the primacy of their national institutions. The untiring efforts of people such as Donnedieu de Vabres and
Sir Hartley Shawcross could not in 1948 push states further toward the establishment of a permanent international penal tribunal. Both men worried
that, without such a court, the Genocide Convention would be yet another
of those high-sounding, meaningless pieces of rhetoric in which international institutions seemed to specialize. Similar fears were expressed about
the Universal Declaration of Human Rights by the highly respected British
scholar Sir Hersch Lauterpacht.[16] Further, it was clear by the end of 1948

that the UN Charter provisions were not working as planned. Neither the standoff in Berlin nor the fighting in Indonesia, to take only two examples, was yielding to United Nations efforts to achieve a negotiated solution. The cooperative behavior on which the organization depended seemed to be more remote than ever. National goals were in the ascendant once again, with the United Nations as a forum where they could be proclaimed. Three years had passed since the end of World War II. The Grotian moment was over.

The events that, after 1948, undercut the expectations of the planners of the United Nations have been thoroughly studied. Here it is only necessary to mention them as a kind of bleak coda to the innovative efforts of the preceding three years. Cold War tensions between the Soviet bloc and the West hamstrung the Security Council and turned the General Assembly into an accusation arena. "Red-hunting" in the secretariat by U.S. authorities demoralized the UN's administrative body. Decolonization struggles in Southeast Asia and Africa, plus continuing battles between Nationalists and Communists in China, made clear the existence of wars beyond the reach or competence of the United Nations. Even the Korean War, which broke out in June 1950, was not the triumph for collective security measures that had been planned. The UN-sponsored international response to North Korea's incursion into South Korea was so dominated by U.S. troops and equipment that the UN part of the operation began to seem like a footnote—and has been treated that way in many subsequent accounts. Further, both at the time and later, there were fierce disagreements over defining North Korea's actions as aggression or, conversely, as part of a long national struggle to free Korea from colonial domination and unify the country. A third point of view, held especially by many top U.S. officials, was that the Korean War was a war to stop the spread of Communist influence in Southeast Asia.[17]

None of these complications had been foreseen by those who planned the United Nations as the institutional expression of a collective will to maintain international peace and security. The lessons they had drawn from World War II simply did not fit the situations that confronted the UN in the latter half of the twentieth century. Even if that organization had had the resources and capabilities that had been planned for it, the difficulties of coping with these events would have been great. The years after 1948 made it increasingly clear that, not only were the resources and capabilities of the United Nations inadequate for the many tasks it faced, but the very presumption on which it was based was false. The charter's assumed commonality of purpose did not exist. As Dag Hammarskjöld, the UN's most eloquent secretary-general, put it in 1958, "we are still far from being prepared for world community."[18] The interdependence of states was a fact of international life, but the shared feelings and purposes of a world community were yet to come.

For Hammarskjöld, this gap between interdependence and community was a cause for determination, not despair. Some had certainly despaired of the fractured, tension-ridden organization that, in 1953, he had agreed to serve. And *serve* is the key word. For Hammarskjöld, *serve* was not just a verb. It was a commitment as well. Until his death in 1961, he devoted his intelligence, his administrative skills, and his formidable capacity for work to the service of the United Nations. He saw the organization as "a bridge which may help us to pass safely over this period of transition," the transition from the interdependence that already was to the community that was yet to be. Further, said Hammarskjöld, since justice was one of the principles undergirding the United Nations, and the maintenance of conditions for justice was one of its purposes, the organization could be the very vehicle to achieve that long-sought goal, the "rule of justice in international life."[19]

With all his faith in the future and in the organization he served, not even Dag Hammarskjöld could see the developments that lay ahead or the multiple ways in which "justice in international life" would be defined and used. The effects of the Grotian moment did not disappear when the moment did. Too many changes had been made in concepts and institutions for them to disappear altogether when national feelings again rose to the fore. What de Vabres, Shawcross, Lauterpacht, and others could not foresee was how long it would take for these changes to make any change in the rigid system of states in which they were embedded. The process by which the work of the Grotian moment effected any change in the system itself was subtle, incremental, and very slow indeed. But it went on. Throughout the following years the process continued. By century's end initial steps had been taken toward the enforcement of peace, international protection of human rights, and the establishment of courts for the prosecution of international crimes. These steps, limited as they were by domestic measures, were far beyond what could have been imagined by the most optimistic in the three-year period following World War II. By continuing efforts begun at The Hague in 1899, by forging and strengthening institutional links between justice and peace, justice and rights, and justice and law, people in that period contributed more than they knew toward the future. In that future, the concept of justice was to be so elaborated and so often appealed to by so many groups that it outpaced all rivals and became the first, the primary, the universal value in a diverse and fractious world.

CHAPTER SIXTEEN

A Home for the Heart

An observer looking back from the end of the twentieth century would surely be struck by the century's violence and by the human upheavals and suffering strewn across its years. There might be, too, a recognition of the damage wreaked on the environment both by wars and by the heedless pursuit of short-term gains and productivity. Less obvious would be a different pursuit, the one that has been the subject of this book. In good times and bad, whatever the focus of activity, no matter the cultural or economic base, there was throughout the century a steady pursuit of justice, however defined. A case could be made that the violence of the century was, in fact, a direct result of these efforts to achieve justice by groups or states that saw no other way than force to achieve the goals that they themselves had defined as just.

The focus of this book has been on the century-long efforts to change that situation by changing the base from which justice is perceived. Instead of a narrow, self-regarding base, an international one. Instead of definitions valid only within one small, self-defined group, definitions on which there could be wide, if not universal, agreement. The efforts have been far too numerous to be set out in detail in any but a multivolume work. The goal here has been to pick those that illustrate the kinds of efforts that have been made, to show the conditions that both stimulated those efforts and set obstacles in their path, and to trace the results of this interaction through time. The crucial period is not the second half of the century, with its prominent and much-studied initiatives but the first half, when the matrix within which later efforts would unfold was given lasting shape. In addition to helping explain the past fifty years, those early years determined the ways used and the directions taken in the latter half of the century as people have continued their quest to define and achieve international justice.

The work of that critically important early period was, in many ways, a continuation of the work begun by the delegates to the Hague Conference in 1899. They, in turn, saw themselves as continuing a work that had been begun even earlier. The ceremony in Delft that was mentioned in the prologue was intended to do more than pay a graceful tribute to the Dutch scholar Hugo Grotius. It was also intended as a reminder that the work that Grotius had begun in the seventeenth century was a work in progress. The tasks of exploration of the conditions for a just war, determination of rules for its conduct, and consideration of the implications of these for international relations in general were not finished when Grotius completed his systematic and learned examination in 1625. This work had to be picked up by each generation and set within the changing context of that generation's times. For Grotius, the context had been the Thirty Years' War and the exceptional brutalities of the scattered and bitter conflicts in that war.

The delegates of 1899 saw themselves as living in more fortunate times. They had the good fortune and the opportunity to concentrate on matters more suited to the general aspects of Grotius's thought than to his thoughts on war, although they, too, had to treat the rules of armed conflict. They did not see attention to considerations of war as their primary task, however. Their task at The Hague was to reduce the risk of war by devising means for the just settlement of disputes between states. Here Grotius could provide inspiration but not guidance. His discussions of such settlement methods as mediation and arbitration were replete with the classical and biblical references expected in the seventeenth century but which, at the end of the nineteenth, were neither useful nor impressive. Cicero and Saint Paul had lost their authority in international affairs. The delegates at The Hague relied, instead, on the examples of recent successful ad hoc arbitrations when it came to the accomplishment of which they were the most proud, the establishment of the Permanent Court of Arbitration. Here, they felt, was the Grotian vision of justice and peace given an institutional form that was fit for the needs of the times. In this compelling vision and not in his somewhat tedious discussions of war lay Grotius's true greatness.[1]

Splitting the thought of Grotius's masterwork, *De Jure Belli*, in this way would not only have been shocking to its author. It would have been almost incomprehensible. For Grotius, the work was one integrated whole, each part related to and necessary for the other parts, and all of it held in perfect balance by the will of God and the laws of nature. To perceive that balance and the relationships that could maintain it was the task of human beings, a task Grotius had carried out to the best of his ability. That ability was truly formidable, as later generations were to affirm. Then, having paid due tribute, they proceeded to drop both God and the laws of nature from international affairs. They entered the twentieth century with the practice of states as their guide. By then, too, the idea of a just war had been dropped or merged into the acknowledged right of states to make war for reasons of state.

Grotius's thought was not so easily dismissed, however. Much of his work on the laws of war and peace, sprawling though it might be and sometimes contradictory, can be seen as the base for modern thought about international affairs. It is illuminating to compare the work of this seventeenth-century scholar with the assumptions that underlay the efforts in the twentieth century to place justice in an international setting and give it a presence there. These assumptions shifted back and forth through the Grotian terrain, now accepting, now rejecting aspects of Grotius's thought, as the changing circumstances of war and peace gave this or that aspect renewed relevance. From 1899, just-war concepts were passé until the violence and frequency of national-interest wars brought them back into the mainstream of thought. Similarly, natural-law standards by which the actions of states and individuals might be judged were thrust aside until the unbridled cruelties of the '30s and '40s made them seem not only useful but essential if any standards were to be maintained. In the latter half of the twentieth century even the Divine was brought back into international affairs. Grotius would have recognized this claim for other-worldly authority, and he could have predicted some of its less-than-happy worldly consequences.

What Grotius could not possibly have predicted was a shift that took place throughout the twentieth century and that affected all efforts to give justice an international base. This was a shift in the source of legitimacy. For Grotius that source was in the past, in biblical and classical texts and in the sayings and actions recorded there. These had so little resonance in international affairs in the twentieth century that they were not even considered. Increasingly, as the century wore on, the source of legitimacy for thought and action became the public. The steps through which this happened, the ways in which public opinion was discerned or expressed and then brought to bear, how this was part of a general democratizing trend that affected even the elite world of international affairs—all this is worthy of study, and the study would surely fill another book. The most that can be done here is to provide anecdotal evidence of the trend. The trend would have surprised Hugo Grotius as much as it annoyed the traditional diplomats at the Hague

Conference of 1899. For years the general assumption about international affairs was that they would be conducted by the elite: aristocrats in Grotius's day, diplomatic and legal experts in the periods up to and including the twentieth century. This being the case, how could the public be involved? Why did they want to be involved, anyway? What was it the public wanted?

By the end of the twentieth century it had become clear that, in some direct or indirect way, the public was going to be involved in international affairs—or at least the portion of the public that was interested in such matters. What would take many more years to work out was how the desires of the public could be fitted into the existing framework of international affairs, or, perhaps, how that framework could be modified to accommodate and express the public's desires.

GOING HOME

Thomas King was eleven years old in 1932 when he wrote a letter to a much-heralded disarmament conference meeting in Geneva under the auspices of the League of Nations. "I understand the Disarmament Conference is bogged down," he wrote. "I have a proposition. Take away the guns of those who want to fight at any price, let them fight with rotten eggs, tomatoes, maybe grapefruit, or popguns."[2]

This letter was put in a glass case with others at the end of a corridor in the Disarmament Building, placed so its message could be read through the glass. It became one of the sights of the conference and provided one of the few occasions for smiles. As the days went on and failure became ever more certain, the occasions for smiling dropped to zero. Much as the delegates might agree with the girl who wrote from Greece that "the lives of animals and plants are sacred, and yet war destroys everything. This is unjust,"[3] they seemed unable to agree on measures that would reassure that little girl, or Thomas King, or any of the millions upon millions who had sent messages to Geneva.

This number is not an exaggeration. The messages came in such abundance that they overwhelmed the staff at the disarmament conference and overflowed the space that had been allotted for them. Thousands of the messages were put into the display case along with Thomas King's letter. Trucks were needed to haul the rest away for storage. There were petitions, telegrams, personal letters, and copies of resolutions and declarations that had been passed by various organizations. Some were painstakingly handwritten, some were printed and bound, some had elaborate seals, some were rolled and tied with ribbon, still others were in specially made cases bearing symbols of peace. They came from Japan, Germany, Austria, Italy, Romania, France, The Netherlands, Belgium, the United Kingdom, Canada, the United States, Australia, Bulgaria, Spain, New Zealand, Switzerland, Czechoslovakia, Sweden, South Africa, the Argentine Republic, Hungary, Portugal, Jamaica, Poland, Yugoslavia, Lithuania, Denmark, Uruguay, the Irish Free State, and Norway, and from organizations such as the International Federation of Teachers or the Women's International League for Peace and Freedom with members in many countries. Not content with informing the conference how many members they represented, many of the groups had gathered individual signatures on the petitions—eight million, for example, on the petition from the Women's International Organizations. But smallness did not stop people from letting their opinions be known. The pupils at Ash Valley School in Kansas and the members of the Rotary Club of Canyon, Texas, were right there along with the big veterans' organizations, church groups, and social democratic parties.[4]

This tremendous outpouring was an embarrassment for the conference delegates. What were they to do with it? How should they respond? The days were long past when they could try to keep their sessions private, as the delegates at the 1899 conference had tried to do. Private sessions had also been the inclination in the early days of the League of Nations, but the pressure for openness was too great. Most League meetings had quickly been opened to the press and the public. For the career diplomats and government officials accredited as delegates to the disarmament conference in 1932, that was as far as openness could or should go. Some of the demands of the petitioners to the conference were beyond all reason, and, surely, beyond the bounds of possibility. Without in the least understanding the technical difficulties involved, some petitioners called for complete, immediate, multilateral disarmament. Others seemed to think that the disarmament conference should address all international problems or even remake the whole international system along new lines. One group called for "replacing force by justice" in the settlement of international disputes. Another called for "the renunciation of the old-fashioned idea of the absolute sovereignty of States." And, in a message particularly upsetting to officialdom, another group wanted the public to be a part of the whole negotiating process: "We demand that the people shall have a share in the election of the delegates."[5]

To the delegates at the disarmament conference, this sweeping approach was a clear indication of the unsuitability of the public for the tricky business of negotiation. The public wanted to move from the darkness of suspicion and fear to the brightness of day in one big jump, when all that could possibly be hoped from such a conference was to light a few lamps in the dark. The committee that was appointed to consider the public's relation to the conference made soothing noises about the importance of the public and its petitions and hopes but came down hard on the side of officialdom all the same. As the committee put it, the conference, after all, was composed "of the plenipotentiary representatives of Governments," and it was hardly suitable that private persons, whatever their personal standing, should either address the conference or have any official part in it whatsoever, "even in the form of petitions." It was decided that they should list and summarize the petitions in the conference's journal and hold a special, definitely unofficial meeting at which a few private individuals might speak.[6]

By the end of the twentieth century, "private persons" were an important part of many international negotiations, so much so that a new worry was generated about the increasing role of nongovernmental organizations in what were still negotiations on behalf of governments. The glimpse that has been given here of the disarmament conference of 1932 suggests the obstacles that have had to be overcome in the intervening years before the private sector was even listened to, much less invited to give advice and provide drafts of agreements for the official negotiators to use. Part of this late opening to the private sector springs from the need for expert advice on increasingly technical subjects of negotiation. But part is also due to the prolonged pressure on international elites to be—or at least to appear—less elite and to let the public know what is going on while it is going on. The opening of the first session of the United Nations General Assembly is a case in point.

In many ways, the League of Nations had seemed remote from the public, a place where diplomats made speeches to advance the interests of their own states and to impress their bosses back home. The founders of the United Nations were determined to avoid giving that impression. The opening session of the General Assembly in London was scripted with the public in mind. The introductory speeches were to be broadcast, which meant that the proceedings had to be tailored to the requirements of the radio networks of 1946. Each official delegate received a copy of the "Programme for the Opening Meeting of the General Assembly," which spelled out not only *what* would happen but exactly *when* it would happen—the "when" being of crucial importance for radio. The program announced that "the first session of the General Assembly shall be convoked for 3:45 P.M. on Thursday, 10 January 1946." Then, allowing for some slippage and for the inevitable late arrival of delegates not familiar with London streets, the tightly crafted session was to get under way:

"It is the present intention that the meeting shall be formally called to order at 4 P.M. and that the meeting shall actually start at 4:03 P.M. precisely, so as to allow radio commentators three minutes to 'build up' their stories." Then the acting president of the assembly was to give his speech, followed by the appearance and speech of Clement Attlee, prime minister of the United Kingdom. "It is probable that his speech will not take more than a quarter of an hour, thus enabling it to fit into the radio timetable."[7] Official awareness of the public had come of age, with some results perhaps not foreseen by its most fervent advocates.

As late as 1946, however, the three basic issues raised by some of the petitioners in 1932 had not been resolved. The role of the public in international affairs, the extent of state sovereignty, and the replacement of force by justice were still live issues. By the end of the twentieth century they still pressed for attention and resolution. Broadcasting the opening session of the General Assembly was a long step forward from keeping the public at arm's length, as at the Hague Conference in 1899 and at the League of Nations in its early days. It was also a long step away from direct public involvement in the choice of international decisionmakers, as one group of petitioners had demanded in 1932. There were no easy or obvious answers to the problem of public participation in these affairs of state, affairs that involved people, like it or not, at a personal level. One method that was tried by the United States government when the United Nations Charter was at the drafting stage was to invite representatives of a number of private organizations to the San Francisco Conference to act as consultants to the official U.S. delegation. By the end of the century, the role of consultant seemed to be the most that governments would grant and the least that the public would accept.

The issue of sovereignty in the international system revolves around the questions of extent. How much is too much? How little is too little? How much sovereignty is consistent with the preservation of the system itself? How little is consistent with the preservation of each individual state? One group of petitioners in 1932 had called on officials to renounce the "old-fashioned idea of the absolute sovereignty of States." Much has been said in this study about sovereignty and its effect on efforts to define and achieve international justice, but official renunciation of the principle has not been part of the story. It was hardly to be expected that the many new states that have entered the international system since 1932 would willingly give up what they had so recently gained, nor were long-established states any more eager to give sovereignty away. What *was* part of the story in the twentieth century was the way efforts at defining and achieving international justice interacted with classical views of the state to make "absolute sovereignty" much less absolute than it was at the beginning of the century. But the question of extent has not been resolved. The interaction process continues, as do its effects on both concepts of sovereignty and concepts of justice.

And, finally, *justice*—that elastic, all-purpose term that has proved to be central in the history of the twentieth century. As a rhetorical device, as a call to unspecified action, the term has no equal. Thus British prime minister Clement Attlee in the broadcast of the opening moments of the new United Nations General Assembly in 1946 stated: "Finally, let us be clear as to what is our ultimate aim. It is not just the negation of war, but the creation of a world of security and freedom, of a world which is governed by justice and the moral law. We desire to assert the pre-eminence of right over might and the general good against selfish and sectional aims."[8]

This study has shown how difficult and tortuous has been the road from grand and vague references such as this to specific international instruments and actions that might lead to "a world which is governed by justice and the moral law." This study has also shown how, despite these difficulties, people have persisted in their efforts to define and achieve justice—that fervently invoked principle—and what changes have occurred in outlook and achievements during the first fifty years of the twentieth century. This effort might well seen as a struggle to move away from a world where wars have to be fought on behalf of justice to a different world, a just world, where, because justice does indeed govern, wars are no longer necessary.

As for what it is the public wants—a question that has bedeviled international policymakers at least since crowds of peace advocates sat themselves down at the doorstep of the 1899 conference—the question cannot be answered in the form in which it is usually put. There are too many publics, and their desires are too diverse, changeable, and, often, contradictory. One public that has been left entirely out of this account is the one that marches to war with high enthusiasm for the cause, whatever that cause might be. This particular public does not camp on the doorsteps of international bodies. For the most part it has little use for international bodies since they are so frequently concerned to dampen down the fires of war and decrease armaments. On the other hand, the causes for which this belligerent public is willing to fight are almost always presented as just causes, and the ensuing battles are portrayed, and seen, as battles for justice.

So justice enters the discussion even here; at a high level of generality, it is fair to say that "the public" wants justice. How that goal is to be defined and achieved is, of course, one of the major questions of the future as it was a major question in the twentieth century. This study has shown how the efforts to achieve that goal in the critical first fifty years of the century have succeeded in two significant ways: they have given the concept of justice an international dimension, and they have given it an institutional presence in international affairs. There have also been conceptual refinements. In the international sphere, justice has been linked to other goals in ways that direct its development along the three different paths mentioned in the previous chapter—peace, rights, and law. To review and emphasize:

The first and oldest link is between justice and peace. The relationship is close, but it is also flexible. At any given period one or the other may predominate. From the 1899 Hague Conference through World War I, justice was seen as the prerequisite for peace. From the end of that war until the beginning of World War II, peace was given priority as the necessary precondition for justice. This see-saw of priorities continued through the remaining years of the century right up to the present, but whichever goal predominates, the connection between justice and peace remains unbroken.

The second link is between justice and rights. The experiences of World War II revealed the inadequacy of international measures for the protection of human beings. So inadequate were the measures and so searing were the experiences that, in the immediate postwar period, rights came to be identified specifically as human rights. The relationship between justice and rights, like that between justice and peace, is a close one, with permeable boundaries and shifting emphases. Whether rights are seen as a deserved matter of justice or the requirements of justice entail an emphasis on rights, the connection between the two is now exceptionally strong.

The third link is between justice and law. This is a complicated relationship with a checkered history. The concept of law, when placed within an international context, changed radically in the twentieth century. In broad terms, the change has been a movement away from a system of voluntary compliance with international rules toward a system in which those rules can be enforced. The link between justice and *enforceable* law was made in the internationally authorized war crimes trials following World War II and given a peacetime stamp of approval in the Genocide Convention. Then, while states continued to pay lip service to the idea, they let the relationship effectively lapse until near the end of the century, when events in the former Yugoslavia forced a reconsideration of how justice could be served through law. By the end of the century the link between justice and law was effective chiefly in the area of international crimes. The states continued to resist it elsewhere, and its application in the field of international crimes has been highly selective. It seems clear, however, that the link between justice and law in the international sphere will endure and perhaps be strengthened in the years to come.

The hypothetical observer mentioned at the beginning of this chapter might or might not perceive the pursuit of justice that characterized the twentieth century and formed the subject of this study. That observer would, however, surely notice how, in the latter half of the century, justice came to be defined in astonishingly broad terms. Even a cursory look at the international instruments that originated in the United Nations General Assembly during those fifty years will demonstrate the range of human desires that can be encompassed in the term *justice*. Justice for children. Justice for women. Justice for the aged, the infirm, the disabled, the mentally retarded. Justice for those unfairly imprisoned as well as for those who have committed crimes. Justice for those who struggle for self-determination and for those who are discriminated against because of race, religion, or ethnic origin. Justice not only for individuals but for whole peoples. Justice for states, most especially for states that are economically disadvantaged. Justice for the environment and for the whole range of life on earth. Justice for the generations yet to come, so that the earth that is passed down to them is not ruined by greed nor devastated by war. Justice, in fact, for everyone and everything on almost every conceivable ground[9]

This list is exactly what it seems, a list of wishes that, short of Paradise, will never be granted or fulfilled. But that is just the point, and it is the final point of this study. The list expresses human longings in a particularly poignant and detailed way. It is not the perfect city of God, nor yet the secularist's perfect society, but it is an expression of the persistent human desire for perfection. By the end of the twentieth century a brief resting place for this desire had been found on the international level. Through long years of struggle, the idea of justice had been elaborated and refined until, by century's end, whether from a religious or a secular perspective, justice had become the heart's true earthly home.

Introduction

1. The International Criminal Tribunal for the Former Yugoslavia (ICTY) was established by the United Nations Security Council in 1993. The first international tribunal for the prosecution of war crimes since the International Military Tribunals at Nuremberg and Tokyo following World War II had for its mandate the prosecution of those "responsible for serious violations of international humanitarian law committed in the territory of the former Yugoslavia since 1991." This included the many different conflicts generated by the break-up of the former Socialist state and covered the war over Kosovo as well. Authorization for the establishment of the ICTY by the council was Chapter VII of the UN Charter and a finding by the council that the situation in the former Yugoslavia constituted a threat to international peace and security.

In 1994, the government of the African state of Rwanda, then with a seat on the UN Security Council, took the initiative in persuading the council that the widespread slaughter of the Tutsi minority by the Hutus in Rwanda also constituted a threat to international peace and security. The outcome was the council's establishment in 1994 of the International Criminal Tribunal for Rwanda (ICTR). Unlike the tribunal for the former Yugoslavia, which took up quarters in The Hague—home to international courts and events discussed in this book—the ICTR has its seat in Arusha, Tanzania. Its prosecutorial mandate covers persons responsible for serious violations of humanitarian law committed in 1994 in Rwandan territory or by Rwandan citizens in neighboring states. The fact that the conflict in Rwanda was not an international conflict gives the establishment of the ICTR special significance.

Many people saw the establishment of these two international criminal tribunals as steps on the way to a permanent international tribunal with power to prosecute violations of international humanitarian law wherever they took place. Since the war crimes trials in Nuremberg and Tokyo, this has been both a long-sought and fiercely resisted goal—subjects covered in this book. The Rome Statute, intended to establish such a court, was signed in 1998 by 120 states (not including the United States). As of April 2002, the statute had finally been ratified by the number of states necessary to bring it into existence. The first prosecutor of the ICTY has written revealingly of the difficulties of getting even that more limited institution up and running. See Richard Goldstone, *For Humanity: Reflections of a War Crimes Investigator* (New Haven: Yale University Press, 2000). William W. Horne, "The Real Trial of the Century," in *War Crimes: The Legacy of Nuremberg*, ed. Belinda Cooper (New York: TV Books, 1999), 120–38, provides useful commentary on the problems of international criminal prosecution.

Prologue

1. Hugo Grotius, *De jure belli ac pacis* (1625). The standard English translation is no. 3 in the Classics of International Law series, ed. James Brown Scott, vol. 2, *On*

the Law of War and Peace, trans. Francis W. Kelsey (Oxford: Clarendon, 1925). A less formal translation, from which quotations in this text are taken, is *The Rights of War and Peace*, trans. A. C. Campbell (Washington, D.C.: M. Walter Dunne, 1901).

2. Andrew D. White, *Autobiography of Andrew Dickson White* (New York: Century, 1905), 2:260. White was head of the United States delegation to the conference.

3. Grotius, *Rights*, bk. 3, chap. 20, sec. 11, para. 4. An account of the ceremony at the Nieuwe Kerk can be found in *Proceedings at the Laying of a Wreath on the Tomb of Hugo Grotius* (The Hague: Martinus Nijhoff, 1899). The agreement for the establishment of the Permanent Court of Arbitration was part of a more general treaty, the Convention for the Pacific Settlement of International Disputes. Because of the similarity of names, it is easy to confuse the Permanent Court of Arbitration, established 1899, with the Permanent Court of International Justice, established 1921. Article 15 of the 1899 convention sets out a critical difference: "International arbitration has for its object the settlement of differences between States by judges of their own choice, and on the basis of respect for law." In other words, the arbiters serve at the pleasure of the disputants and for that dispute only. The bench of the Permanent Court of International Justice, on the other hand, was composed of judges who served for nine years after being elected by the assembly and the council of the League of Nations. Here was a standing institution, available at all times to states involved in a dispute, as is its successor, the International Court of Justice, established 1945. For more on the context of this approach to dispute settlement, see Francis Anthony Boyle, *Foundations of World Order: The Legalist Approach to International Relations, 1898–1921* (Durham, N.C.: Duke University Press, 1999).

4. The diary of Andrew D. White, chief U.S. delegate, is the source for this behind-the-scenes look at the conference. It was included in White's *Autobiography*, 2:250–354, and was also published separately as *The First Hague Peace Conference* (Boston: World Peace Foundation, 1912). The work of the conference, in both plenary and committee sessions, can be followed in *The Proceedings of the Hague Peace Conferences: The Conference of 1899* (New York: Oxford University Press, 1920). For an evaluation by modern international lawyers, see George H. Aldrich and Christine M. Chinkin, eds., "Symposium: The Hague Peace Conferences," *American Journal of International Law* 94 (January 2000): 1–98.

5. *Proceedings*, 17.

6. Ibid., 14.

7. Ibid., 517.

8. Frederic de Martens, the Russian delegate, was instrumental in securing agreement on the laws of land warfare. His plea for unanimity on the laws and on their incorporation into the manuals of the signatory states can be found in *Proceedings*, 518. Geoffrey Best, *Humanity in Warfare* (New York: Columbia University Press, 1980), places the 1899 convention on the rules of land warfare, and the similar 1907 convention, in the overall context of multiple efforts to restrain and govern the use of force.

9. *Trial of the Major War Criminals before the International Military Tribunal* (Nuremberg: Secretariat of the International Military Tribunal, 1948), 22:475. This reference by the Nuremberg tribunal to the Hague rules of land warfare can also be found in *Nazi Conspiracy and Aggression, Opinion and Judgment* (Washington, D.C.: Government Printing Office, 1947), 62. Citations in the war crimes trials were to

the 1907 Hague Convention with the same title and covering the same subject matter as the convention of 1899. Since the delegates of 1899 drafted the convention on which the states could finally agree, and since the 1907 convention made only slight alterations, I have felt free to give the credit to the delegates of 1899. For an article-by-article comparison of the two conventions, see James Brown Scott, ed., *The Hague Conventions and Declarations of 1899 and 1907* (New York: Oxford University Press, 1915), 100–39. To be precise, the rules on which the delegates agreed are not listed in the conventions themselves but rather in annexes that follow the main body of the conventions.

10. "Regulations Respecting the Laws and Customs of War on Land," Annex to the 1899 Convention, art. 46.

11. *Proceedings*, 486, 488.

12. Ibid., 595.

Chapter One

1. Isaiah 1:18, RSV.

2. League of Nations, *Official Journal*, 1934, 21.

3. Ibid.

4. Hugo Grotius, *The Rights of War and Peace*, trans. A. C. Campbell (Washington, D.C.: M. Walter Dunne, 1901), bk. 1, chap. 2, sec. 1, para. 2.

Chapter Two

1. League of Nations, *Official Journal*, 1931, 2379.

2. Andrew W. Cordier and Wilder Foote, eds., *Public Papers of the Secretaries-General of the United Nations*, vol. 3, *Dag Hammarskjöld, 1956–1957* (New York: Columbia University Press, 1973), 309. An excellent biography that focuses on Hammarskjöld's years at the United Nations is Brian Urquhart, *Hammarskjöld* (New York: Knopf, 1972).

3. Permanent Court of International Justice, Advisory Committee of Jurists, *Procès-Verbaux of the Proceedings of the Committee, June 16th–July 24th, 1920 with Annexes* (The Hague: Van Langenhuysen Bros., 1920), 23.

4. *New York Times*, 29 Dec. 1934, p. 15, col. 3. Regarding the names of Japanese leaders, I have followed their practice in this period, putting surnames last in the Western style.

5. League of Nations, *Official Journal*, 1929, 976–77.

6. Harold Butler, *The Lost Peace* (London: Faber & Faber, 1941), 49.

7. Comment at a symposium on world organization, Princeton University, April 1941, printed in *International Conciliation*, pamphlet 372 (September 1941), 642.

8. *New York Times*, 13 Nov. 1955, p. 88, col. 4; *New York Times*, 17 Feb. 1946, sec. 6, p. 24, col. 1; Sara Wambaugh, *Plebiscites since the World War* (Washington, D.C.: Carnegie Endowment for International Peace, 1933), 1:355. For a full account of this failed effort to settle the Chilean-Peruvian boundary dispute through a plebiscite, see 1:331–410.

9. Lilian T. Mowrer, *Journalist's Wife* (New York: William Morrow, 1937), 331.

10. Emery Kelen, *Peace in Their Time* (London: Victor Gollancz, 1964), 3.

11. Alois Derso and Emery Kelen, *Le testament de Genève* (Paris: Georges Lang, 1931), 8. Translated from the French.

12. Salvador de Madariaga, *Morning without Noon: Memoirs* (London: Saxon House for D.C. Heath, 1974), 3.

13. Ibid., 3.

14. *The Forum* 80 (1928): 755, 907–11; *The Forum* 81 (1929): 301, 368.

15. Max Huber, "In Memoriam," introduction to Åke Hammarskjöld, *Juridiction Internationale* (Leyden: Sijthoff, 1938), 56.

16. Cordier and Foote, *Public Papers of the Secretaries-General,* 3:708.

17. Åke Hammarskjöld, "The Permanent Court of International Justice and Its Place in International Relations," speech of 29 April 1930, printed in *Journal of the Royal Institute of International Affairs* 9 (July 1930): 473.

18. Ibid.

19. Alfred Thayer Mahan, "The Peace Conference and the Moral Aspect of War," In *Lessons of the War with Spain* (Boston: Little Brown, 1899), 236–37.

20. Hammarskjöld, "Permanent Court of International Justice," 473.

Chapter Three

1. This chapter is based on a study of policy statements and justifications for action offered by the states that were active in international affairs in the 1930s. It is not an attempt to give the conceptual frameworks described here the kind of analysis appropriate to a work of political philosophy. Rather, the intent is to provide a roadmap for the reader's use and orientation in the often-bewildering terrain of national argument and justification.

Chapter Four

1. George Washington, Farewell Address, 17 September 1796, in *American Historical Documents*, ed. Harold C. Syrett (New York: Barnes & Noble, 1960), 146. For a clear twentieth-century statement of Washington's eighteenth-century warning, see the speech against Senate approval of the Versailles treaty by Idaho senator William E. Borah, 19 November 1919, ibid., 348–53.

2. Quoted in Stephen Bonsal, *Suitors and Suppliants* (New York: Prentice-Hall, 1946), 132.

3. Address to a joint session of Congress, 8 January 1918 (the Fourteen Points speech), in Arthur S. Link, ed., *The Papers of Woodrow Wilson* (Princeton: Princeton University Press, 1984), 45:537–38. See also the address of 11 February 1918, ibid., 46:321, for the clear statement, " 'Self-determination' is not a mere phrase. It is an imperative principle of action." For a summary of the complex negotiations at Paris regarding the various claimants to territory or statehood, see Sara Wambaugh, *Plebiscites since the World War* (Washington, D.C.: Carnegie Endowment for International Peace, 1933), 1:12–45.

4. For the Koreans, see Bonsal, *Suitors and Suppliants*, 222–26.

5. Quoted in ibid., 226. For Finnish recognition see Malbone W. Graham, *The Diplomatic Recognition of the Border States*, pt. 1: *Finland*, Publications of the University of California at Los Angeles in Social Sciences, vol. 3 (Berkeley: University of California Press, 1936), 136–43.

6. The three elements of statehood were enshrined in Article 1 of the Convention on the Rights and Duties of States (1933), *League of Nations Treaty Series* (Lon-

don: Harrison and Sons, 1920–46), 165:19. Karl Doehring's discussion of the state in the authoritative *Encyclopedia of Public International Law* (Amsterdam: Elsevier, 1987), 10:423–28, also relies on the doctrine of the three elements. To avoid the charge of oversimplification, Doehring subjects each of the elements to a "detailed and subtle interpretation" (424). Even so, the result is a definition that presents the ideal, formal case, modified only slightly by Doehring's reluctant acknowledgment of the role played by politics in the recognition of statehood.

7. Malbone W. Graham, *The League of Nations and the Recognition of States*, Publications of the University of California at Los Angeles in Social Sciences, vol. 3 (Berkeley: University of California Press, 1933), 50 (Ireland), 51 (Circassia-Daghestan), 52 (Egypt), 53 (Azerbaijan). Emir Faisal's statements on behalf of the Arabs are quoted in Bonsal, *Suitors and Suppliants*, 37, 38.

8. Graham, *League of Nations*, 51.

9. For a detailed account, see the studies by Malbone Graham listed above. Arno J. Mayer was one of the first to point out the effect at the peace conference of the fear of Bolshevism in *The Politics and Diplomacy of Peacemaking* (New York: Knopf, 1967). A few of the successor states, such as Armenia and the Ukraine, did receive tentative recognition, but the recognition was rendered null when they were overrun by armed forces and incorporated into neighboring states. For a comparison of League practices with those of the United Nations in its early days, see Aleksander W. Rudzinski, "Admission of New Members: The United Nations and the League of Nations," *International Conciliation*, pamphlet 480 (April 1952): 141–96.

10. League of Nations, *The Records of the Second Assembly* (1921), *Meetings of the Committees* (Geneva, 1921), 2:159.

11. E. Brian Titley, *A Narrow Vision: Duncan Campbell Scott and the Administration of Indian Affairs in Canada* (Vancouver: University of British Columbia, 1986), 110–34.

Chapter Five
1. By far the best, most detailed account of the Manchurian Incident is Seki Hiroharu, "The Manchurian Incident," trans. Marius B. Jensen, in James William Morley, ed., *Japan Erupts* (New York: Columbia University Press, 1984), 140–230. This account sets the incident in the context of tensions within the Kwantung Army and the complicated relationship of the Japanese military to the Japanese government. The explosion itself is described on 225–30.

2. League of Nations, *Official Journal, 1932*, Special Supplement 111, 32–33, 35, 40, 47.

3. Ibid., 47.

4. League of Nations, "Appeal by the Chinese Government," *Report of the Commission of Enquiry* (Geneva, 1 October 1932), 129. Lord Lytton was chair of this commission, and the report is usually known by his name. "Appeal by the Chinese Government" is the League title for its activity and references regarding the Manchurian Incident.

5. See, e.g., a detailed study of the responses of the League and major Western powers to the events in eastern Asia in the early thirties: Christopher Thorne, *The Limits of Foreign Policy* (London: Hamish Hamilton, 1972). The problems set for national policymakers by an event with far-reaching international implications are ex-

plored by Warren Cohen in "American Leaders and East Asia, 1931–1938," in *American, Chinese, and Japanese Perspectives on Wartime Asia, 1931–1949*, ed. Akira Iriye and Warren Cohen (Wilmington, Del.: Scholarly Resources, 1990), 1–27.

6. The photographs were reproduced in Chester H. Rowell, "What Does Japan Want?" *Asia* 32 (April 1932): 216.

7. "Swift News from the Far East," *Asia* 32 (June 1932): 353.

8. Kentaro Kaneko, "Roosevelt on Japan," *Asia* 32 (November 1932): 539, 541.

9. Kikujiro Ishii, *Viscount Ishii's Addresses Delivered in America, May 1933* (n.p., 1933), 38.

10. *New York Times*, 20 December 1931, p. 19, col. 1.

11. J. H. W. Verzijl, "Along the Scaffolding of the Edifice of the International Legal Order," speech delivered 3 June 1930 in Utrecht, printed in *International Law in Historical Perspective*, vol. 1, *General Subjects* (Leyden: Sijthoff-Leyden, 1968), 369.

12. George H. Blakeslee and Nathaniel Peffer, *The Lytton Report*, a New York luncheon discussion, 5 November 1932, Foreign Policy Association Pamphlet 86 (New York: Foreign Policy Association, December 1932), 6–7.

13. Quoted in the biographical sketch of Nathaniel Peffer in Stanley Kunitz and Howard Haycraft, eds., *Twentieth Century Authors, 1942* (New York: H. W. Wilson, 1942).

14. Blakeslee and Peffer, *Lytton Report*, 11–12.

15. Ibid., 13.

Chapter Six

1. For a scholarly account of the Balkan wars, see Barbara Jelavich, *History of the Balkans*, vol. 2, *Twentieth Century* (Cambridge: Cambridge University Press, 1983), 95–100. For the wars in relation to broader issues, see the chapter titled "The End of Ottoman Rule in Europe," 2:79–105.

2. Nicholas Murray Butler to Elihu Root, 19 July 1913, Papers of the Carnegie Endowment for International Peace (hereafter, CEIP), Division of Intercourse and Education, bound volume, "Paris Office Accounts, 1913." The CEIP papers are in the Department of Special Collections, Butler Library, Columbia University.

3. Butler's optimistic projection for completion and publication of the commission's report is in his letter of 21 July 1913 to Baron d'Estournelles de Constant, chair of the Commission. Ibid.

4. Leon Trotsky, *The Balkan Wars, 1912–1913: The War Correspondence of Leon Trotsky*, ed. George Weissman and Duncan Williams (New York: Monad, 1980), 145. Trotsky covered the Balkan wars as a correspondent for a Russian newspaper. Joyce Cary's experiences as a volunteer can be followed in *Memoir of the Bobotes* (Austin: University of Texas Press, 1960).

5. Mowrer's dispatch of 15 December 1912 was published in the *Chicago Daily News*, 2 January 1913. Reprinted in Paul Scott Mowrer, *The House of Europe* (Boston: Houghton Mifflin, 1945), 171.

6. Samuel T. Dutton to Nicholas Murray Butler, 20 September 1913, CEIP papers, Division of Intercourse and Education, bound volume, "Balkan Commission, 1913–1915." Paul Scott Mowrer also describes conditions in the refugee camps. See his *House of Europe*, 185, 190.

7. Nicholas Murray Butler to Baron d'Estournelles de Constant, 21 July 1913,

CEIP papers, Division of Intercourse and Education, bound volume, "Paris Office Accounts, 1913."

8. Baron d'Estournelles de Constant, introduction to *Report of the International Commission to Inquire into the Causes and Conduct of the Balkan Wars* (Washington, D.C.: Carnegie Endowment for International Peace, 1914), 5–11. See also George F. Kennan's introduction to the reprint of the 1914 report, *The Other Balkan Wars* (Washington, D.C.: Carnegie Endowment for International Peace, 1993), 6–7. The report of yet another commission of inquiry, dispatched by the Carnegie Endowment and the Aspen Institute to investigate yet another outbreak of Balkan violence, is *Unfinished Peace: Report of the International Commission on the Balkans* (Berlin and Washington, D.C.: Aspen Institute and the Carnegie Endowment for International Peace, 1996).

9. For an example of a successful commission of inquiry, see Dorothy V. Jones, *Code of Peace* (Chicago: University of Chicago Press, 1991), 26–28.

10. Samuel T. Dutton to Nicholas Murray Butler, 23 July 1913, CEIP papers, Division of Intercourse and Education, bound volume, "Balkan Commission, 1913–1915."

11. Estournelles de Constant, introduction, *Report of the International Commission*, 5.

12. Kennan, *Other Balkan Wars*.

13. Convention with Respect to the Laws and Customs of War on Land (1899), in Clive Parry, ed., *Consolidated Treaty Series* (Dobbs Ferry, N.Y.: Oceana, 1979), 187:431.

14. "Report of the Commission of Enquiry into the Incidents on the Frontier between Bulgaria and Greece," League of Nations, *Official Journal*, *1926*, 205.

15. League of Nations, *Official Journal*, *1925*, 1696–97.

16. League of Nations, *Official Journal*, *1926*, 196. For a biographical sketch of Horace Rumbold see the entry by James Marshall Cornwall in *The Dictionary of National Biography*, *Supplement* (London: Oxford University Press, n.d.), vol. 6.

17. "Report of the Commission of Enquiry," 204.

18. Ibid., 172–77, 581, 584–85. At the time, troubles at home made warfare with each other an unattractive prospect for both Greece and Bulgaria. Alexander Zankov in Bulgaria and General Theodore Pangalos in Greece had each been recently installed following a military coup d'état that negated the results of national elections, and each was deeply engaged in pursuing domestic enemies and consolidating power. That, rather than any sense of international responsibility, may have prompted compliance with the League of Nations. However that may be, had the League not provided an opportunity for a face-saving retreat, the war might well have continued. So, intentionally or not, Greece and Bulgaria handed the League a victory that enhanced its reputation and strengthened its authority.

19. League of Nations, *Official Journal*, *1925*, 1716.

20. Count Coudenhove-Kalergi, *An Idea Conquers the World* (London: Hutchinson, 1953), 123.

21. League of Nations, *Official Journal*, *1925*, 1714, 1715.

22. For a summary of the work of the five League commissions of inquiry, see F. P. Walters, *A History of the League of Nations* (London: Oxford University Press, 1952), 1:103–5, 159–61, 302–5, 305–10, 311–15.

23. The cholera attempt was made public in 1994 in an interview in Japan with Prince Mikasa, youngest brother of Emperor Hirohito. The interview was widely reported in the Western press. See, for example, the *Economist*, 9 July 1994, 34, and the *Chicago Tribune*, 7 July 1994, 14.

24. Thomas Hobbes, *Leviathan*, chap. 13, sec. 63, para. 2.

25. League of Nations, "Appeal by the Chinese Government," *Report of the Commission of Enquiry* (Geneva, 1 October 1932) (hereafter Lytton Commission Report), 9–10.

26. Ibid., "Itinerary in the Far East of the League of Nations Commission of Enquiry," 140–48. See also Map 13 accompanying the report: "Principal Route Map Showing Itineraries of the Commission in the Far East."

27. Ibid., 132–39. For Lytton's evaluation of the commission's work, see his "Lessons of the League of Nations Commission of Enquiry in Manchuria," *New Commonwealth Quarterly* 3 (December 1937): 1–16.

28. The successful League administration of a small area in South America is treated in detail in chapter 8 of this book.

29. Quoted in Edgar Snow, *Far Eastern Front* (New York: Harrison Smith and Robert Haas, 1933), 128.

30. Ibid., 86.

31. Ibid., 88. In his presentation at the Foreign Policy Association luncheon in New York, George H. Blakeslee, technical adviser to the Lytton Commission, also mentions these handbills. See George H. Blakeslee and Nathaniel Peffer, *The Lytton Report*, Foreign Policy Association Pamphlet 86 (New York: Foreign Policy Association, December 1932), 4.

32. Lytton Commission Report, Supplementary Documents (League Series Publication C.663.M.320. 1932. VII. Annexes), Annex B, "List of Interviews," 15–21.

33. Henry Kittredge Norton, "The Japanese Monroe Doctrine at Work," *Asia* 32 (1932): 542–45, 592–96. For a brief biography of Araki, see the *Biographical Dictionary of Japanese History* (Tokyo: Kodansha International, 1978).

Chapter Seven

1. Quoted in Herbert B. Elliston, "Realities in Manchuria," *Asia* 32 (January 1932): 5. For an in-depth treatment of the whole Asian situation during this critical period, see Akira Iriye, "Japanese Aggression and China's International Position 1931–1949," in *The Cambridge History of China*, ed. John K. Fairbank and Albert Feuerwerker, vol. 13, *Republican China 1912–1949*, pt. 2 (Cambridge: Cambridge University Press, 1986), 492–546.

2. League of Nations, *Official Journal, 1932*, Special Supplement 111, 71.

3. Ibid., 27.

4. Clarence K. Streit, "The Far Eastern War in Geneva," *Asia* 33 (February 1933): 80, 84.

5. Ibid., 128.

6. League Special Supplement 111 (1932), 33.

7. F. P. Walters, *A History of the League of Nations* (London: Oxford University Press, 1952), 1:33–65, discusses in detail the drafting of the Covenant of the League of Nations. The ethical heritage that helped shape the covenant is discussed in Dorothy V. Jones, *Code of Peace* (Chicago: University of Chicago Press, 1991), 22–

50. Excerpts from relevant documents can be found in Ruth B. Henig, ed., *The League of Nations* (New York: Barnes & Noble, 1973), 19–44.

8. League Special Supplement 111 (1932), 60.

9. George Bronson Rea backed Japan in this controversy. His arguments can be found in League of Nations, *Official Journal, 1933*, Special Supplement 112, 44–52.

10. League Special Supplement 111 (1932), 56.

11. Ibid., 41.

12. Warren F. Kuehl, ed., *Biographical Dictionary of Internationalists* (Westport, Conn.: Greenwood, 1983), has biographical sketches of the Japanese delegates mentioned in the text: Makino, 467–68; Nitobe, 542–43; Sugimura, 704–6; Ishii, 380–81; Sato, 652–54; Adachi, 4–5.

13. Names of the Japanese delegates to the special League Assembly session, 1932–33, that considered the Lytton Report can be found in League Special Supplement 111 (1932), 11. Delegate Kanji Ishiwara's part in planning the military action that has become known as the Manchurian Incident emerges in scattered references in the chapter of that name by Seki Hiroharu in James William Morley, ed., *Japan Erupts* (New York: Columbia University Press, 1984), esp. 202–230.

14. League Special Supplement 111 (1932), 41, 42.

15. League Special Supplement 112 (1933), 23.

16. Ibid.

17. League Special Supplement 111 (1932), 51.

18. Ibid., 61, 38, 36, 43, 44, 45.

19. Ibid., 31.

20. Walters, *History of the League*, 1:301. Much of the help was devoted to settling refugees. See, for example, League of Nations, *Official Journal, 1926*, minutes of the council, 1244–47, 1394–98.

21. League Special Supplement 111 (1932), 51.

22. Ibid.

23. War Minister Sadao Araki stood trial before the International Military Tribunal for the Far East, the body that conducted the trial of the leading Japanese charged as war criminals. He was found guilty on two counts connected with the charge of waging aggressive war and was sentenced to life imprisonment (he was released from prison in 1955 and later pardoned). Yosuke Matsuoka, who had carried the burden of the Japanese defense at the League, was charged for his later activities as an architect of Japanese expansion and alliance with the Axis powers (the Tripartite Pact). In poor health, he died shortly after the trial began. Shigeru Honjo, commander of the Japanese Army in Manchuria at the time of the Manchurian Incident, was also charged as a war criminal. He committed suicide rather than face trial. For a summary of this trial, usually called simply the Tokyo War Crimes Trial, see John Alan Appleman, *Military Tribunals and International Crimes* (1954; reprint, Westport, Conn.: Greenwood, 1971), 237–64. The definitive account of the Tokyo trial remains to be written. The available literature (sparse compared to that for the trial of the major German war criminals at Nuremberg) is very uneven. It is particularly inadequate when treating the international law of the period and the development of that law during the interwar years. A straightforward journalistic account is Arnold C. Brackman, *The Other Nuremberg* (New York: Morrow, 1987). Richard Minear did much spade work in hard-to-use documents to produce one of the first scholarly ex-

aminations of the trial, *Victor's Justice: The Tokyo War Crimes Trial* (Princeton: Princeton University Press, 1971). The title faithfully conveys his point of view. Essential for any future work on the trial is John W. Dower, *Embracing Defeat* (New York: Norton, 1999), 443–84. Dower's account of the trial is extremely valuable because of his broad and sensitive use of Japanese sources. His unquestioning reliance on the dissenting opinion of Radhadinod Pal, the Indian judge on the Tokyo tribunal, is considerably less valuable. A more nuanced reading of Pal's dissent and of the trial itself can be found in Tim Maga, *Judgment at Tokyo: The Japanese War Crimes Trial* (Lexington: University Press of Kentucky, 2001). Finally, whereas the proceedings before the international military tribunal that conducted the trial of the major German war criminals in Nuremberg were published shortly after that trial and widely disseminated, it was not until 1981 that the proceedings of the Tokyo War Crimes Trial were published: R. John Pritchard and Sonia M. Zaide, eds., *The Tokyo War Crimes Trial* (New York: Garland, 1981). These volumes are still not widely available, a fact that helps explain the late start on scholarly treatment of this trial.

24. League of Nations, *Official Journal, 1932*, Special Supplement 101, 50.

25. League of Nations, *Official Journal, 1932*, Records of the 13th Ordinary Session of the Assembly, 28.

Chapter Eight

1. Emery Kelen, *Peace in Their Time* (London: Gollancz, 1964), 253–66; *Le livre d'or de l'exposition coloniale internationale de Paris, 1931* (Paris: Librairie ancienne Honoré Champion, 1931); John E. Findling, ed., *Historical Dictionary of World's Fairs and Expositions, 1851–1988* (Westport, Conn.: Greenwood, 1990), 261–65.

2. Arnold J. Toynbee, *Survey of International Affairs, 1930* (London: Oxford University Press, 1931), 135–42; Arnold R. Verduin, trans., *Manual of Spanish Constitutions, 1808–1931* (Ypsilanti, Mich.: University Lithoprinters, 1941), 86. References in League of Nations documents to Briand's plan of union are so scattered that it is hard to get a clear picture of its reception and final disposition. Toynbee's summary is helpful here. For a copy of the plan see John Wheeler Bennett, ed., *Documents on International Affairs, 1930* (London: Oxford University Press, 1931), 61–73.

3. Preamble, The Covenant of the League of Nations, in *The League of Nations*, ed. Ruth B. Henig (New York: Barnes & Noble, 1973), 179.

4. Victor Mogens, *Greenland: The Norwegian-Danish Conflict* (Oslo: Morten Johansens Boktrykkeri, 1931), 36.

5. The Danish application was filed 11 July 1931, just one day after the Norwegian proclamation of sovereignty. For the application see Publications of the Permanent Court of International Justice, ser. C, *Pleadings, Oral Statements and Documents*, "Legal Status of East Greenland" (hereafter, PCIJ, ser. C, "E. Greenland"), no. 62, 11. A year later, in a development not treated in the text, Norway extended the area of its claim on the east coast of Greenland. This claim, which Denmark also disputed, gave rise to a separate case, "Legal Status of the South-Eastern Territory of Greenland." The two cases were eventually joined by the court, but arguments were heard first in the case first filed, the East Greenland case. After judgment was rendered in that case, the second was withdrawn. The several legal actions brought in connection with the latter case appear in PCIJ, ser. C, "Legal Status of the South-Eastern Territory of Greenland," no. 69.

6. The pleadings and documents in the case fill six volumes in PCIJ, ser. C, "E. Greenland," nos. 62–67. Danish arguments can be followed in their written application and initial statement, no. 62, 9–114; in their written reply to the Norwegian counter-case, no. 63, 619–980; and in their oral presentations, no. 66, 2619–2915. For the Norwegian arguments see no. 62, 115–610, no. 63, 981–1470, and no. 66, 2916–3281. Subheadings in no. 67, the table of contents volume, facilitate picking out particular strands of thought in these lengthy proceedings. For the supporting documents submitted by Denmark, see no. 64, and for those submitted by Norway, see no. 65.

7. See, e.g., Yosuke Matsuoka, *Japan's Case, as Presented before the Special Session of the Assembly of the League of Nations* (Geneva: Japanese Delegation to the League of Nations, 1933).

8. The history portion of Norway's argument can be found in PCIJ, ser. C, "E. Greenland," no. 62, 115–372. A seven-chapter analysis of the relevant law is at 373–610.

9. The Danish view of the facts in the case is in ibid., 12–114, and their analysis of the relevant law is in no. 63, 712–980. For a sample of the argument regarding the well-being of the natives, see no. 64, 1482–97.

10. *A Hundred Pictures from Greenland* (Copenhagen: Royal Danish Ministry for Foreign Affairs, 1932), n.p.

11. For brief biographies of De Visscher, see Arthur Eyffinger, *The International Court of Justice, 1946–1996* (The Hague: Kluwer Law International, 1996), 333, and the De Visscher entry by Sally Marks in Warren F. Kuehl, *Biographical Dictionary of Internationalists* (Westport, Conn.: Greenwood, 1983), 207–8.

12. PCIJ, ser. C, "E. Greenland," no. 66, 2794, translated from the French.

13. De Visscher, *Theory and Reality in Public International Law*, trans. P. E. Corbett (French edition, 1953; Princeton: Princeton University Press, 1957), xi.

14. PCIJ, ser. C, "E. Greenland," no. 66, 2794.

15. PCIJ, ser. E, no. l, *Annual Report of the Permanent Court of International Justice* (Leyden: Sijthoff, n.d.), 11; PCIJ, Ser. E., no. 7, *Seventh Annual Report* (Leyden: Sijthoff, n.d.), 19.

16. PCIJ, ser. C, "E. Greenland," no. 66, 2592.

17. The proposed customs union was abandoned by Germany and Austria on 3 September 1931 and two days later the court issued its advisory opinion regarding the legality of the union. See Manley O. Hudson, ed., *World Court Reports* (Washington: Carnegie Endowment for International Peace, 1934–43), 2:711. One of the most controversial actions by the court, this opinion has stimulated an enormous literature, much of it critical.

18. PCIJ, ser. A/B, *Judgments, Orders and Advisory Opinions*, fasc. 53, "Legal Status of Eastern Greenland," 75. For the entire judgment plus supporting documents, *see* 22–147.

19. "When Nations Invoke the Law in Court," *New York Times*, 13 Sept. 1931, sec. 5, p. 6.

20. Ibid.

21. Anthony Patric, *Chicago Daily Tribune*, 12 May 1933, p. 10.

22. Art.5(2), Rules of the Court, in PCIJ, ser. D, *Statute and Rules of Court and Other Constitutional Documents, Rules or Regulations*, no. 1 (2nd ed.), 25.

23. PCIJ, ser. E, No. 7: *Seventh Annual Report*, 20.

24. Åke Hammarskjöld, "The Late President Adatci [Adachi]," *American Journal of International Law* 30 (1936): 115–16.

25. PCIJ, Advisory Committee of Jurists, *Procès-Verbaux of the Proceedings of the Committee, June 16th–July 24th 1920 with Annexes* (The Hague: Van Langenhuysen Bros., 1920), 11.

26. For the work of the Mixed Commission and the Arbitral Tribunal in Upper Silesia, see Georges Kaeckenbeeck, *The International Experiment of Upper Silesia* (London: Oxford University Press, 1942). Kaeckenbeeck, a Belgian, was president of the Arbitral Tribunal. Felix Calonder, a Swiss, was president of the Mixed Commission. International involvement in the Saar can be followed in Sarah Wambaugh, *The Saar Plebiscite* (Cambridge: Harvard University Press, 1940). The Letitia dispute is covered briefly by F. P. Walters, *A History of the League of Nations* (London: Oxford University Press, 1952), 2:536–40. Notes 27–33 give the sources for the more detailed treatment of the Letitia dispute.

27. League of Nations, "Appeal by the Chinese Government," *Report of the Commission of Enquiry* (Geneva, 1 October 1932) (Lytton Commission Report), 129; "General Treaty for Renunciation of War as an Instrument of National Policy" (the Pact of Paris), League of Nations Treaty Series 94, 63.

28. The Japanese ambassador was also present at the meeting, but Japan did not send a note to Peru. As a signer of the Pact of Paris, Japan may not have wanted to call official attention to the pact's provisions at the same moment that it was engaged in breaking them in China. For Stimson's efforts to gather international support behind the Pact of Paris in the Letitia controversy see *Foreign Relations of the United States* (hereafter, *FRUS*) 1933, vol. 4, *The American Republics* (Washington, D.C: Government Printing Office, 1950), 421–23; for the responses of European powers see 449–50, 455–56, 458–59, 464. Bryce Wood, *The United States and Latin American Wars, 1932–1942* (New York: Columbia University Press, 1966), 169–251, sets out the Letitia negotiations, dispatch by dispatch, through the whole twenty-two months of the controversy.

29. The commissioners were from Spain, Brazil, and the United States. This account of their work in Letitia is drawn from the detailed reports that they sent to the council of the League. The reports can be found in League of Nations, *Official Journal, 1934,* 21–25, 912–47. The incident centering on the Peruvian flag is on 928.

30. Bryce Wood discusses possible factors in Peru's eventual willingness to come to an agreement in his *Latin American Wars,* 241–46. For the Colombian delegate's comments, see *Bulletin of the Pan American Union* 68 (July 1934): 547.

31. Ibid.; for the protocol, see 549–55.

32. League of Nations, *Official Journal, 1934,* 944.

33. Hugh Robert Wilson, *Diplomat between the Wars* (New York: Longmans, Green, 1941), 262.

34. For the battles of Nanawa and Campo Via, see Bruce W. Farcau, *The Chaco War: Bolivia and Paraguay, 1932–1935* (Westport, Conn.: Praeger, 1996), 129–40, 149–64; and David H. Zook Jr., *The Conduct of the Chaco War* (n.p.: Bookman Associates, 1960), 142–90. Walters, *History of the League,* 2:526–36, summarizes mediation efforts, especially those of the League, and Wood, *Latin American Wars,* 19–166, provides a detailed look at other efforts, particularly those of the United States, to end the war.

35. League of Nations, *Dispute between Bolivia and Paraguay: Report of the Chaco Commission* (Geneva, 1934), 34.

36. League of Nations, *Report of the Chaco Commission*, 56.

37. Walters, *History of the League* 2:526.

38. League of Nations, *Report of the Chaco Commission*, 7.

39. League of Nations, *Official Journal*, 1933, 758.

40. League of Nations, *Report of the Chaco Commission*, 54; Zook, *Conduct of the Chaco War,* 47–48.

41. League of Nations, *Report of the Chaco Commission*, 57. The Mohegan comment is quoted in James Axtell, *The European and the Indian* (New York: Oxford University Press, 1981), 140. For the casualty figures see Zook, *Conduct of the Chaco War,* 240–41. Geoffrey Parker discusses the Western way of war in his introduction to *The Cambridge Illustrated History of Warfare*, ed. Geoffrey Parker (Cambridge: Cambridge University Press, 1995), 2–9, as does John Keegan in *A History of Warfare* (New York: Vintage, 1994), esp. 3–24, 386–92. On page 391 Keegan presciently observes, "The triumph of the Western way of warfare [in the world beyond Europe] was, however, delusive. Directed against other military cultures it had proved irresistible. Turned in on itself it brought disaster and threatened catastrophe."

42. The text of the Protocol of Peace can be found in *Bulletin of the Pan American Union* 69 (July 1935): 518–20.

43. For the Treaty of Peace, see *Bulletin of the Pan American Union* 72 (September 1938): 453–54. The ceremony in Buenos Aires is described on 497–502.

44. League of Nations, *Report of the Chaco Commission*, 34.

Chapter Nine

1. The process of change is discussed in more detail in Dorothy V. Jones, "The League of Nations Experiment in International Protection," *Ethics & International Affairs* 8 (1994): 77–95.

2. "Note by the Secretary-General . . . ," League of Nations, *Official Journal, 1933,* 929; the quotation from the petition of Franz Bernheim is on 933.

3. Part 3, Division 1 of the German-Polish Convention (the Geneva Convention), printed in Georges Kaeckenbeeck, *The International Experiment of Upper Silesia* (London: Oxford University Press, 1947), 601. Kaeckenbeeck's account of this international experiment is thorough and thoughtful. It deserves far wider notice than it has had for its reflections on the complexities of international administration.

4. *Official Gazette of the Control Council for Germany*, Control Council Law No. 1 (29 October 1945), 6; for the statement from the Bernheim petition, see League of Nations, *Official Journal, 1933,* 932.

5. Ibid., 930, 932, 933.

6. Ibid., 833.

7. For Lester's comment concerning difficulties, see ibid., 835; for the excerpt from the Lester committee report, see 839.

8. For the list of actions by Germany that ran counter to its pledges, see ibid., 930. In the copy of the Geneva Convention printed in Kaeckenbeeck, *Upper Silesia*, the protective provisions are on 602–3, 610, 612, and 614.

9. For von Keller's objections, see League of Nations, *Official Journal, 1933,* 839–40.

10. Ibid., 840.
11. Ibid.
12. Ibid., 840–41.
13. Ibid., 841.
14. Ibid., 842.
15. Ibid.
16. Ibid., 842, 847.

Chapter Ten

1. Bernheim Petition, League of Nations, *Official Journal, 1933*, 933.
2. Raul Hilberg, *The Destruction of the European Jews* (New York: Holmes & Meier, 1985), 1:88. In chapter 5, "Expropriation," 83–154, Hilberg traces in painstaking detail the initial stages in the campaign that eventually reduced European Jewish communities to a few scattered remnants.
3. William E. Dodd Jr. and Martha Dodd, eds., *Ambassador Dodd's Diary, 1933–1938* (New York: Harcourt, 1941), 20.
4. "Final Report by the Right Honourable Sir Nevile Henderson, G.C.M.G., on the Circumstances Leading to the Termination of His Mission to Berlin, September 20, 1939," British Command Paper 6115 (London: His Majesty's Stationery Office, 1939), 4.
5. Ibid., 3–4.
6. *The Diaries of a Cosmopolitan, Count Harry Kessler, 1918–1937*, ed. and trans. Charles Kessler (London: Weidenfeld and Nicolson, 1971), 8. Count Kessler's diaries were published in the United States under the title *In the Twenties* (New York: Holt, Rinehart and Winston, 1971).
7. Fritz Tobias, *The Reichstag Fire* (New York: Putnam, 1964), gives a flavor of the passions involved in the question of responsibility, as well as providing a detailed account of who, what, where, when, and how.
8. Arthur Garfield Hays, *City Lawyer* (New York: Simon & Schuster, 1942), 343.
9. Ibid.
10. Striking photographs of activities based on National Socialist definitions of what was and was not German can be found in *Archives of the Holocaust*, vol. 1: *Bildarchiv Preussischer Kulterbesitz, Berlin*, pt. l: *1933–1939* (New York: Garland, 1990), 25–56.
11. *The Burning of the Reichstag: Official Findings of the Legal Commission of Inquiry* (London: Relief Committee for the Victims of German Fascism, 1933), 24.
12. An example of dramatic coverage can be found in the sober pages of the *Economist*, which, from 30 September to 30 December, 1933, gave the Reichstag fire trial extensive space, often presenting testimony in dialog form.
13. Three of the men, including Dimitrov, were released at the end of February, two months later, in a prisoner exchange. The fourth man, Ernst Torgler, who had been leader of the parliamentary Communists in the Reichstag, was not released until the middle of 1935.
14. Douglas Reed, *The Burning of the Reichstag* (New York: Covici-Friede, n.d. [1934?]), 37.
15. Yves Beigbeder, *Judging War Criminals: The Politics of International Justice* (New York: St. Martin's, 1999), 137–45.

16. *Foreign Relations of the United States 1934*, vol. 2, *Europe, Near East, and Africa* (Washington, D.C.: U.S. Government Printing Office, 1951), 509–12.

17. Ibid., 509, 510–11.

18. *New York Times*, 8 March 1934, p. 14, col. 3.

19. Ibid., col. 7.

Chapter Eleven

1. *New York Times*, 8 March 1934, p. 15, col. 3. It is only fair to note that even privately organized protests against human rights abuses were selective. The government of the Soviet Union got off lightly in this respect although its policies in the purge trials and the collectivization campaign trampled all over human rights and caused widespread deaths and suffering. It is also fair to note that anti-Semitism in this period was not confined to Germany, but, in different strengths and at different levels, could be found throughout Eastern Europe and in the West as well. The anti-Semitic policies of the National Socialists found prepared ground.

2. Arthur Garfield Hays discusses these cases in his autobiography, *City Lawyer* (New York: Simon and Shuster, 1942).

3. Ernst Fraenkel, *Der Doppelstaat* (1940), published in English as *The Dual State*, trans. E. A. Shils (New York: Oxford University Press, 1941). Fraenkel distinguished between the Prerogative State and the Normative State. In the first, the government is unrestrained by legal limits in its exercise of power and use of violence. The Normative State has an elaborate system of statutes, court decisions, and administrative bodies to support legal guarantees for its citizens. An excellent introduction to the complicated legal situation under the National Socialists is Michael Stolleis, *The Law under the Swastika* (Chicago: University of Chicago Press, 1998). For a personal and poignant reflection on the masquelike quality of daily life under the National Socialists, see Stefan Lorant, *I Was Hitler's Prisoner* (New York: Putnam, 1935), esp. 316.

4. Negley K. Teeters, *Deliberations of the International Penal and Penitentiary Congresses, 1872–1935* (Philadelphia: Temple University Bookstore for the American Prison Association, [1949?]), 179–80.

5. A. M. Klein, "The Hitleriad," in *The Poets of the Year: 1944* (New York: New Directions, 1944), 22.

6. *New York Times*, 21 September 1933, p. 9, col. 2.

7. Sir Jan Simon van der Aa, ed., *Proceedings of the XIth International Penal and Penitentiary Congress Held in Berlin, August 1935* (Bern, Switzerland: Bureau of the International Penal and Penitentiary Commission, 1937), 23, 24.

8. The Nuremberg laws were being prepared in the Interior Ministry, rather than the Ministry of Justice, and Guertner may or may not have known about them. This diffusion and confusion of responsibilities was typical at the upper levels of the National Socialist regime. Guertner certainly knew about the anti-Semitic legislation already in place when he spoke to the congress.

9. Van der Aa, *Proceedings of the XIth International Penal and Penitentiary Congress*, 5. The German text of Guertner's talk can be found in *Das neue Strafrecht* (Berlin: R. v. Decker's Verlag, 1936).

10. Van der Aa, *Proceedings of the XIth International Penal and Penitentiary Congress*, 9.

11. Ibid., 10.

12. Ibid., 18.

13. Ibid., 20, 6.

14. Ibid., 14.

15. There is a biographical sketch of Guertner in Robert S. Wistrich, *Who's Who in Nazi Germany* (1982; reprint, London: Routledge, 1995), 92–93.

16. Van der Aa, *Proceedings of the XIth International Penal and Penitentiary Congress*, 448.

17. Ibid., 24, 25.

18. For the discussion, see ibid., 168–212, 226–36; for the question that generated such extended discussion and disagreement, see 575. Geoffrey Bing, a British delegate, published a scathing account of the congress in *The Penal Reformer* (January 1936), but this was, of course, after the proceedings were over and he had left Germany. There were undoubtedly criticisms voiced during the congress, but—at least in the official account—they were effectively muted by professional protocol.

19. Van der Aa, *Proceedings of the XIth International Penal and Penitentiary Congress*, 602. For a description of the entire trip, see "The Tour for Purposes of Study," 599–615.

20. Ibid., 603.

21. Wolfgang Sofsky, *The Order of Terror: The Concentration Camp*, trans. William Templer (Princeton: Princeton University Press, 1993).

22. Henry Friedlander and Sybil Milton, eds., *Archives of the Holocaust*, vol. 1, pt. 1, *Bildarchiv Preussischer Kulterbesitz, Berlin*, ed. Sybil Milton and Roland Klemig (New York: Garland, 1990), photos 76–87. There is a biographical sketch of Theodor Eicke in Wistrich, *Who's Who in Nazi Germany*, 51–52.

23. Sofsky, *Order of Terror*, 28–43, has a good short account of the confusing early history of the concentration camp system within Germany. For those who want more detail, Sofsky's source notes and bibliography provide guidance to the abundant literature on the subject.

24. Fredrik Stang, chair of the Nobel Committee, speech of 10 December 1936, in *Nobel Lectures, Peace*, vol. 2, *1926–1950*, ed. Frederick W. Haberman (Amsterdam: Elsevier for the Nobel Foundation, 1972), 207, 209. The Nobel Peace Prize for 1935 had been reserved and was awarded to Ossietzky in 1936. The response of the German government was to forbid German citizens' acceptance of any of the Nobel prizes. For more on the life of Ossietzky see Irwin Abrams, *The Nobel Peace Prize and the Laureates* (Boston: Hall, 1988), 125–28. Istvan Deak, *Weimar Germany's Left-Wing Intellectuals* (Berkeley: University of California Press, 1968) puts Ossietzky in his intellectual context.

25. Sofsky, *Order of Terror*, 32–34.

26. Friedlander and Milton, *Archives of the Holocaust*, vol. 7, *Columbia University Library, New York: The James G. McDonald Papers*, ed. Karen J. Greenberg, 244. For McDonald's comments on the disadvantages of being separated from the League, see 240.

27. Ingo Müller, *Hitler's Justice: The Courts of the Third Reich*, trans. Deborah Lucas Schneider (Cambridge: Harvard University Press, 1991), 39–41.

28. *Trials of War Criminals before the Nuernberg Military Tribunals under Control*

Council Law No. 10, vol. 3, *The Justice Case* (Washington, D.C.: U.S. Government Printing Office, 1951), 1081–87, 1118–28, 1200.

29. For a list of those attending the congress, see Van der Aa, *Proceedings of the XIth International Penal and Penitentiary Congress*, 537–70. The list is organized by country. Biographical sketches of the Germans mentioned in the paragraph can be found in Wistrich, *Who's Who in Nazi Germany*: for Theodor Eicke, see 51–52; for Otto Thierack, see 256–57; for Hans Frank, see 62–63; for Kurt Daleuge, see 35–36.

Chapter Twelve

1. Nicholas Politis, *La justice internationale* (Paris: Hachette, 1924), 255; *Les nouvelles tendances du droit international* (Paris: Hachette, 1927), 6–7, 40–41, 92. For a biographical sketch of Politis, see Warren F. Kuehl, *Biographical Dictionary of Internationalists* (Westport, Conn.: Greenwood, 1983), 580–82. Scattered references in Dorothy V. Jones, *Code of Peace* (Chicago: University of Chicago Press, 1991), suggest the importance of this little-known man in the interwar period.

2. Robert H. Jackson," The Challenge of International Lawlessness," speech before the American Bar Association, 2 October 1941, Indianapolis, printed in *International Conciliation* pamphlet no. 374 (November 1941): 683.

3. Twenty-four men were indicted in the trial. Gustav Krupp was separated from the proceedings because he was not physically or mentally fit to stand trial. Robert Ley committed suicide in the prison at Nuremberg. Martin Bormann was tried in absentia. The remaining twenty-one were Hermann Goering, Rudolf Hess, Joachim von Ribbentrop, Wilhelm Keitel, Ernst Kaltenbrunner, Alfred Rosenberg, Hans Frank, Wilhelm Frick, Julius Streicher, Walter Funk, Hjalmar Schacht, Karl Doenitz, Erich Raeder, Baldur von Schirach, Fritz Sauckel, Alfred Jodl, Franz von Papen, Arthur Seyss-Inquart, Albert Speer, Constantin von Neurath, and Hans Fritzsche. The chief instigator of terror, Adolf Hitler, had committed suicide in the closing days of the war, as did other top officials such as Joseph Goebbels and Heinrich Himmler. For a thorough account of the trial by a member of the U.S. prosecution team, see Telford Taylor, *The Anatomy of the Nuremberg Trials* (Boston: Little Brown, 1992).

4. Airey Neave, *Nuremberg* (London: Hodder and Stoughton, 1978), 71.

5. Reports of trials in the various cities mentioned in the text can be found in United Nations War Crimes Commission, *Law Reports of Trials of War Criminals* (London: His Majesty's Stationery Office for the United Nations War Crimes Commission, 1949); and Sir David Maxwell Fyfe, ed., *War Crimes Trials* (London: William Hodge, 1948–1952). These are major sources, but they are only two of thousands of accounts and discussions of war crimes trials, particularly those following World War II. A guide to the literature is Norman E. Tutorow, *War Crimes, War Criminals, and War Crimes Trials* (New York: Greenwood, 1986). Annotations make this an especially useful work, but it needs to be brought up to date. Basic sources for the Tokyo trial of the Japanese leaders charged as major war criminals can be found in chap. 7, n. 23. Basic sources for the major Nuremberg trial are *Trial of the Major War Criminals before the International Military Tribunal, Nuremberg* (Nuremberg: Secretariat of the International Military Tribunal, 1947–49); *Nazi Conspiracy and*

Aggression (Washington, D.C.: Office of United States Chief of Counsel for Prosecution of Axis Criminality, U.S. Government Printing Office, 1946–47).

6. The figure on the number of trial proceedings comes from two sources: "Progress Report of War Crimes Trials from Data Available on March 1st, 1948," in United Nations War Crimes Commission, *History of the United Nations War Crimes Commission and the Development of the Laws of War* (London: His Majesty's Stationery Office, 1948), 518 (1,991 cases), and United Nations War Crimes Commission, *Law Reports*, vol. 15, *Digest of Laws and Cases* (London: His Majesty's Stationery Office, 1949), xvi (2,003 cases). The commission was an international body established by the Allies in 1943 as an information-gathering agency. No Russian trials are included in this total, since the Russians did not participate in the commission's work. In the introduction to Tutorow, *War Crimes*, 4–8, there is a higher estimate of the number of trials held by the Allies and also by the Germans under the denazification program—a program that is outside the scope of this book. The total given in the text for the number of trials is undoubtedly low. A higher figure would, however, only reinforce the points being made.

7. For debates among American policymakers, see the detailed account by Bradley F. Smith, *The Road to Nuremberg* (New York: Basic, 1981). Smith's *The American Road to Nuremberg* (Stanford, Calif.: Hoover Institution Press, 1982) contains documents illustrating the development of U.S. policy.

8. Sir Jan Simon van der Aa, ed., *Proceedings of the XIth International Penal and Penitentiary Congress Held in Berlin, August 1935* (Bern: Bureau of the International Penal and Penitentiary Commission, 1937), 10, 454.

9. Major G. I. A. D. Draper, counsel for the prosecution, in Fyfe, ed., *War Crimes Trials*, vol. 7, *The Velpke Baby Home Trial*, ed. George Brand (London: William Hodge, 1950), 338.

10. Ibid., 203.

11. Ibid., 328.

12. Ibid., 330.

13. Ibid., 343. These were the only death sentences handed down in the case. Disposition of the other six defendants is as follows: one died during the course of the trial, one was dismissed from the case, two were acquitted, and two were given prison sentences of fifteen and ten years, respectively. See ibid., 111, 294, 342–43.

14. Answers to the question of why the National Socialists were successful in Germany are so numerous that they constitute a field of study in themselves—one that is beyond the scope of this book. The chapter titled "Democracy and Dictatorship, 1918–45" in Mary Fulbrook, *A Concise History of Germany* (Cambridge: Cambridge University Press, 1990), 155–203, usefully summarizes both the events of the regime and the arguments about it. See also her thoughtful concluding chapter, "Patterns and Problems of German History," 247–50. Her bibliography for the Nazi period provides leads to other, more specialized works. A later work that deserves special mention is Daniel Jonah Goldhagen, *Hitler's Willing Executioners* (New York: Knopf, 1996) because of the controversy over its central thesis that the "eliminationist antisemitism" of ordinary Germans provided the motivation for them to participate in the National Socialist program of genocide against the Jews. References to other works and other explanations can be found in Goldhagen's notes.

15. Brand, *Velpke Baby Home Trial*, 138.

16. Ibid., 305.

17. *Trials of War Criminals before the Nuernberg Military Tribunals under Control Council Law No. 10*, vol. 3, *The Justice Case* (Washington, D.C.: U.S. Government Printing Office, 1951), 127, 289–91. The extent, nature, and effectiveness of internal resistance to the National Socialist regime are hotly debated. A way into the subject is Michael Geyer and John W. Boyer, eds., *Resistance against the Third Reich, 1933–1990* (Chicago: University of Chicago Press, 1994).

18. Fyfe, ed., *War Crimes Trials*, vol. 4, *The Hadamar Trial*, ed. Earl W. Kintner (London: William Hodge, 1949), 14.

19. Ibid., 175. For a detailed and scholarly account of the National Socialist program of killing Germans deemed unproductive and undesirable, see Michael Burleigh, *Death and Deliverance* (Cambridge: Cambridge University Press, 1994).

20. Brand, *Velpke Baby Home Trial*, 103, photos facing 128, 192, 258–59, 264.

21. Kinter, *Hadamar Trial*, 164.

22. Quoted in a letter from the bishop of Limburg to the Reich minister of justice, 13 August 1941, document 615-PS, exhibit no. USA-717, *Trial of the Major War Criminals*, 5:364; Burleigh, *Death and Deliverance*, 144–61; Robert S. Wistrich, *Who's Who in Nazi Germany* (1982; reprint, London: Routledge, 1995), 20, 31–32.

23. Brand, *Velpke Baby Home Trial*, 171.

24. For a carefully reasoned argument that the charge of crimes against humanity was applicable to actions in Germany prior to World War II, as well as during that war, see the argument by Telford Taylor, prosecutor in the trial of the German industrialist Friedrich Flick, in *Trials under Control Council Law No. 10*, vol. 6 (The Flick Trial) (Washington, D.C.: U.S. Government Printing Office, 1952): 76–91. The judges disagreed; see 1212–16.

Chapter Thirteen

1. David Maxwell Fyfe, ed., *War Crimes Trials*, vol. 4, *The Hadamar Trial*, ed. Earl W. Kintner (London: William Hodge, 1949), 3–5.

2. For more on the legal orientation of the people who actually planned and conducted the war crimes trials, see Dorothy V. Jones, "Power and Responsibility in International Criminal Law," in *Power and Responsibility in World Affairs: Reformation vs. Transformation*, ed. Cathal J. Nolan (forthcoming). G. I. A. D. Draper, a lawyer prominent in the preparation of the British trials, later commented, "I did not know what a war crime was. I had never even studied public international law at the university. I knew a little about the law of mortgages, but I was told it was really irrelevant when dealing with the Belsen concentration camp." Draper, *Reflections on Law and Armed Conflicts* (The Hague: Kluwer Law International, 1998), 116. Draper was not alone in his ignorance, nor was he alone in seeking the help of those who were trained in international law. Robert Jackson, the U.S. chief prosecutor, when in London in the summer of 1945 for the drafting of the charter of the international military Tribunal, sought the advice of Hersch Lauterpacht, Cambridge professor and influential scholar of international law. The official U.S. approach to the trials can be followed in Bradley F. Smith, *The Road to Nuremberg* (New York: Basic, 1981). The British side, and in particular, the contribution of the United Nations War Crimes Commission, can be found in Arieh J. Kochavi, *Prelude to Nuremberg: Allied*

War Crimes Policy and the Question of Punishment (Chapel Hill: University of North Carolina Press, 1998). As regards "the Geneva Convention" referred to by both the defense and the prosecution, there were actually two Geneva conventions, both signed in 1929, one covering the treatment of prisoners of war and one the care of the sick and wounded. See "Convention Relative to the Treatment of Prisoners of War" and "Geneva Convention for the Amelioration of the Condition of the Wounded and Sick in Armies in the Field," 27 July 1929, League of Nations Treaty Series 118: 305–36, 345–97. Copies of these conventions can also be found in the useful compilation edited by Dietrich Schindler and Jirí Toman, *The Laws of Armed Conflicts*, 3d ed. (Dordrecht, The Netherlands: Martinus Nijhoff, 1988), 325–34, 339–64.

  3. *Trial of the Major War Criminals before the International Military Tribunal* (Nuremberg: Secretariat of the International Military Tribunal, 1948), 5:365–66; Kinter, *Hadamar Trial*, 14.

  4. Leon Jaworski, *Confession and Avoidance* (Garden City, N.Y.: Anchor Press/Doubleday, 1979), 108, 204.

  5. Kinter, *Hadamar Trial*, 5–6.

  6. Ibid., 7. The rule is Article 46 of the annex to the 1907 Hague Convention Respecting the Laws and Customs of War on Land. Article 46 of the annex to the 1899 Convention, on which the 1907 Convention is based, says "religious convictions and liberty" instead of "religious convictions and practice." Otherwise, the wording is the same.

  7. Kinter, *Hadamar Trial*, 7.

  8. This is stated in Article 1 of both the 1899 and the 1907 Conventions.

  9. For war crimes proceedings in German courts after World War I, see Claud Mullins, *The Leipzig Trials* (London: H. F. & G. Witherly, 1929).

  10. For the Laternser statement, see Kinter, *Hadamar Trial*, 220. Hermann Jahrreiss made his statement when appearing as an expert witness at one of the twelve subsequent trials conducted by the Americans under the authority of Control Council Law No. 10. See *Trials of War Criminals before the Nuernberg Military Tribunals under Control Council Law No. 10*, vol. 3, *The Justice Case* (Washington, D.C.: U.S. Government Printing Office, 1951), 281.

  11. Article 1, Agreement of August 8, 1945, U.S. Department of State, *Report of Robert H. Jackson, United States Representative to the International Conference on Military Trials, London, 1945*, Publication 3080, International Organization and Conference Series II, European and British Commonwealth 1 (Washington D.C.: U.S. Government Printing Office, 1949): 420. This volume is a documentary record of the negotiations in London where representatives of the United States, Great Britain, the Soviet Union, and France worked out arrangements for the establishment of the International Military Tribunal to try the major German war criminals. The nineteen other states who agreed to the provisions worked out in London: Australia, Belgium, Czechoslovakia, Denmark, Ethiopia, Greece, Haiti, Honduras, India, Luxembourg, Netherlands, New Zealand, Norway, Panama, Paraguay, Poland, Uruguay, Venezuela, Yugoslavia.

  12. Kinter, *Hadamar Trial*, 12. Those who dismiss these trials as "victors' justice" seem to be operating on the concept of law put forward here by the prosecutor at the Hadamar trial, namely that law, to be authoritative, must be issued by a sovereign

body. The implication of "victors' justice" is, of course, that the victorious Allies made a charade of legality to cover their determination to punish the defeated. People who use the label usually have not bothered to distinguish national law from international law, and thus they miss the larger legal issues at stake in these trials. A good corrective is Gary Jonathan Bass, *Stay the Hand of Vengeance: The Politics of War Crimes Trials* (Princeton: Princeton University Press, 2000).

13. Kinter, *Hadamar Trial*, 7–8. For an expression of similar views by Robert H. Jackson, chief U.S. prosecutor at the trial of the major German war criminals, see Jackson, "Report to the President of the United States, June 7, 1945," in *The Nürnberg Case* (New York: Knopf, 1947), 14, 15.

14. Kinter, *Hadamar Trial*, 243.

15. Ibid., 14, 246; Michael Burleigh, *Death and Deliverance*, (Cambridge: Cambridge University Press, 1994), 273; *Trial of the Major War Criminals*, vol. 22 (Nuremberg: Secretariat of the International Military Tribunal, 1948), 400. Seven years after Jodl's execution at Nuremberg, a German court found him not guilty of crimes under international law and exonerated him posthumously.

16. Specialists will recognize that this brief statement of the charges in the Nuremberg war crimes trial is an oversimplification based on the charter of the international military tribunal. The statement in the text does not go into the charges of participation in a common plan or conspiracy, does not mention the attempt in the trial to brand specified organizations as criminal, and does not distinguish between the Nuremberg trial, in which crimes against humanity was a separate charge, and the Tokyo trial, in which it figured only when linked to the charge of war crimes.

17. Jaworski, *Confession and Avoidance*, 116.

18. Kinter, *Hadamar Trial*, 7–8.

19. Ibid., 6.

20. *Trial of the Major War Criminals*, 3:103.

21. Ibid., 22:427, 462. Also quoted in *Nazi Conspiracy and Aggression* (Washington, D.C.: Office of United States Chief of Counsel for Prosecution of Axis Criminality, U.S. Government Printing Office, 1946–47), 16, 49. The judges' reasoning was a two-stage process: Was aggressive war a crime? And had the defendants engaged in or conspired to engage in such a war?

22. The judges for France were Henri Donnedieu de Vabres (alternate, Robert Falco); for Great Britain, Sir Geoffrey Lawrence (alternate, Sir Norman Birkett); for the Soviet Union, Major General I. T. Nikitchenko (alternate, Lieutenant Colonel A. F. Volchkov); for the United States, Francis Biddle (alternate, John J. Parker). Early on, it was agreed that the alternates would be full participants in the proceedings with the right to put questions in court and to vote in the private discussions of the judges. They did not cast votes in the final judgment and sentencing, but this was a formality since they had taken full part in the discussions through which these final decisions were made.

23. This is an abbreviated account of the tribunal's judgment in the Nuremberg war crimes trial. The account omits some points of legal interest, particularly in regard to the prosecution's attempt to categorize certain specified organizations as criminal. For the entire judgment see *Trial of the Major War Criminals*, 22:411–589, or *Nazi Conspiracy*, which prints the judgment in full. Telford Taylor has an extended account of the judgment and sentencing in his *Anatomy of the Nuremberg Trials* (New

York: Knopf, 1992), 546–603, as do Ann Tusa and John Tusa, *The Nuremberg Trial* (New York: Atheneum, 1984), 446–74.

24. Telford Taylor, *Final Report to the Secretary of the Army on the Nuernberg War Crimes Trials under Control Council Law No. 10* (1949; reprint, Buffalo, N.Y.: William S. Hein, 1997), 107–12, 221–23. John Alan Appleman, *Military Tribunals and International Crimes* (1954; reprint, Westport, Conn.: Greenwood, 1971), 139–233, discusses each of the twelve subsequent trials and gives much factual detail such as the names of the judges, defendants, and lawyers, the charges that were made, and the outcomes.

25. These twelve judges came from eleven different states: Connecticut, Colorado, Indiana, Iowa, Louisiana, Minnesota, North Dakota, Ohio, Oregon, Tennessee, and Washington. Some federal judges had accepted invitations to preside at the trials but were prevented from doing so by a ruling of Fred M. Vinson, Chief Justice of the U.S. Supreme Court, which forbade any federal judges taking part in the trials.

26. Neither the International Criminal Court for the Former Yugoslavia nor the International Criminal Tribunal for Rwanda has jurisdiction over the crime of aggression. The Rome Statute for the International Criminal Court does give that court such jurisdiction, but, since the drafters could not agree on the definition of *aggression,* effective jurisdiction is in the future tense. After the court is established, the states parties have seven years in which to agree on a definition and amend the statute to reflect that agreement.

27. Robert H. Jackson, *The Case against the Nazi War Criminals* (New York: Knopf, 1946), 90.

Chapter Fourteen

1. The Moscow Declaration, 1 November 1943, in *Foreign Relations of the United States 1943,* vol. 1, *General* (Washington, D.C.: U.S. Government Printing Office, 1963): 769.

2. David Maxwell Fyfe, ed., *War Crimes Trials,* vol. 1, *The Peleus Trial,* ed. John Cameron (London: William Hodge, 1948), xiv–xv.

3. "The Challenge of International Lawlessness," speech by Jackson at the anual meeting of the American Bar Association, Indianapolis, 2 October 1941, printed in *International Conciliation* pamphlet 374 (November 1941), 691.

4. After the trials, David Maxwell Fyfe became active in the movement to articulate and secure human rights in Europe. See the entry on Fyfe by R. F. V. Heuston in *The Dictionary of National Biography, 1961–1970* (London: Oxford University Press, 1970), 408–9.

5. Telford Taylor, *Anatomy of the Nuremberg Trials* (New York: Knopf, 1992), 120; Francis Biddle, *In Brief Authority* (Garden City, N.Y.: Doubleday, 1962), 380–81; Rebecca West, *A Train of Powder* (New York: Viking, 1945), 18–19; Airey Neave, *Nuremberg* (London: Hodder and Stoughton, 1978), 227–28, 234–35; Henri Donnedieu de Vabres, "Un traité multilatéral pour la définition de l'aggresseur," in *L'Année politique française et étrangère* 8 (1933): 400–404.

6. *Introduction à l'étude du Droit pénal international* (Paris: Sirey, 1922). For a comprehensive list of de Vabres's publications, see the festschrift *Les principaux aspects de la politique criminelles moderne* (Paris: Editions Cujas, 1960), 3–13.

7. Otto Stahmer, Motion Adopted by All Defense Counsel, 19 November 1945, in *Trial of the Major War Criminals*, (Nuremberg: International Military Tribunal, 1947), 1:170.

8. Quincy Wright, "Legal Positivism and the Nuremberg Judgment," *American Journal of International Law* 42 (1948): 405.

9. Quoted in Taylor, *Anatomy of the Nuremberg Trials*, 551.

10. Fyfe, ed., *War Crimes Trials*, vol. 1, *The Peleus Trial*, 45.

11. Fyfe, ed., *War Crimes Trials*, vol. 2, *The Belsen Trial*, ed. Raymond Phillips (London: William Hodge, 1949), 486, 487, 503.

12. *Trial of the Major War Criminals*, 17:478–79.

13. David Maxwell Fyfe, ed., *War Crimes Trials*, vol. 4, *The Hadamar Trial*, ed. Earl W. Kinter (London: William Hodge, 1949), xv–xvi.

14. For Jackson's comments regarding the opposition of older international lawyers, see his MS diary, entry for 22 May [1945], Box 95 of the Robert H. Jackson papers, Manuscript Division, The Library of Congress, Washington, D.C.

15. Ibid, entry for 10 May 1945 (TS diary); for Jules Basdevant see the entry in Warren F. Kuehl, ed., *Biographical Dictionary of Internationalists* (Westport, Conn.: Greenwood, 1983), 58–59.

16. Ibid., entries for 10 May and 22 May 1945. For de Vabres's discussion of what he called "*un Droit des gens nouveau,*" see his *Le procès de Nuremberg* (Paris: Editions Donat, 1947), 50–74. His discussion of the Nuremberg charge, crimes against peace, is on 223–33.

17. Vespasien V. Pella, "Le professeur Henri Donnedieu de Vabres," *Revue internationale de Droit pénal* 22 (1951): 443.

18. De Vabres, *Le procès de Nuremberg*, 283.

19. Jean Graven, ed., *Actes de Vᵉ Congrès International de Droit Pénal* (Paris: Librairie du Recueil Sirey, 1952), 16, 130–39, 152; *The Charter and Judgment of the Nürnberg Tribunal*, Memorandum submitted by the UN Secretary-General (Lake Success, N.Y.: United Nations [A/CN.4/5], 1949), 15–30. For subsequent attempts to codify international criminal law and establish an international criminal court, see Roger S. Clark, "The Influence of the Nuremberg Trial on the Development of International Law," in George Ginsburgs and V. N. Kudriavtsev, *The Nuremberg Trial and International Law* (Dordrecht, The Netherlands: Martinus Nijhoff, 1990), 249–63.

20. Ivan S. Kerno, "In Memoriam: Vespasian V. Pella, 1897–1952," *American Journal of International Law* 46 (1952): 709–10.

21. For contemporary statements of opposition to an international criminal court by the president of the American Bar Association, see Frank E. Holman, *The Proposal for an "International Bill of Rights"* (Seattle: Argus, 1948), and *Our Common Heritage* (Seattle: Argus, 1949). In the early stages of discussion of an international bill of rights, there was talk of an international court in which such rights could be enforced. It was this that stimulated Holman's and the ABA's opposition.

Chapter Fifteen

1. For the final session of the League Assembly, see League of Nations, *Official Journal*, Records of the Twentieth (Conclusion) and Twenty-First Ordinary Sessions of the Assembly [1938, 1946] (Geneva, 1946). Louis Cheronnet, *The Palace of*

the League of Nations (Paris: *L'Illustration*, 1938), has abundant interior and exterior photographs of the League building.

2. Resolution 95(I), affirming the Nuremberg principles, and 96(I), declaring genocide an international crime, were adopted by the General Assembly on 11 December 1946. See United Nations, *Official Records of the Second Part of the First Session of the General Assembly*, Verbatim Record, 23 October–16 December 1946, 1135, 1144. John P. Humphrey, "The UN Charter and the Universal Declaration of Human Rights," in *The International Protection of Human Rights*, ed. Evan Luard (New York: Praeger, 1967), 39–58, is a succinct account of early United Nations efforts in the field of human rights.

3. The term *Grotian moment* was coined by Richard Falk, a scholar of international law and commentator on the contemporary scene. For a number of years he has been developing the concept and applying it in different ways in response to perceived political necessities. See his *Law in an Emerging Global Village: A Post-Westphalian Perspective* (Ardsley, N.Y.: Transnational, 1998), esp. 3–29. References in that work will direct the interested reader to earlier formulations.

4. Joseph Paul-Boncour, address to the League Assembly, 10 April 1946, League of Nations, *Official Journal*, *1946*, 37.

5. United Nations Charter, Article 27(3).

6. Andrei Gromyko, address to the final session of the San Francisco Conference, 26 June 1945, in *Documents of the United Nations Conference on International Organization, San Francisco, 1945* vol. 1, *General* (London and New York: United Nations Information Organizations, 1945), 664. The unspoken aspect of this provision was that the great powers would never be the target of military action authorized by the Security Council, since no great power was likely to vote in favor of action against itself. As one of the readers of this book in manuscript form pointed out, this provision was actually a step backward from the use-of-force provisions in the covenant of the League of Nations, wherein no exception was made for the great powers of those days.

7. United Nations Charter, Chapter VII, "Action with Respect to Threats to the Peace, Breaches of the Peace, and Acts of Aggression."

8. *Dumbarton Oaks: Proposals for the Establishment of a General International Organization*, Sen. Doc. 245, 78 Cong., 2d sess., Ch. I.1, Ch. II.6b, Ch. V.1, Ch. VI B.1, Ch. VIII B.1, Ch. VIII B.5. United Nations Charter Art. 1.1, Art.2.6, Art. 11.1, Art. 11.2, Art. 24.1, Art. 39, Art. 43. The sense of the cited passages is the same in the Dumbarton Oaks Proposals and in the UN Charter. Where the wording differs, I have chosen the charter's words, but the differences are slight. The phrase "the maintenance of international peace and security" is especially abundant in the Charter. I have not cited all its appearances.

9. Jan Christian Smuts, address to the sixth plenary session of the San Francisco Conference, 1 May 1945, in *Documents of the United Nations Conference*, 1:425.

10. Harry S. Truman, welcoming address to the delegates at the San Francisco Conference, 25 April 1945, ibid., 113.

11. For a discussion of some of the ideas behind the changes made at San Francisco, see Dorothy V. Jones, "Sober Expectations: The United Nations and a 'Sensible Machinery' for Peace," in *The Dumbarton Oaks Conversations and the United Nations, 1944–1994*, ed. Ernest R. May and Angeliki E. Laiou (Washington, D.C.:

Dumbarton Oaks Research Library and Collection, 1998; distributed by Harvard University Press), 9–14. The proceedings at San Francisco can be followed in detail in the sixteen-volume set from which the quotations in the text are taken, *Documents of the United Nations Conference* (see n. 6 above). Detailed enough for most purposes is the coverage provided by Leland M. Goodrich and Edvard Hambro, *Charter of the United Nations: Commentary and Documents*, rev. ed. (Boston: World Peace Foundation, 1949).

12. The Convention on Rights and Duties of States can be found in the *League of Nations Treaty Series* (London: Harrison and Sons, 1920–46), 165:19–31. Article 1 of the League of Nations Covenant makes explicit the right of withdrawal from the organization. No such provision is included in the United Nations Charter, but discussions at San Francisco made it clear that members states retained that right. As the delegates of some states pointed out, if the right of withdrawal were prohibited or limited in any way, the constitutions of their countries would prohibit them from signing the charter. For discussion of this point, see Goodrich and Hambro, *Charter of the United Nations*, 142–45.

13. A postwar development that is not covered here was the movement to revise and expand the rules governing the conduct of war. Four treaty agreements, usually called the Geneva Conventions, were worked out in the immediate postwar period at meetings in Geneva, Switzerland, sponsored by the International Committee of the Red Cross. They have been signed and ratified by most of the world's states. They are: Convention for the Amelioration of the Condition of the Sick and Wounded in the Field; Convention for the Amelioration of the Condition of the Wounded, Sick and Shipwrecked Members of the Armed Forces at Sea; Convention Relative to the Treatment of Prisoners of War; and Convention Relative to the Protection of Civilian Persons in Time of War. For the texts in English and French, see *United Nations Treaty Series* 75: 31–69, 85–123, 135–243, 287–393. A thorough account of the 1949 Geneva Conventions and their place in the development of the laws of war can be found in Geoffrey Best, *War and Law since 1945* (Oxford: Clarendon Press, 1994), 80–179.

14. Copies of the Universal Declaration of Human Rights abound. Two sources are Irving Sarnoff, comp. and ed., *International Instruments of the United Nations* (United Nations Publication No. E.96.I.15, 1997), 85–87; Ian Brownlie, ed., *Basic Documents on Human Rights*, 3d ed. (Oxford: Clarendon, 1992), 21–27. In his introduction Brownlie points to other sources and to commentaries. For an insider's view of the drafting of this much-discussed and -studied document, see John P. Humphrey, *Human Rights and the United Nations: A Great Adventure* (Dobbs Ferry, N.Y.: Transnational, 1984), 14–77. Humphrey was director of the Division of Human Rights in the United Nations Secretariat during this period and was intimately involved at all stages of the drafting, revision, and adoption of the declaration.

15. Article 6 of the Genocide Convention. Copies of the convention can be found in Sarnoff, *International Instruments of the United Nations*, 83–84, and Brownlie, *Basic Documents on Human Rights*, 31–34. Nehemiah Robinson has an exhaustive, committee-by-committee account of the drafting of the Convention in *The Genocide Convention: Its Origins and Interpretation* (New York: Institute of Jewish Affairs, World Jewish Congress, 1949.)

16. Hersch Lauterpacht, "The Universal Declaration of Human Rights," in *The*

British Yearbook of International Law, 1948 (London: Oxford University Press, n.d.), 354–81. Lauterpacht noted that such a declaration might have a beneficial effect if issued by groups whose purpose was to influence public opinion, but "when emanating from Governments it is a substitute for a deed" (372). Lauterpacht's own views on the need for enforceable human rights provisions can be seen in his *An International Bill of the Rights of Man* (New York: Columbia University Press, 1945).

17. Only the Soviet boycott of the UN Security Council allowed that body to authorize a military response to North Korea's action—another complication in this complicated mix. For an account of the Korean War from an international perspective, see William Stueck, *The Korean War: An International History* (Princeton: Princeton University Press, 1995), an exhaustively researched, multiarchival work. Bruce Cumings, *The Origins of the Korean War* (Princeton: Princeton University Press, 1981, 1990), is indispensable for an account from a nationalist perspective. For the conceptual roots of United States policy in the Korean War, see Frank Ninkovich, *Modernity and Power* (Chicago: University of Chicago Press, 1994), esp. 186–207.

18. Address to members of both Houses of Parliament, London, 2 April 1958, in Andrew W. Cordier and Wilder Foote, eds., *Public Papers of the Secretaries-General of the United Nations*, vol. 4, *Dag Hammarskjöld, 1958–1960* (New York: Columbia University Press, 1974), 46.

19. Ibid.; Preamble and Art. 1, United Nations Charter; Cordier and Foote, *Public Papers of the Secretaries-General* (New York: Columbia University Press, 1975), 5:546.

Chapter Sixteen

1. This attitude is reflected in the tributes paid to Grotius at the 1899 Independence Day celebration in Delft. See *Proceedings at the Laying of a Wreath on the Tomb of Hugo Grotius* (The Hague: Martinus Nijhoff, 1899).

2. Quoted in Emery Kelen, *Peace in Their Time* (London: Gollancz, 1964), 238.

3. Ibid.

4. Lists of the communications received by the conference, along with a brief summary of contents, can be found in League of Nations, Conference for the Reduction and Limitation of Armaments, *Journal*, 4 February–6 August 1932. The treatment in the text only hints at the richness of this source.

5. Ibid.: Union of Austrian Peace Societies (23 February 1932), 141; the National Council of the National Federation of Ex-Service Men and Victims of the War (France) (30 April 1932), 477; International Council of the International Union of Antimilitarist Ministers and Clergymen (The Netherlands) (7 May 1932), 516.

6. Report of the Committee for the Preliminary Examination of Petitions from Private Organisations, Disarmament Conference, *Journal* (4 February 1932), 22. The indefatigable Lord Robert Cecil was one of the speakers at the ad hoc, strictly unofficial meeting on February 6. Most delegates did not attend this meeting, although Arthur Henderson, the chair of the conference, presided out of a feeling of sympathy for this outpouring of public concern.

7. Programme for the Opening Meetings of the General Assembly, memorandum issued by the executive secretary on instructions of the temporary president of

the General Assembly, United Nations, *Journal of the General Assembly*, pt. 1, 3–4. The assembly met in London from 10 January to 14 February 1945.

8. Ibid., 41.

9. See Irving Sarnoff, *International Instruments of the United Nations* (United Nations Publications, E.96.I.15, 1997), especially the instruments listed under these headings: "Human Rights," "Economic and Development Issues," and "Social Issues."

A BIBLIOGRAPHIC NOTE
ON THEORIES OF JUSTICE

The notes for *Toward a Just World*, while providing sources for citations, also function as guides to further research. Readers will find many titles of books and articles that are relevant to and expand on subjects discussed in the text. Often, too, the notes themselves expand the discussion of a subject mentioned but not further developed in the text since extended treatment there would interrupt the flow of the narrative. Thus the notes, besides supporting the argument of the book, also deepen the argument and point beyond themselves to related and relevant subjects. One thing the notes do not do, however. They offer little help to readers who might want to explore justice in a philosophical, rather than a political setting. This bibliographic note suggests some works to fill that gap. The richness and complexity of recent philosophical debates on justice can help bring into sharper focus the achievements of the nonphilosophers whose struggles are detailed in this book.

Much modern discussion of the subject begins with John Rawls, *A Theory of Justice* (Cambridge: Harvard University Press, 1971). Rawls's purpose is to take the familiar theory of the social contract as set out, for example, by Rousseau or Kant and move it to a higher level of abstraction. Two later works have made his theory more relevant to international affairs: *The Law of Peoples* (Cambridge: Harvard University Press, 1999), and *Justice as Fairness: A Restatement* (Cambridge: Harvard University Press, 2001). For another source, see "The Law of Peoples," in *On Human Rights: The Oxford Amnesty Lectures, 1993*, ed. Stephen Shute and Susan Harley (New York: Basic, 1993), 42–82.

A good introduction to the debates that have filled the pages of philosophical and international affairs journals since Rawls published his theory in 1971 is Harold J. Berman, "Individualistic and Communitarian Theories of Justice: An Historical Approach," in Berman, *Faith and Order: The Reconciliation of Law and Religion* (Atlanta, Ga.: Scholars, 1993), 231–76.

Part of the richness of modern philosophical debates on justice is surely due to Michael Walzer's contributions and the moral passion that informs his work. See especially *Spheres of Justice: A Defense of Pluralism and Equality* (New York: Basic, 1983), in which Walzer subjects the idea of distributive justice to penetrating analysis. His *Just and Unjust Wars: A Moral Argument with Historical Illustrations* (New York: Basic, 1977) arose from his opposition to the Vietnam War, but the distinctions he makes regarding just and unjust uses of force have relevance far beyond that particular war.

One more title and readers will be well on their way to seeing this subject's fascination and complexity. From the philosophic side, Onora O'Neill, in *Bounds of Justice* (New York: Cambridge University Press, 2000), attempts to bridge the gap between justice in a philosophical setting and justice in a political setting—in other words, to offer practical guidelines for choices.

The debate goes on, as it has gone on since the days of Plato and Aristotle. The needs of the twentieth century gave the debate a particular urgency as changes in communication, economic exchanges, and population movements put pressure on older concepts of what might be required for justice to prevail in the world—a world that now contains many new and fragile states. As Terry Nardin has observed in his *Law, Morality, and the Relations of States* (Princeton: Princeton University Press, 1983), the controversy about the meaning of justice in international affairs has occupied most of the twentieth century. And on page 255 he adds, "The argument has not of course been primarily about a word, but rather about what sort of international order would count as just and about what sort of international conduct a just order would require of states and individuals."

This book, *Toward a Just World*, gives some of the answers that were worked out during the first fifty years of the twentieth century, answers we are living with today.